Improving
Organizational
Effectiveness
Through
Transformational
Leadership

Improving Organizational Effectiveness

Through Transformational Leadership

Edited by **Bernard M. Bass**
and **Bruce J. Avolio**

SAGE Publications
International Educational and Professional Publisher
Thousand Oaks   London   New Delhi

For information address:

SAGE Publications, Inc.
2455 Teller Road
Thousand Oaks, California 91320

SAGE Publications Ltd.
6 Bonhill Street
London EC2A 4PU
United Kingdom

SAGE Publications India Pvt. Ltd.
M-32 Market
Greater Kailash I
New Delhi 110 048 India

Printed in the United States of America

Library of Congress Cataloging-in-Publication Data

Main entry under title:

   Improving organizational effectiveness through transformational
leadership / edited by Bernard M. Bass, Bruce J. Avolio.
      p. cm.
   Includes bibliographical references and indexes.
   ISBN 0-8039-5235-X.—ISBN 0-8039-5236-8 (pbk.)
   1. Organizational effectiveness. 2. Leadership. I. Avolio,
Bruce J. II. Title.
HD58.9.B37   1994
658.4'09—dc20   93-30874
                                                                      CIP

94 95 96 97 10 9 8 7 6 5 4 3 2 1

Sage Production Editor: Megan M. McCue

Contents

Preface

In late 1990, Dr. Gian Franco Gambigliani asked the editors to organize a series of papers that would provide policy makers and program designers at Fiat and its 300 companies the latest information about selected issues in human resources management. He especially wanted information on how transformational leadership might contribute to organizational change. These papers would augment Fiat's efforts to develop transformational leadership among its managers and senior executives and could be dovetailed with other efforts—such as its total quality program—to generate a synergistic acceleration of Fiat's changes and improvements.

One goal of this project was to generalize the model of transformational leadership beyond the immediate effects expected from the training program to its diffusion throughout the organization. In this vein, the range of topics included in this volume signify the potential "second-order" effects that can accrue by providing organizational leaders with an alternative philosophy and way of thinking about leadership.

The chapters in this volume were written by the editors and colleagues in the Center for Leadership Studies at the State University of New York at Binghamton, as well as by theorists at the University of Georgia, Concordia University, and Florida International University.

The editors express their appreciation to Ileana Martinez, Bev Watson, Wendy Kramer, Sharon Potochniak Burdick, and Cheryll Hague, along with the help of Center for Leadership Studies research assistants Wendy

Wright, Natalie Adams, and Brian Moore for their work in preparing the manuscripts.

Finally, we dedicate this book to Gian Franco Gambigliani and Giovanni Testa for their support and trust in our work, their desire to set the highest challenges and standards, their constant rethinking of better ways to train leaders, and their immense consideration and friendship throughout our working relationship.

BERNARD M. BASS
BRUCE J. AVOLIO

1

Introduction

BERNARD M. BASS

BRUCE J. AVOLIO

Center for Leadership Studies,
School of Management, SUNY Binghamton

EXECUTIVE SUMMARY

The purpose of this book is to show how the concepts of the full range
of leadership—transactional and transformational—can apply to specific areas of leadership, management, and organizational development.
Transactional and transformational leadership are introduced within the
framework of a full-range model of leadership that includes the highly
inactive and ineffective laissez-faire (LF) leadership to the highly active
and effective inspirational and, ideally, influential leadership. This
model is concisely applied to research, development, and training that
have already appeared. Brief summaries of the chapters that follow are
provided.

When a human resources director for a newly organized assembly
plant was asked how the new organization came about, he said
it began with a vision. The vision was subsequently modified and shared
by management and employees. The director was describing one aspect
of transformational leadership: the new leadership that must accompany
good management but goes beyond the importance of leaders simply
getting the work done with their followers and maintaining quality
relationships with them.

During the last two decades, theories about transformational leadership have taken shape. Evidence about these theories has been amassed

for all levels of organization and society and not just for charismatic leaders of social movements and organizations.

In physics, a new theory is usually tested by colleagues within a few years, sometimes even within a few months. Applications may appear in new technologies shortly afterward. In social science, theories are seldom adequately tested. They are likely to hang around as long as the originator is active. Adaptations take decades. Thus the theories of team participation that originated in the 1930s resulted in a mass of research in the 1950s; for the most part, they are just now being applied to the wholesale restructuring of many industrial firms.

One exception has occurred with transformational leadership. First mention of it appeared in Downton's *Rebel Leadership* (1973), a sociological treatise, and independently in James McGregor Burns' seminal 1978 conceptualization.[1] In 1985, Bass presented a formal theory of transformational leadership as well as models and measurements of its factors of leadership behavior.[2] These were refined further by Bass and Avolio and their colleagues from a variety of evaluative investigations and the development of a model—the full range of leadership development—and an assessment and training program in transformational leadership.[3]

Meanwhile, at least 25 independent dissertations and numerous other research projects were completed in the United States and elsewhere.[4] And, starting in 1989, just four years after the appearance of *Leadership and Performance Beyond Expectations*, Fiat, an Italian multinational conglomerate of 250,000 employees, launched programs to present the *full range of leadership program* (FRLP) to 200 of its *alta direcciones* (top executives) and many of its 4,000 *direcciones* (middle managers) and 20,000 supervisors. A parallel program supported by the Kellogg Foundation also was initiated at the Center for Leadership Studies; by 1993, it was completed with close to 400 leaders. These leaders were drawn from all sectors of local communities, including education, health care, arts, industry, and government.

Transformational leadership is seen when leaders:

- stimulate interest among colleagues and followers[5] to view their work from new perspectives,
- generate awareness of the mission or vision of the team and organization,
- develop colleagues and followers to higher levels of ability and potential, and
- motivate colleagues and followers to look beyond their own interests toward those that will benefit the group.

Transformational leaders motivate others to do more than they originally intended and often even more than they thought possible. They set more challenging expectations and typically achieve higher performances.

Transformational leadership is an expansion of *transactional* leadership. Transactional leadership emphasizes the transaction or exchange that takes place among leaders, colleagues, and followers. This exchange is based on the leader discussing with others what is required and specifying the conditions and rewards these others will receive if they fulfill those requirements.

Transformational leaders do more with colleagues and followers than set up simple exchanges or agreements. They behave in ways to achieve superior results by employing one or more of the "Four I's"[6]:

1. **Idealized influence**. Transformational leaders behave in ways that result in their being role models for their followers. The leaders are admired, respected, and trusted. Followers identify with the leaders and want to emulate them. Among the things the leader does to earn this credit is considering the needs of others over his or her own personal needs. The leader shares risks with followers and is consistent rather than arbitrary. He or she can be counted on to do the right thing, demonstrating high standards of ethical and moral conduct. He or she avoids using power for personal gain and only when needed.

2. **Inspirational motivation**. Transformational leaders behave in ways that motivate and inspire those around them by providing meaning and challenge to their followers' work. Team spirit is aroused. Enthusiasm and optimism are displayed. The leader gets followers involved in envisioning attractive future states. The leader creates clearly communicated expectations that followers want to meet and also demonstrates commitment to goals and the shared vision.

3. **Intellectual stimulation**. Transformational leaders stimulate their followers' efforts to be innovative and creative by questioning assumptions, reframing problems, and approaching old situations in new ways. Creativity is encouraged. There is no public criticism of individual members' mistakes. New ideas and creative problem solutions are solicited from followers, who are included in the process of addressing problems and finding solutions. Followers are encouraged to try new approaches, and their ideas are not criticized because they differ from the leaders' ideas.

4. **Individualized consideration**. Transformational leaders pay special attention to each individual's needs for achievement and growth by acting as coach or mentor. Followers and colleagues are developed to

successively higher levels of potential. Individualized consideration is practiced as follows: New learning opportunities are created along with a supportive climate. Individual differences in terms of needs and desires are recognized. The leader's behavior demonstrates acceptance of individual differences (e.g., some employees receive more encouragement, some more autonomy, others firmer standards, and still others more task structure). A two-way exchange in communication is encouraged, and "management by walking around" work spaces is practiced. Interactions with followers are personalized (e.g., the leader remembers previous conversations, is aware of individual concerns, and sees the individual as a whole person rather than as just an employee). The *individually considerate* leader listens effectively. The leader delegates tasks as a means of developing followers. Delegated tasks are monitored to see if the followers need additional direction or support and to assess progress; ideally, followers do not feel they are being checked on.

Several thousand leaders in the private sector and community leaders in the public sector have been trained using the model of the full range of leadership.[7] This model includes the Four I's of transformational leadership as well as transactional leadership behavior and laissez-faire or nonleadership behavior.

Transactional leadership occurs when the leader rewards or disciplines the follower depending on the adequacy of the follower's performance. Transactional leadership depends on contingent reinforcement, either positive *contingent reward* (CR) or the more negative active or passive forms of *management-by-exception* (MBE-A or MBE-P). CR has been found to be reasonably effective, although not as much as the Four I's, in motivating others to achieve higher levels of development and performance. With this method, the leader assigns or gets agreement on what needs to be done and promises rewards or actually rewards others in exchange for satisfactorily carrying the assignment.

Management-by-exception tends to be more ineffective but required in certain situations. In MBE-A, the leader arranges to actively monitor deviances from standards, mistakes, and errors in the follower's assignments and to take corrective action as necessary. MBE-P implies waiting passively for deviances, mistakes, and errors to occur and then taking corrective action. The LF style is the avoidance or absence of leadership and is, by definition, the most inactive—as well as the most ineffective according to almost all research on the style. As opposed to transactional leadership, laissez-faire represents a nontransaction.

Fundamental to the full-range leadership training effort is that every leader displays each style to some degree. An optimal profile is shown

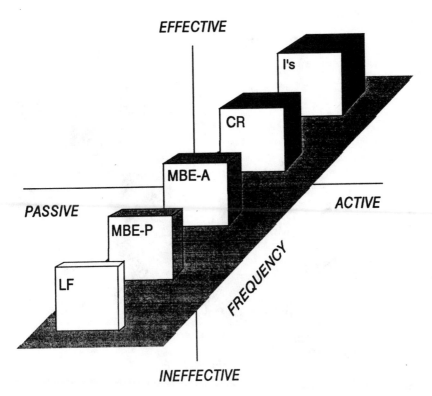

Figure 1.1 Optimal Profile

in Figure 1.1. The third dimension of this model (depth) represents how frequently an individual displays a particular style of leadership. The active dimension helps clarify the style, and the effectiveness dimension broadly represents the impact of the leadership style on performance.

In Figure 1.1, the leader infrequently displays LF leadership and increasing frequencies of the transactional leadership styles of MBE-P, MBE-A, and CR. This optimal profile shows the transformational Four I's as they are most frequently displayed.

In contrast, the poorly performing leader's profile, tending toward inactivity and ineffectiveness, is opposite that of optimal leaders (see Figure 1.2).

Many research studies have been completed in business and industry, government, the military, educational institutions, and nonprofit organizations, all of them showing that transformational leaders, as measured by the survey instruments derived from the Bass and Avolio model, were more effective and satisfying as leaders than transactional

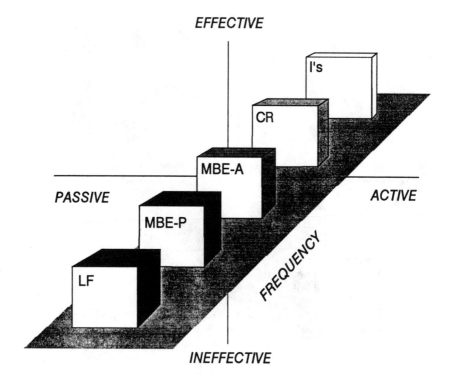

Figure 1.2   Suboptimal Profile

leaders, although the best of leaders frequently do some of the latter but more of the former. Follow-up investigations have shown that developing transformational leadership with training in the Four I's can enhance effectiveness and satisfaction as a leader.[8] Hence, the optimal and suboptimal models depicted in Figures 1.1 and 1.2 represent the full range of styles and the impact on effectiveness found in these previous investigations.

This book shows how transformational leadership is expected to contribute to an organization's efforts to improve its operations and the best use of its human resources. (These innovations are even seen to occur in organizations that do not explicitly recognize that transformational leadership is involved.)

Each chapter deals with a different aspect of the organization and how it is affected by influence processes that are associated especially with frequent transformational leadership. In each instance, the end goal is to develop a highly committed work force that is more eager and willing to take on the challenges in the last decade of this century and into the next millennium. As we will see, employee commitment, involvement, and loyalty, coupled with enlightened management, are fundamental to long-range organizational improvement.

In Chapter 2, Karl Kuhnert focuses attention on the delegation process. He shows, as with transformational leadership in general, the connection of the delegation process with the moral development of the leader. The concept of delegation is expanded beyond traditional definitions and is included as part of the overall developmental strategy for elevating the needs and potential of both leader and follower in the organization.

We have found transformational leadership to varying degrees at every level in the organization from the informal leadership that takes place in team activities to the leadership displayed by chief executive officers. Moreover, as we move up the organizational pyramid, such leadership can indirectly influence increasing numbers of both levels and employees. In Chapter 3, Francis Yammarino describes how leadership may cascade downward in the organization through many levels as well as bypass levels. As a consequence, the transformational leader can exert influence indirectly at an organizational distance by the behaviors and actions that serve as role models and by the culture that is developed to support the leader's vision and mission. Moreover, such indirect influence is also exerted upward in the system in ways described by Yammarino.

Organizations increasingly are coming to depend on self-managed but fully led multifunctional teams to get tasks done effectively. In Chapter 4, David Atwater and Bernard Bass lay out what a half century of research on small group behavior tells the team leader who would be transformational. In Chapter 5, David Waldman reviews current examples of how transformational leadership of multifunctional teams more effectively promotes research, innovation, and change.

In Chapter 6, Bernard Bass considers the linkages between transformational leadership and decision making in teams and organizations.[9] He connects his model of organizational decision making with the Avolio and Bass model of transformational leadership. This combined leadership and decision-making framework highlights the impact of transformational leadership on the information-processing strategies of leaders, teams, and followers in the organization. The framework also shows the procedures that leaders, teams, and followers go through to make effective decisions.

The authorities, Deming and Juran, heavily emphasize the importance of leadership to total quality improvement but do not say much about the actual or specific leadership required. In Chapter 7, Bruce Avolio supplies the linkages between transformational and transactional leadership and quality-improvement programs, offering strategies for merging these respective areas to enhance the leadership and quality-improvement efforts underway today in many firms, agencies, and institutions.

The last three chapters expand into detailed examinations of what firms are doing to promote innovation and change in their human resources programs and policies that can contribute to the emergence of more transformational leadership. In Chapter 8, Leanne and David Atwater review organizational change efforts, current innovations, and selected benchmark companies. In addition to reviewing these successful organizational efforts, the authors also detail the criteria for change that are used by these respective organizations and the methods used for such appraisals.

K. Galen Kroeck in Chapter 9 further examines the principles and applications of the transformational leadership model, focusing attention on examples of reorganizing, "right-sizing" efforts and accompanying human resources programs and practices. His chapter focuses on redirecting organizations from managing work force numbers to a longer-term strategy of human resource staffing whereby the organization continuously "right sizes" its work force to the organization's current demands and future aspirations.

The chapter that follows Kroeck's deals with applications of transformational leadership and related innovations; these are relevant to the diffusion of transformational leadership that seeks to improve organizational performance in the 1990s. In Chapter 10, Avolio and Bass sum up the efforts of the preceding chapters. To remain competitive in a world of rapidly changing technology, changing work force expectations, and cheaper off-shore labor, leadership—particularly transformational leadership—is required at all levels in the firm and must be diffused into more traditional areas of organizational functioning to have the best effect. Avolio and Bass add a special concern for the role of training and development in the diffusion effort and the integration of individual development and organizational development.

The full-range model of transformational, transactional, and nontransactional leadership has been introduced in this chapter. In the following chapters, the model generates implications for development and change in the individual leader and his or her associates, the team, the organization, and the full range of leadership. We begin now by examining the delegation process as it appears at different levels of the full range of leadership as a contribution to the development of leaders and their associates.

Notes

1. Burns, J. M. (1978). *Leadership.* New York: Harper & Row; Downton, J. V. (1973). *Rebel leadership: Commitment and charisma in the revolutionary process.* New York: Free Press.

2. Bass, B. M. (1985). *Leadership and performance beyond expectations.* New York: Free Press.

3. Bass, B. M., & Avolio, B. J. (1990). *Multifactor leadership questionnaire.* Palo Alto, CA: Consulting Psychologist Press.

4. For example, see Deluga, R. J. (1988). Relationship of transformational and transactional leadership with employee influencing strategies. *Group & Organization Studies, 13,* 456-467.

5. *Follower* will be used in this book in its most general sense. In formal organizations, those who are influenced by leaders may include subordinates, supervisees, and direct reports, as well as colleagues. *Associates* will imply followers or colleagues or both. If the influence is upward in the organization, then the follower is the leaders' boss. In social and political movements, followers may include constituents, adherents, disciples, partisans, and supporters.

6. Avolio, B. J., Waldman, D. A., & Yammarino, F. J. (1991). Leading in the 1990s: The Four I's of transformational leadership. *Journal of European Industrial Training, 15*(4), 9-16.

7. See Bass (1983), Chapter 9, and Avolio, B. J., & Bass, B. M. (1990). *The full range of leadership program: Basic and advanced manual.* Binghamton, NY: Bass, Avolio, & Associates.

8. Bass, B. M., & Avolio, B. J. (1990). The implications of transactional and transformational leadership for individual, team, and organizational development. *Research in Organizational Change and Development, 4,* 231-272.

9. Bass, B. M. (1983). *Organizational decision making.* Homewood, IL: Irwin.

2

Transforming Leadership

DEVELOPING PEOPLE
THROUGH DELEGATION

KARL W. KUHNERT

Department of Psychology, University of Georgia

EXECUTIVE SUMMARY

Because of such influences as downsizing, restructuring, and greater international competition for products and services, organizational leaders over the past decade have had to rethink radically how to manage their people and institutions. With fewer employees required to share greater work loads, many of these leaders have had to stretch the capacity of their human resources to keep pace with rapid changes in the market. To address these ongoing changes and to capitalize on an organization's human assets, leaders must continuously develop their people to higher levels of potential. This chapter explores the process of *delegation*, one of the least appreciated and most misunderstood ways of developing people. Specifically, the chapter will show how three different leadership models consistent with the full-range model of leadership can be used to understand how transformational leaders use delegation to develop their people. In terms of the full-range model presented in Chapter 1, much of the discussion in this chapter will focus on life-span development as it relates to individualized consideration.

Delegation and Development

The professional development of employees is big business world-wide. Traditionally, professional development has been conceptualized as training opportunities provided outside the immediate work environment. Recent estimates of annual corporate investment in classroom training in the United States reach approximately $40 billion. This is a staggering figure given that most of what a manager learns (as much as 70% to 80%) comes from on-the-job experiences and practices. Knowing that development and learning are primarily the result of job experience, it becomes obvious that what one is able to learn directly results from the opportunities made available on the job. It is not surprising, then, that individuals who receive greater opportunities and get more meaningful assignments throughout their careers will be more likely to develop and grow professionally, eventually becoming leaders in their own right.[1]

One common way for organizations to expose potential leaders to development opportunities is through rotating job assignments. Often these assignments are in highly visible positions in different departments across the organization and usually are for a specified period of time. The purpose of such assignments is to test the capabilities of the leader in an attempt to transform potential, perhaps latent, talent into actual talent.[2] The costs of such programs, however, are considerable. Relocation expenses, salary increases, losses in efficiency and errors during the learning process, and the cost of failure in a new assignment all contribute to the high price of development.[3] Too often, the strategy underlying the use of job rotation for development is short-term and is disrupted as the needs of the organization change. That is why we must look for other strategies to develop personnel.

Delegation is another way to do so. Defined simply, it is the assignment of responsibility or authority to another; it is a frequently used management tool in organizations around the world.[4] Delegation has been conceptualized as a time-management tool,[5] a decision-making process,[6] or a way of getting more things done through others, especially under such conditions as those described at the outset of this chapter.[7] However, few authors have viewed delegation as a way of developing and transforming employees to higher levels of ability and potential.

Although delegation can ease the job of managing and increase the effectiveness of the manager, this is a relatively narrow view of delegation. Some of the more forward-looking authorities mention that delegation can develop individuals' skills and enhance individual involvement. Nonetheless, there is virtually no discussion of what is getting developed through delegation or how or why some leaders seem to be able to develop the potential in others while other leaders cannot.

As with other, more traditional concepts, we examine in this chapter the process of delegation using the full-range perspective.

Delegation and the Development Leader

To understand the process of delegation, we must first examine in greater detail the orientation or perspective of the delegating manager or leader. As noted in Chapter 1, Burns and Bass's[8,9] comprehensive views of leadership identified two types of leadership: nontransactional-transactional and transformational. Transactional leadership occurs when one person takes the initiative in making contact with others for the purposes of an exchange of something valued; that is, leaders approach followers with an eye toward negotiation. Focus of the leader can be either to correct a problem or to establish an agreement to increase the probability of achieving positive results—for example, a constructive transaction. Transformational leadership, on the other hand, is based on more than the compliance of followers or the establishment of agreements: It involves shifts in followers' beliefs, values, needs, and capabilities. Thus from the standpoint of theory building, these two orientations toward leadership offer striking contrasts in philosophy toward development and delegation.

More recently, Kuhnert and Lewis[10] have expanded on Burns and Bass's work by incorporating a developmental framework that identifies three distinct leadership models within the transactional and transformational paradigm. According to their framework, each successive model has its own frame of reference and represents unique ways of understanding leader behavior and, in turn, the impact of the leader's behavior on followers and colleagues. It is through each of these models that we can explore a leader's central preoccupations, focal tasks, and expectations. This information can be extremely helpful in clarifying a developmental view of delegation.

The purpose of presenting these views of delegation through the three models is to help you understand your own personal beliefs about delegation. Ultimately, you can see how this fits with your leadership orientation, whether it occurs in an individual or team context. Leadership and delegation are viewed here through three lenses at different levels of development.

It is important to confront the philosophy and behavior that each model advocates and contrast them with the leader's beliefs and ways of delegating duties, responsibilities, and learning experiences. In applying these models, you may ask: Do I agree with one model more than another? Which model describes the way I think about delegation? Which model offers the surest path toward the development of people who work with me?

Applying Three Leadership Models to Delegation

Model I: The Transactional Operator

The first leader type can be called the *transactional operator*. As Table 2.1 shows, a transactional operator is an individuals who has a personal agenda that is pursued without true concern for the welfare of others. These others are seen as instrumental or detrimental to the accomplishment of the operator's own goals. The operator is, fundamentally, a purely transactional person: He or she enters into agreements to satisfy his or her own personal agenda. This is not to say that all transactional leaders are self-serving and interested only in their own personal initiatives and goals. Rather, at the *lowest* level of development they would concern themselves only with their own personal needs.

Unfortunately, people do not often trust operators: They believe that operators will go beyond permissible bounds to satisfy their own needs. Common wisdom is that an operator is secretly "looking out for number one" despite occasional appearances to the contrary. However, this rather negative view of operators is perhaps too narrow. Successful Model I individuals usually are very good at planning, organizing, directing, and controlling. In fact, Model I individuals may be highly task-oriented, as well as self-interested, and thus can be reasonably effective leaders. They can be positive and productive by expecting and demanding results. Whether they stay within the boundaries of acceptable behavior depends on their values and motives. Also, followers may feel that they have been fairly treated as long as there are enough rewards to go around.

What distinguishes these leaders is not that they have self-serving personal agendas, but that they can pursue tasks and goals only in a way that reflects a characteristically one-sided, narrow view of the world. Their critical shortcoming is an idiosyncratic perspective of the world. They find it impossible to subordinate their goals and agendas to the good of other individuals, the group, or the organization. The limitation of the operator is an inability to internalize another person's view of him or her, and, in the extreme, a lack of concern for such views. This lack of empathic ability makes it impossible for such operators to participate fully in those collective processes that are so essential to the higher order forms of leadership along the full range that we have labeled as transformational leadership, or leadership that is characterized by mutual trust and team spirit. As a consequence, operators are limited in their ability to develop others through delegation. They use delegation

TABLE 2.1 Model I: The Transactional Operator

Major Attributes

- Operates out of own needs and agenda.
- "Manipulates" others and situations.
- Seeks concrete evidence of success.

View of Others

- Others seen as facilitators or obstacles to meeting own goals.
- Others seek own payoffs and can be manipulated with that knowledge.

Leadership Philosophy

- Play by my rules and I will get you what you want.

Follower Philosophy

- Let me know what you want and I will get it for you (if you take care of my needs).

Major Blind Spots in Delegation

- Cannot suspend agenda or coordinate agenda with others.
- Cannot think of others as thinking about him; lack of trust.
- Does not understand that some people will forego immediate payoffs to maintain a relationship of mutual trust or respect.

---

to serve their own purposes, not to develop followers to higher levels of potential.

For operators, delegation is a purely transactional process in that they are likely to delegate responsibility to others in exchange for fulfilling an actual or perceived agreement that emphasizes control, accountability, and clear lines of authority. Although the agreement may be in both parties' best interests, it is not certain how long a transactional leader can continue to strike such a bargain. If, after a time, the operator can no longer reward the individual for entering into agreements, the individual will likely begin to resent the delegation. One reason that delegation is often seen as a "dumping process" is that operators give to their associates those tasks that leaders find undesirable while keeping for themselves tasks that afford the most personal enjoyment, visibility, or payoff, whether it be short- or long-term. When followers and colleagues see delegation in this light, they view it as merely a transfer of tasks, often undesirable ones, rather than as a tool for developing their individual skills, even when such tasks could be viewed in that manner. This can result in a loss of respect for the operator and resentment for what others see as the operator's failure to recognize their potential. There also is a loss because of the failure on the operator's part to apply the full potential of followers to the challenges confronting the organization. This lack of internal perspective and concern for others can have very damaging effects on employees at very early stages in their careers.

Because of the operator's inability to trust others, delegation may be perceived as a risk. Delegation for the transactional operator may trigger feelings of loss of power, authority, meaning, personal expression, and personal achievement. The delegation process is thus seen as a subtraction from one's assets. In other words, what is delegated is seen as removed from the operator's power rather than as something gained: the bringing together of leaders and employees to define tasks, increase productivity, and meet organizational goals. The operator's perspective ignores the role of the leader as "coach" and makes it impossible for the operator to provide associates with the support and guidance necessary to see a task through to completion; the operator thus wholly lacks the facility of development. Remember, the operator is the way he or she is because of a lack of capability, which has not been developed.

Examples of Operator (Model I) Leader Delegation

Andres could not let go of much of what he had to do although he was overloaded with assignments. He was afraid that if he delegated too many of his duties to others, then his boss would believe he was shirking his responsibilities. Furthermore, he usually felt he could get the work done better and in less time if he did it himself, so he delegated tasks only when absolutely compelled to do so.

Beatrice was likewise overloaded, but gave tasks to her followers only if two conditions prevailed: If she felt it would not take too much of her time to explain to them what had to be done and if she judged they would complete the tasks without complaining that they were underpaid because of the additional work.

Charles dumped work on followers whenever possible to lighten his own work load and checked carefully to see that others completed delegated assignments as directed, promising them recognition for success, and reproof for failure. All of these leaders demonstrated a view of others that was dominated by external contingencies, which characterizes the transactional operator.

Model II: The Team Player

The second type of leader is the *team player*. Table 2.2 outlines the strengths and limitations of being a team player and shows that the team player's stock-in-trade is connection and relationships with others. Team players define themselves by how others view them, are motivated to maintain good interpersonal relations among members of the work team or with individual colleagues, and are highly sensitive to how others feel. For the team player, task outcomes or consequences are important for what they reveal about working relationships and for what they contribute to the group's sentiments and feelings of camaraderie. Critical for the team player is how people simultaneously feel about one another on the team. Do they work toward a common goal? Is there a special feeling of satisfaction in working with other team members? Do they perform out of a feeling of mutual respect? Is there a satisfactory degree of team loyalty? The team player is transactional to the extent that his or her efforts are stimulated mainly by his or her need for affection from others; he or she can be seen as transformational to the degree that team outcomes take center stage. Yet what others think of the team player dominates this leader's actions, so he or she is driven by external contingencies like the operator.

With the ability to establish positive interpersonal roles and connections, team players are able to motivate associates through trust, respect, and consideration. For team players, effective delegation is a two-way process that encourages an open exchange of ideas and problem perspectives. In contrast with operators, they are less likely to be directive in style. They understand that people will sometimes delegate responsibility as a means of pursuing group goals, sharing knowledge, and fostering achievements that will engender shared trust and loyalty. For the team player, delegation may also be a way to communicate trust in other team members and respect for their level of skills. The very act of delegating tasks to employees shows that these leaders trust their associates, respect their skills, and have confidence in their abilities and potential for contributing to the organization. Thus delegation for the team player is a way of building and maintaining interpersonal relationships. In turn, team players do not view the delegation of tasks by the manager or leader as an "off-loading" of undesirable responsibilities. They can receive both good and poor task assignments, which may or may not have high payoffs. This view stems from the level of trust established in the team's relationships.

Although team players can delegate through transactional agreements, they also can capitalize on mutual feelings of trust, respect, or affection in the exercise of leadership. Leaders who are team players (Model II) have a broader perspective of delegation than do their operator (Model I) counterparts. Whereas operators are constrained to view the world as a place in which delegation is done to gain personal

TABLE 2.2 Model II: The Team Player

Major Attributes

- Very sensitive to how he or she is viewed or experienced internally by others.
- Self-definition derives in part from how he or she is experienced by others.
- Lives in a world of interpersonal roles and connections.

View of Others

- Thinks others define themselves by how he or she experiences them, so feels responsible for others' self-esteem.

Leadership Philosophy

- Show associates consideration and respect and they will follow you anywhere.
- The "unit" and team morale are paramount.

Follower Philosophy

- I will do what it takes to earn your respect, but in return you must let me know how you feel about me.

Major Blind Spots in Delegation

- Unable to define self independent of others' view or independent of role expectations.
- Unable to make difficult decisions that entail a loss of respect.

advantage, team players see delegation as a way of strengthening relationships, as well as improving follower contributions and satisfaction. This does not suggest that personal gain would not be desirable, but that it is not predominant in the leader's thinking.

Despite the broader and added influence possessed by team players in comparison with operators, team players also have a critical flaw. Their perspectives are unduly influenced by concerns for their relationships, connections, and loyalties. In other words, team players are disproportionately controlled by others' views of them. Because follower acceptance and support are paramount for team players, they are unlikely to delegate problems that may entail a loss of respect. It is unlikely that team players would delegate authority that might undermine the work teams' cohesiveness, even where a temporary loss of cohesiveness may be necessary to achieve a particular critical task. Team players can and do delegate for the development of followers, but the delegated activities are concentrated on the enhancement of the interpersonal commitments among the work group members and not to foster autonomy, individuality, and growth. Teams may be strengthened, but the leadership does not transform its individual members. To sacrifice team goals for the good of specific individuals is a difficult, if not impossible, assignment for Model II leaders.

Examples of Team Player (Model II) Leader Delegation

Dan kept his team informed about any new assignments that his boss asked him whether he could handle. He would turn to his team to ask if he should accept the new responsibilities and if the team would be ready, willing, and able to help him. Delegation of assignment was accomplished through negotiation with his goal of avoiding dissatisfaction for any of his associates.

Emilia complained to her team members about being overloaded and asked them if it was all right to off-load some of these tasks to them. Emilia would complete the tasks if she sensed any resistance from her followers.

Frank met weekly with his team to discuss new assignments that were allocated on the basis of consensual discussions. Frank was determined that all members were always satisfied with their assignments. Maintaining group harmony was quite important to him.

In the context of the full-range model, our team leader is demonstrating an integration of contingent reward and individual consideration. Yet such leaders have not established a stronger inner sense of direction or belief that characterizes the higher end of the full-range model of leadership.

Model III: The Transformational "Self-Defining" Leader

The third model of leadership is not simply an alternative to the others, it transcends them. As summarized in Table 2.3, Model III describes the characteristics and outlook of "self-defining" leaders. Such leaders tend to be self-defining by having strong internalized values and ideals. They are able and willing to forgo personal payoffs and, when necessary, to risk loss of respect and affection to pursue actions that they are convinced are right. These leaders have a sense of self-worth that is self-determined: not in a self-serving way, but in a manner that allows them to make tough, unpopular decisions. They exhibit a strong sense of inner purpose and direction, which often is viewed by others as the great strength of their leadership.

Such transformational, self-defining, leaders are able to energize followers to take actions that support higher purposes rather than their own self-interest, and they are able to create an environment in which people are encouraged to address problems and opportunities with

TABLE 2.3 Model III: The Transformational "Self-Defining" Leader

Major Attributes
- Concerned about values, ethics, standards, and long-term goals.
- Self-contained and self-defining.

View of Others
- Able to grant others autonomy and individuality.
- Concerned about others without feeling responsible for their self-esteem.

Leadership Philosophy
- Articulates clear long-term standards and goals.
- Bases decisions on broad view of the situation, not just immediate factors.

Follower Philosophy
- Give me autonomy to pursue broad organizational goals.
- Do not ask me to compromise my own values or standards of self-respect, unless it is for the good of the group or organization.

Major Blind Spots in Delegation
- Can be too self-contained and reluctant to delegate.
- May become isolated in leadership role.

creativity and personal commitment. Because self-defining leaders are guided by their internal values and standards rather than their needs, relationships, or purely external standards, they are able and quite likely to base their delegation decisions in a much broader context. They can consider the long-term goals and interests of the organization, as well as of the individual, rather than being shackled by immediate or short-range goals. Thus the self-defining leader is the first leader who comfortably can delegate autonomy and individuality to others and develop them in ways that can enhance learning and build a high-performance team and work environment. Unlike operators, who delegate to accomplish certain goals to enhance their own worth, or team players, who delegate to feel appreciated by their colleagues and to maintain their own self-esteem, self-defining leaders are transformational in the confidence with which they delegate to accomplish higher-order objectives. In the process, they help to move associates closer to becoming self-defining, transformational leaders themselves.

Note that delegation in exchange for personal gain or for work team cohesion is not discarded as one moves from transactional to transformational leadership. Obviously, we all are transactional in pursuit of personal goals at one time or another. Many of us cultivate team play. Through self-definition, however, the transformational leader is able to construct a broader understanding and perspective of development. This leader has the ability to see the organization's larger mission, as well as followers' needs and demands. Specifically, the transformational, self-defining leader can separate the needs of individual followers from the needs of the leader and the team and, at critical times, align many of those needs to maximize both performance and development.

Examples of Self-Defining (Model III) Leader Delegation

Gloria discussed with each of her department members their career plans in the organization and whenever possible assigned them tasks that fit their career plans as well as contributed to the organization's needs to get the work done expeditiously. Emphasis in these discussions was on continuously striving to improve performance potential.

Henry focused the attention of each of his team members on the importance of taking on challenging assignments that met not only their own needs, but also those of team members and ultimately those of the organization.

Ignacio was willing to put in the extra time to coach those of his colleagues who otherwise might not be able to do the job as well as he could do it if he did not delegate the work to them. He also was willing to risk early mistakes to develop associates who could do the work better in the future. He worked with others to establish a long-term perspective on what they could achieve in their careers individually and collectively by enhancing one another's perspectives and potential.

Models Parallel Moral Development

The three models of leadership discussed above parallel three stages of moral development. Model I operators are arrested in their development at the level of judging what is right and wrong in terms of whether what is done is a gain or loss, a reward or punishment for themselves. They are purely transactional in their approach. It is the least mature stage of development. Model II team players judge on the basis of what others will think of their actions as leaders; in the extreme, they are constrained by such judgments. Model III self-defining leaders are most mature in their moral and cognitive development. They are most transformational. They are more prepared to take full responsibility for their actions, judging what is right or wrong in terms of balance and integration of conflicting individual, team, organizational, and societal interests. Their basis for evaluation and decision making is likely to be internal standards that are considered right or morally correct. They will more likely choose courses of action not because they necessarily serve their own best interests or the current interests of the followers, but because the choice is the right thing to do.

Note that Model III leaders have the capacity to view the world at a higher level of morality. Yet for many reasons they may choose to operate at a lower level. Thus given the available evidence on the moral development of leaders, we can say that Model III leaders have the capacity to base their decisions on the interests of the group rather than on their own interests. However, under pressure or for reasons beyond their control, they may choose to operate as Model I or II leaders. The lack of maturity and capability of Model I leaders significantly reduces the probability that they will make decisions for the good of the group.

Effective Delegation for Development

One purpose of presenting these three models is to help managers classify others and thus determine their stage of development. The next question is, How do these models of leadership help managers become better delegators? The three models presented above represent successive stages in the potential development of every person. In other words, how you delegate says a good deal about your own level of development as a leader. Thus each model has important implications for the development of others and, more generally, for the development of leader effectiveness.

In applying this developmental framework, managers must realize that no model of leadership or of delegation is necessarily sufficient. The appropriate leadership and delegation style is a function of the leader, the associate's needs and abilities, and the leader's objectives. This view thus may help to explain why any one approach to delegation may be inappropriate for a given situation or inadequate for the development of all associates.

For example, in an environment that calls for highly structured planning and careful control, the operator's style of leadership and delegation may be most appropriate in the short term. But if the environment is one that values and requires a cohesive team spirit and significant cooperation, then the team player's style of leadership and delegation may be most appropriate. In an organization that highly values individuals who work interdependently toward common goals, then the transformational leader is the one who fits most readily. What is important is not that there is one correct style, but the ability of the leader to distinguish the appropriate style for the environment and to make choices about the leadership and delegation approach that is most likely to fit the context. Ultimately, a leader needs to be able to operate at the level of Model III, even though the leader might sometimes consider Models I and II appropriate. Only the self-defining leader can operate at all three levels.

In addition to the environment, leaders must understand that the developmental level of followers also affects the appropriate leadership and delegation style. An approach may not work because followers have not reached a phase in their own development where they understand and are motivated by higher-level considerations. This is not the fault of the leader or the environment. For example, individuals who are operators may not be in a position to benefit from delegated activities that focus primarily on cooperation and group goals. To motivate these people, the leader may initially have to appeal to their basic and lower-level transactional nature by emphasizing the advantage of such activities in terms of their personal interests, rather than appealing to their status on a mutually supportive team. Ultimately, however, development of those individuals to a level on the full range must come from delegation of those activities that drive them to confront the limitations of their own self-interests and to see how there may be greater gains through a broader perspective.

Although both the environment and the individual will influence the appropriate leadership and delegation styles, what should also be clear is that the leader's capacity to make choices among the appropriate styles also is paramount. Unfortunately, in the paradigm presented, Model I leaders are not able to make such a choice because they have not developed to a level that allows for an understanding of the perspective of Model II or Model III leaders. Similarly, Model II leaders are unable to fully understand Model III leadership, although they remain able to reflect on and appreciate Model I perspectives. Thus, only the Model III leader has the capacity to understand and make choices among the three models.

The Model I and Model II leaders' inabilities to reflect on all three models of leadership ultimately limits their capacity to delegate effectively as a means of developing employees. For example, leaders who are operators will not recognize the opportunities for followers' professional development that may result from delegation. Because the perspective of such leaders is their own personal agenda, they will be unable to recognize the overall value of delegation to individuals or to the organization as a whole. The value in delegation can accrue only from personal payoff to the leader.

At the next level, leaders who are team players will recognize the advantages to followers of delegation, but only if such delegation can be viewed as fair and does not risk violating team cohesion. Values of team players are shared values, or those that are derived from their connection to the group. Team players will embrace organizational values if their team adopts those values as standard. If team players perceive a growing divergence between the interests of their own unit and those of the organization at large, then organizational values are likely to be sacrificed.

The same risk does not exist with Model III transformational leaders. For these leaders, delegation becomes a question of defining and providing followers with opportunities to engage in activities that explore the compatibility between organizational and personal standards and strongly held values. In other words, transformational leaders are able to delegate activities and tasks that may be contrary to their individual agendas or that may be perceived as inequitable to other team members, if such delegation ultimately will increase the individual's professional development while enhancing organizational functioning. Often, what may be perceived by followers as inequitable is not when considered through the leader's long-term vision of developing followers to their highest potential.

The only way to help a follower develop is to understand how he or she views the world and then help him or her in confronting experiences that illustrate the limitations of that view. Thus, the ability to fully use delegation as a developmental tool requires that leaders understand that delegation of specific types of activities is necessary if followers are to advance to the next level of development. Delegation by abdication of responsibility will not develop others.

From the viewpoint of organizational growth and maturity, the development of employees who are able to become self-defining or transformational leaders is fundamental to long-range survival. In other words, leaders must aspire to more than just getting others to follow: They must see the development of their associates as their personal responsibility if the organization is to grow and maximize its potential. It is not enough to motivate operators to be good managers; they also must learn how to be a part of the shared commitment and mutual trust of a work team. Similarly, team players must transcend their loyalty to the work team by embracing and articulating organizational values. According to Chester Barnard, the ultimate moral act of the executive is to delegate responsibly because "organizations can only endure in accordance with the breadth of morality by which they are governed."[11]

This chapter has explored delegation as a method of professionally developing employees within the context of the full-range model of leadership. Three different leadership models have been proposed by which to understand delegation. Each model starts with different attributes of leaders based on their perspective-taking abilities and leadership philosophies. Differences in these models lead to very different orientations toward delegation.

The transactional operators of Model I, for example, are motivated by self-interest and see others as similarly motivated; delegation is thus a means of influence, control, and personal gain. Although not rejecting this perspective, the team players of Model II are able to define themselves through the eyes of others and use delegation as a way to gain trust, commitment, and loyalty among group members. The transformational, self-defining leaders of Model III take the team players' views a step farther, believing that the needs of their teams are best served through the attainment of individual needs that serve worthwhile purposes. Such leaders thus can see delegation as a means of individual as well as organizational development because they know that exceptional organizational performance rests on the entire organization's creativity and dedication to its mission. In sum, transformational, self-defining leaders realize their responsibility for the development of future leaders.

In the final analysis, how one leads says much about how one delegates, how one delegates says much about the quality of the people being led, and the quality of followers says much about a leader. A leader thus must know him- or herself before the development of others through delegation can be understood. It is through the process of delegation that one is revealed as a leader. Ultimately, delegation is not only a tool to be used in the professional development of followers, but also a way to develop oneself as a leader.

We next examine how the full range of leadership can be direct or indirect.

Notes

1. Tritt, F. (1978). Delegation—the essence of management. *Personnel Journal*, pp. 528-530. This article outlines reasons for delegation.

2. Jennings, G. (1971). *The mobile manager*. New York: Free Press. This is one of the first books to comment on the importance of assigning managers to challenging tasks that benefit the organization.

3. McCall, M. W., Lombardo, M. M., & Morrison, M. (1988). *The lessons of experience: How successful executives develop on the job*. Lexington, MA: Lexington.

4. Nelson, R. B. (1988). *Delegation: The power of letting go*. Glenview, IL: Scott, Foresman. The author of this book presents the essential steps of delegation and explains how to avoid crucial mistakes in order to achieve desired results.

5. Jenks, J. M., & Kelly, J. M. (1985). *Don't do. Delegate!* Toronto, CA: Franklin Watts.

6. Carrie, R. L. (1986). Predictors and consequences of delegation. *Academy of Management Journal, 29*, 754-774. This work found that supervisors' perceptions of subordinates, the volume of supervisors' workloads, and the importance of decisions were significant predictors of delegation.

7. LeBoeuf, M. (1979). *Working smart: How to accomplish more in half the time*. New York: Warner. The author explores various strategies for improving managerial skills.

8. Burns, J. M. (1978). *Leadership*. New York: Harper & Row. This book sketches the leadership styles of many political leaders.

9. Bass, B. M. (1985). *Leadership and performance beyond expectations*. New York: Free Press. The author explores transformational leadership and its impact on followers.

10. Kuhnert, K. W., & Lewis, P. L. (1987). Transactional and transformational leadership: A constructive/developmental analysis. *Academy of Management Review, 12*, 648-657.

11. Wolf, W. B. (1973). *Conversations with Chester I. Barnard*. Ithaca, NY: Cornell University Press. The author interviews Barnard.

3

Indirect Leadership

TRANSFORMATIONAL LEADERSHIP AT A DISTANCE

FRANCIS J. YAMMARINO
Center for Leadership Studies,
School of Management, SUNY Binghamton

EXECUTIVE SUMMARY

Direct leadership, or the relationships and interactions between a focal leader and his or her immediate followers (or direct reports), has been the subject of extensive research for leaders at various organizational levels and in a multitude of settings. In contrast, our knowledge and understanding of *indirect leadership*, or the influence of a focal leader on individuals not reporting directly to him or her, is much more limited. Studies of the effects of this "leadership at a distance" have typically focused on world class leaders or chief executive officers (CEOs) of major corporations. But indirect leadership is not confined to the realm of these highly visible leaders. Rather, leaders at all levels in organizations can influence the development and effectiveness of individual followers at lower levels regardless of whether the followers report directly to those leaders. By extension, indirect leadership can be displayed upward by followers to higher-level leaders and horizontally across co-workers and units. The purpose of this chapter is to suggest some ways that transformational leaders, regardless of their organizational position, can use the Four I's—individualized consideration, intellectual stimulation, inspirational motivation, and idealized influence—to influence others from a distance. Transformational leadership at a distance is discussed in terms of two models of indirect leadership and three key facets of indirect leadership. The intended outcomes are the development of others, the creation of new leaders, and the fostering of performance beyond expectations at various organizational levels by the focal leader regardless of his or her position. The key point of this chapter is that transformational leadership is not only direct and top-down, but also can be observed in organizations indirectly, from the bottom up, and horizontally.

Introduction

This chapter's focus is on *indirect* leadership or the influence of a focal leader on the development and performance of individuals who do *not* report directly to that leader. More specifically, the intent is to discuss this "leadership at a distance" in terms of transformational leadership and its constituent Four I's of individualized consideration, intellectual stimulation, inspirational motivation, and idealized influence. Through their use, transformational leadership is discussed as a philosophy and approach for a leader to employ for developing followers, transforming these followers into leaders, and fostering the performance of followers that transcends expected or established standards. The leaders here are not only those at the highest managerial levels in organizations, but also those who are both formal and informal, regardless of their position or rank. Such leaders have opportunities through their transformational behaviors to develop followers at organizational levels that do not directly report to them. By extension, indirect leadership is also viewed in terms of *upward* influence (that is, followers or leaders affect leaders at higher levels) and *horizontal* influence (that is, followers or leaders influence others such as co-workers from a distance).

This chapter has four objectives. First, we will examine transformational leadership and indirect leadership. Second, we will then take an overview of relevant work on indirect leadership; two resulting models of this phenomenon are presented. Third, we will see extensions of indirect leadership via upward and horizontal influence. Fourth and finally, key facets of indirect leadership built on the Four I's will be described for developing others from a distance.

Transformational and Indirect Leadership

Transformational leadership and the Four I's that it comprises have been the subject of extensive research and writing.[1] Transformational leadership goes beyond the attempts of some leaders to satisfy the current needs of followers by focusing on transactions or exchanges through contingent reward behavior. Transformational leaders instead attempt to raise the needs of followers and promote positive change for individuals, groups, and organizations. Instead of responding to his or her own immediate self-interests and those of followers, the transformational leader arouses heightened awareness and interests in the group or organization, increases confidence, and moves followers gradually from concerns for existence to concerns for achievement and growth. In short, transformational leaders develop their followers to the point where followers are able to take on leadership roles and perform beyond established standards or goals.

To accomplish this transformation of individuals, groups, and organizations, transformational leaders rely on the four sets of behaviors that we already have identified as the Four I's of transformational leadership. Clearly, these can be used to develop immediate followers as well as others at levels removed from the focal leader.

In the same way, some authorities have referred to transformational leadership behaviors as embodied in the Four I's and related concepts as *leadership* rather than simply *management*.[2] John Kotter defined the latter as coping with complexity by means of planning and budgeting, organizing and staffing, and controlling and problem solving. Alternately, he indicated that the former as coping with change by means of setting a direction (vision), aligning people to that direction (communicating the vision), and motivating and inspiring people (moving toward the vision)—that is, transformational leadership. Likewise, Abraham Zaleznik argued that managers and leaders have different focuses; they think, work, and interact with others differently; and have different personalities and developmental experiences. He viewed leadership as the willingness of people in higher-level positions to use their power in the best interests of their employees and their organizations. Zaleznik noted that this implies a variety of crucial differences between leaders and managers. For example, a manager is concerned with how decisions get made and how communication flows, whereas a leader is concerned with what decisions get made and what gets communicated. A manager focuses on process, while a leader focuses on imaginative ideas and stimulating others to work hard and create a new reality from those ideas. Clearly, in discussing leaders, Kotter and Zaleznik are describing transformational leaders whose behaviors can influence the development of both immediate followers and others at a distance.

Note, however, that most of the research and writings on transformational leadership focus on the influence of such leaders on their *immediate* groups of followers. So, it is well documented that transformational leaders have a positive and direct effect on the development and performance of both their direct reports and work units.[3] Moreover, there have been some attempts to assess the indirect influences of such leaders on individuals one or more levels removed from them. These studies of indirect transformational leadership, or transformational leadership at a distance, however, have generally been limited to world class leaders such as Mahatma Gandhi, Winston Churchill, Dag Hammarskjöld, and Martin Luther King, Jr., or highly visible CEOs such as Lee Iacocca (Chrysler), Jack Welch (General Electric), and John DeButts (AT&T). Little is known about indirect leadership in general and indirect transformational leadership in particular for focal leaders who do not hold these prominent positions. Moreover, little has been written about the influence of followers on leaders at a distance or about the influence of individuals on others horizontally, again at a distance. Nevertheless, some information is available that is relevant to the current discussion.

Direct Leadership

Leaders can directly interact with their immediate followers. Here we see supervisors in direct contact with their subordinates face-to-face, by telephone, or in memo. There are no human or mechanical intermediaries to filter the interaction. Characteristics of such direct interaction are:

1. Communication ordinarily can be two-way.
2. Leader and followers know one another personally and must be prepared for their interactions to be consistent with their particular and unique relations.
3. The number of followers per leader must be highly limited.
4. Leadership works directly with followers to enhance their willingness and ability to do their assignments efficiently.
5. Interactions can frequently be spontaneous, reactive, adaptive, and not necessarily require long-term commitments.
6. The authenticity of favorable impressions will depend on face-to-face evaluation.

Indirect Leadership Through Intermediaries

Leadership can be indirect and filtered through intermediaries. Thus, second-line supervisors may influence operating employees in their departments by directly interacting with first-line supervisors who in turn directly interact with the operating employees. Or, as will be discussed later, some of these levels may be bypassed.

The numbers of intermediaries multiply for the leader in larger multilevel hierarchies. Characteristics of such mediated leadership include the following:

1. Two-way communication is more difficult; one-way communication becomes more common.
2. Leader and followers are less likely to know one another personally.
3. The number of followers per leader can be expanded; this is accompanied by expansions in the number of intermediaries.
4. The interactions are likely to be less spontaneous.
5. Less short-term, momentary issues are likely to be involved.
6. Spontaneous action and reaction become difficult if not impossible.
7. The leader has to consider more factors that are likely to be beyond his or her control.
8. Intermediate filtering has to be monitored.
9. Manipulative impression management can be practiced.

Indirect Leadership via Mass Media

Leadership also can be brought about through the intermediation of mass media. The politician or leader of a large organizational conglomerate needs to be able to influence his or her large population of constituents or thousands of employees through the mediation of bulletins, videotapes, or other mass media and staged events. Communications are one-way for the most part. Even with live audiences, follower questioning is limited. Impression management is the rule rather than the exception. Follower reactions are gained from surveys, staff interviews, and expert advice. But in addition, the leader here must create a following and be able to extrapolate from events, experiences, and advice to sense employees' collective mood. This mood must then be addressed with conviction.[4]

Direct leadership and leadership mediated through others or mass media can display the full range of leadership illustrated in Table 3.1.

Models of Indirect Leadership

The vast literature on leadership, summarized by Bernard M. Bass,[5] is replete with studies of and conclusions about direct leadership and the direct influences of transformational leaders on their immediate followers. A general model of *direct leadership* is presented in Figure 3.1, which shows three levels of management in an organization and the direct influences of higher-level individual leaders on lower-level leaders. These direct leadership effects are essentially manifested in two ways in the organization or larger collective of individuals.

First, leader-follower relationships are direct and may occur in groups comprising a focal leader and his or her immediate subordinates. Thus, as depicted in the figure, Boss A forms a group with Managers B and C; Manager B forms a group with Supervisors D and E; and Manager C forms a group with Supervisors F and G. Transformational leadership behaviors and influences, for example, occur within each group such that a focal leader develops his or her immediate followers as a group. For example, a focal leader may provide the responsibility to head a new project at different times to all of his or her immediate followers, thus using delegation to develop his or her group of followers in a similar manner.

Second, leader-follower relationships are direct and may occur in dyads (one-to-one relationships) comprising a focal leader and each of his or her direct reports. Therefore, as the figure also depicts, Boss A forms dyads with Managers B and C; Manager B forms dyads with Supervisors D and E; and Manager C forms dyads with Supervisors F and G. In this case, transformational leadership behaviors and influences occur within each dyad such that a focal leader develops his or her immediate followers in a one-to-one way. For example, a focal leader may provide an opportunity to head a new project to one follower, and may allow another follower to make a presentation to a group of potential customers. This decision to differentiate developmental experiences between followers is linked to individualized consideration. Note, however, that for both the group- and dyad-based views of direct leadership, Boss A's leadership behaviors and influences relative to Supervisors D to G are irrelevant. The behaviors and influences may be nonexistent, or they have been ignored for a variety of reasons in much previous work.[6] Nevertheless, it is known from previous leadership work that an upper-level boss can establish a role model of exceptionally high standards for his or her division that transcends all levels of management. Therefore, in both leadership research and training programs, it is surprising that this form of indirect influence rarely receives proper attention.

Let us now turn to the case where connections between leaders at one level and followers at one or more levels removed have been examined—that is, the case of *indirect* leadership, or the relationships between Boss A and Supervisors D, E, F, and G of Figure 3.1. As mentioned, most previous work on such relationships is derived from studies of world class transformational leaders or highly visible transformational CEOs. The

TABLE 3.1 Leadership and Media

Nontransactional or Transactional Type	Direct	Indirect	
		Mediated via Others	Mediated via Mass Media
Laissez-Faire	I'm sorry that I can't help you at all with your problem.	The boss hinted to me that he was not really interested in seeing you about your problem because he didn't think he could help.	Our strategy is dictated by the fact that problems often disappear if left alone.
Passive Management by Exception	Let me know if you can't manage it yourself.	I'll see your staff if they really think it is necessary.	If it ain't broke, don't fix it.
Active Management by Exception	There are too many flaws in this design. You should use the procedures we've discussed to produce an accurate design.	I judge from the file of customer complaints that your department needs to be more concerned about product quality.	If someone isn't watching the store, we'll be robbed.
Contingent Reward	I'll see that those of you who finish on time will get to select your next project.	I'd like to propose that to improve your people's turnaround time on orders, we arrange a gain-sharing bonus for everyone in your department.	Our policy is to give a fair day's pay for a fair day's work.

Transformational	Direct	Indirect	
		Mediated via Others	Mediated via Mass Media
Individualized Consideration	Here's an assignment that will help you understand how our organization works.	A policy will be introduced to require that all employees in your organization learn multiple job roles to enhance their development potential.	We continuously work to better align our staff's interest with the organization's interest.
Intellectual Stimulation	Are you sure that's the root of the problem or should we broaden our perspectives?	Let's ask each employee at every level what one thing would make it possible for him or her to do his or her job better.	Never kill an idea.
Inspirational Motivation	I know your work, and I'm convinced you can do it.	I'm proud of the organization we've built together.	We are going to be the best of the breed in our industry.
Idealized Influence	We must continue to follow his or her vision and to maintain the trust we have in one another.	Consider each day how your actions symbolize the organization's values in everything you do.	We've been started on our way; now it is up to us to fulfill the vision.

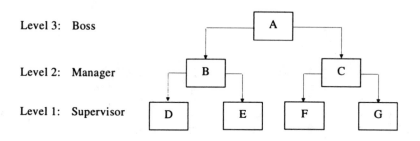

Level 3: Boss

Level 2: Manager

Level 1: Supervisor

Groups in collective[1]:   A-B/C; B-D/E; C-F/G
Dyads in collective[2]:   A-B, A-C; B-D, B-E; C-F, C-G

Figure 3.1   A General Model of Direct Leadership

NOTES: [1] Letter before dash denotes leader; letters after dash denotes group of followers.
[2] Letter before dash denotes leader; letter after dash denotes follower in each dyad.

leadership tenure of such individuals typically involved dramatic organizational, national, or international changes, including the development and implementation of a vision, a realignment of values and
norms, and promoted change of the status quo. The context in these
cases is generally broad-ranging, a crisis is often present, and the
resultant changes are system-wide in terms of both mission and culture.
These transformational leaders addressed the crises and motivated all
followers—whether immediate or more distant—to pursue alternative
and creative courses of action that resulted in dramatic and successful
societal or organizational change. Additional evidence for these cases
of indirect leadership can be observed in the alignment of followers
with the vision and mission at varying levels of organizations or soci-
eties. Further details and results of these studies can be found in the
previously cited work. At this point, it suffices to say that the leaders
displayed behaviors represented by the Four I's of transformational
leadership and influences on both immediate and distant followers'
development and performance were extraordinary.

But what is known about the indirect transformational leadership of
individuals who are neither world class leaders nor CEOs? Are division
directors, general managers, first-line supervisors, or project and team
leaders also capable of influencing followers who are not their direct
reports or immediate subordinates? In other words, is our current
knowledge about the effects of indirect leadership generalizable or
relevant for focal leaders who are not at the very top of organizations

or social movements? Although a dearth of research is available on these issues, there are some suggestions that, in general, leadership effects can be manifested at levels removed from a focal leader regardless of his or her position, and that, in particular, transformational leadership at any level has influences at lower levels beyond immediate followers.

Cascading and Bypass Models of Indirect Leadership

To focus the discussion, we will examine two general models of indirect leadership. In both cases, the relevant research has focused on transformational or transformational-like leadership behaviors of individuals in a variety of positions at various organizational levels. Thus, these models suggest two views of indirect transformational leadership that are applicable for focal leaders at higher and lower levels in organizations. The two general models of indirect leadership are referred to as the *cascading model*[7] and the *bypass model*.[8] Both are shown in Figure 3.2.

The cascading model of indirect leadership has considerable support in the literature on leadership. "Cascading" refers to the modeling of behavior of leaders at successively lower levels of management. (This model directly contrasts the "alternating" model in which strong leaders at one level generate weak leaders at a lower level, who in turn permit the development of strong leaders at a level below.) As a result, from a cascading perspective, a focal leader at a particular level has influence on followers at lower levels beyond his or her direct reports—that is, indirect leadership. As depicted in the left portion of Figure 3.2, Boss A has a direct influence and relationship (the solid line) with Managers B and C, who then model the behaviors of Boss A. In turn, Supervisors D and E model the behaviors of Manager B, and Supervisors F and G model the behaviors of Manager C. Clearly, Supervisors D and E experience the direct leadership of Manager B, and Supervisors F and G experience the direct leadership of Manager C (not shown in the figure). However, the leadership of Managers B and C is actually a manifestation of Boss A's leadership. Thus, Supervisors D, E, F, and G are influenced indirectly by Boss A through Managers B and C. This indirect leadership of Boss A on Supervisors D, E, F, and G is depicted by dashed lines. In this case, the supervisors have been developed indirectly by Boss A; the boss's leadership has cascaded down through at least two levels of the organization. In essence, one or more boss-supervisors groups based on indirect leadership have been established within the larger organizational collective. Working through direct

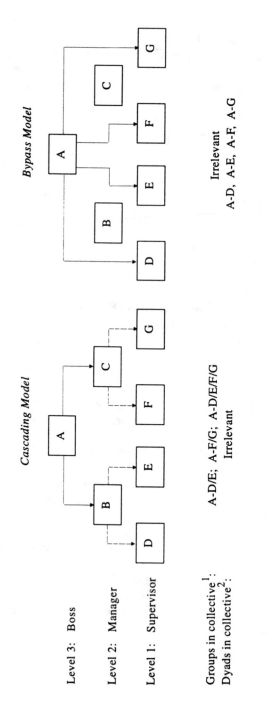

Figure 3.2 Two General Models of Indirect Leadership

NOTES: The dashed lines represent the indirect influence of the Boss on the Supervisor through the Managers.

[1] Letter before dash denotes leader; letters after dash denote group of followers.

[2] Letter before dash denotes leader; letter after dash denotes follower in each dyad.

relationships with the managers, Boss A has indirect leadership effects on a one-to-group basis with the supervisors. For example, through observation in meetings and informal interactions and modeling of behaviors, Supervisors D, E, F, and G may adopt the transformational style of Boss A.

More specifically, Bernard Bass has reviewed research on goal setting, rewards, and punishments that indicates that those outcomes at one (higher) level generally are followed by similar and related goals, rewards, and punishments at successive lower levels. J. M. Burns noted that dedication, caring, and participative behaviors by transformational leaders are multiplied outward from the leaders at various other levels by their disciples. Likewise, Bass and his colleagues have demonstrated the cascading effects of transformational leadership from one level to the next and so on.

Note that the cascading model may work in conjunction with differential selection processes in organizations. For instance, a supervisor at a lower level can be self-selected, selected by the higher-level manager, or selected by the organization (in effect, by the boss) to match and be compatible with his or her manager. Alternatively, particular leadership behaviors (for example, those that are transformational) may be reinforced by the norms and culture of the organization or its various subunits. Therefore, cascading as a form of indirect leadership may be the result of modeling (e.g., supervisor identifies with and adopts the manager's or boss's leadership behavior); selection (as noted above); the subculture of norms, beliefs, and values in which leaders operate; or some combination of the three.

The second model of indirect leadership, the bypass model, also has support in the literature on leadership. "Bypass" refers to a level of management being skipped in terms of relationships between leaders and followers. In other words, a focal leader's leadership behaviors influence nonimmediate subordinates—that is, indirect leadership—without operating through his or her direct reports. As depicted in the right portion of Figure 3.2, Boss A exerts indirect leadership with his or her nonimmediate followers by forming direct relationships (solid lines) with Supervisors D, E, F, and G. These relationships are dyadic or one-to-one in nature, and so may not all necessarily be of the same quality; a boss may be responding to different needs of each supervisor. For example, although Boss A develops Supervisors D, E, F, and G on a one-to-one basis, Supervisor D may require more time and support than Supervisor G from Boss A. Thus, the dyad of Boss A and Supervisor D may operate quite differently from that of Boss A and Supervisor G within the larger organizational collective. It is important to note that

Boss A does not bypass Managers B and C in terms of all behaviors or issues. Rather, for some issues or developmental purposes, Boss A may work through the managers (as in the cascading model in the left portion of the figure), while in other instances Boss A may use a bypass approach to indirect leadership. In essence, in the bypass model, managers are skipped in order for multiple boss-supervisor dyads to operate in which the boss engages in direct one-to-one relationships with individuals at removed levels. For example, Boss A may serve as the mentor for Supervisor D or the organizational champion for the work of Supervisor G instead of those roles being fulfilled by Managers B and C, respectively.

More specifically, MacDonald Dumas, Fred Dansereau, and their colleagues have demonstrated the operation of the bypass model in organizations on leadership dimensions similar to individualized consideration and inspirational motivation as well as in terms of the measured effectiveness of followers. They found, as will be explained, that this model of indirect leadership was more likely to operate in differing degrees in production, adaptive (e.g., research and development, or R&D), and managerial areas of organizations rather than in maintenance (e.g., quality control) and technical support (e.g., design and engineering) areas.

The bypass model, involving considerable "social distance" between leaders and followers, worked particularly well in explaining dyadic relationships in adaptive and managerial collectives or settings. The bypass model can be expected to operate more frequently when roles (jobs) are completely isolated and insulated from the continuous technological process. (Previous work in such settings has suggested that individuals farther away hierarchically from the focal leader tend to identify to a greater extent with the leader than those individuals in close proximity to the leader who have had an opportunity to more adequately evaluate and interact with the leader.) Likewise, in terms of the bypass model in Figure 3.2, the role of the manager (the second-level leader in the figure) in leadership-related matters can be expected to decrease as the distance of the unit from the continuous technological process increases, to the point where the boss (Level 3 in the figure) may be a more relevant focus of attention for leadership influences on the supervisor (Level 1). Thus in terms of training, in units closer to the technological process (e.g., production units), the focus of leadership training should be manager-supervisor dyads or relationships between first- and second-level leaders. In units that are far removed from the technological process (e.g., R&D units), boss-supervisor dyads or relationships between third- and first-level leaders ought to be the focus of leadership-training programs.

Summary

To summarize, the key ideas for indirect leadership thus far are as follow:

- Transformational leaders need not occupy the highest or most prominent positions to influence others.
- Transformational leaders can occupy a variety of positions at various levels of organizations and be formal or informal leaders.
- Transformational leadership can be top-down and either indirect or direct.
- Indirect transformational leadership can be understood in terms of both the cascading and bypass models.

Extensions of the Indirect Models

Upward Influence of Leadership

Whether direct or indirect, leadership is difficult to comprehend without understanding *followership*—that is, the compliance of followers, which is instrumental to the completion of tasks and the socioemotional acceptance of the leadership effort. Thus, followers (subordinates) can influence leaders in a variety of ways. For example, they can control the nature of the feedback from their leaders, their expectations can affect the performance of their leaders, and their perceptions can constrain or enhance the potential for their leaders' success.[9] In other words, followers may exert a considerable amount of *upward influence* on their leaders that is an important contribution to organizational effectiveness. Kipnis and his colleagues[10] identified key upward-influence tactics of followers, including assertiveness, reasoning, bargaining about the exchange of benefits, appealing to higher authority, forming coalitions, and using friendliness, ingratiation, and flattery. These tactics have been demonstrated in a variety of research efforts and have been shown to alter the behavior of leaders, impact their performance, and affect organizations' success.

Upward influence, as addressed in previous leadership work, is thus a *reverse* form of direct leadership. In other words, in terms of Figure 3.1, the directional arrows are reversed so that Supervisors D and E have a direct upward influence on Manager B, Supervisors F and G have a direct impact on Manager C, and Managers B and C have a direct influence on Boss A. For example, Supervisor D may discover a cost-saving production process that permits Manager B to shift resources to other areas or individuals, enhancing the unit's overall effectiveness. But it is also possible that Supervisor D's innovation may permit Boss A to redirect resources and so on under his or her control. Therefore the possibility for reverse and indirect upward influence also exists.

In particular, *reverse cascading* and *reverse bypass* models of indirect upward influence are plausible. These models are presented in Figure 3.3. Note that the directions of these arrowheads are reversed from those in Figure 3.2. Likewise, the potential for group-based and dyad-based upward influences at a distance are depicted in Figure 3.3. From the perspective of the reverse cascading model, the supervisor with a new piece of information, a great innovation, or a particular expertise, can have a profound direct effect on his or her immediate manager as well as a significant indirect influence on his or her boss. In this case, one or more groups within the larger organizational collective may experience improved effectiveness. From the perspective of the reverse bypass model, the information, innovation, or expertise of the supervisor may have a significant and direct effect on his or her boss, bypassing the manager between them. In this case, one or more dyads within the larger organizational collective may benefit with enhanced success and performance. In both cases, however, reverse and indirect (upward) influence will occur only in organizations where a boss listens to the ideas of his or her supervisors or where supervisors are willing to offer ideas to a boss. For both models, the key point is that followers can influence leaders at a distance in various ways and these influences impact the effectiveness of the organization. Thus, leadership can be bottom-up and indirect as well as top-down and direct.

Horizontal Influence of Leadership

A final extension of the models of indirect leadership concerns *horizontal influence* in organizations. Such influences and relations can take a variety of forms such as co-workers or peers influencing other co-workers or peers, staff units affecting line units, or the workings of interfunctional teams and committees comprising representatives from several areas in an organization. Again, in all of these cases the potential exists for both direct and indirect horizontal influences. The examples of direct horizontal influences are legion: A co-worker shares his or her time-saving idea with a fellow co-worker who begins to use it; a supervisor tells a fellow supervisor about his or her bonus system, which is then implemented; the human resources management department makes a change in hiring policy that affects the operation of other departments in an organization. But such influences need not necessarily be direct or outside the realm of leadership.

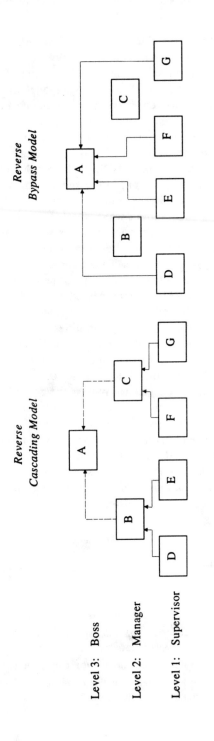

Figure 3.3 Two General Models of Indirect Upward Influence

NOTE: Dashed lines represent indirect influence of supervisors on boss through managers.

Thus it is possible to consider two general models of indirect horizontal influence. These models, again extensions of the cascading and bypass models, are presented in Figure 3.4. To simplify the presentation, a special committee is the focus for each model. Such a committee might be a task force, a problem-solving group, an interfunctional team, or a quality circle comprising one representative (e.g., leader) from several different areas. Four areas are noted in Figure 3.4: production (PROD), research and development (R&D), marketing and sales (MKT), and human resources management (HRM). All contribute members, most likely of similar rank and position, to the special committee displayed at the center of each model. These members then can have horizontal influence in at least two indirect ways. First, from the perspective of the cascading model, committee members sent by a unit can have a direct horizontal influence on the other committee members who in turn can influence their respective units. Thus a committee member can have an indirect influence on units other than his or her own via the committee. For example, the HRM unit may have developed a new leadership training program that the HRM committee member shares with the rest of the special committee. The other committee members can take this program back to their respective units for implementation. Second, from the perspective of the bypass model, a committee member may have a direct influence on units other than his or her own as a result of committee involvement and yet still bypass the committee. For example, an HRM committee member may use his or her status as a committee member to gain entry to other units directly for the purpose of implementing a new leadership-training program. For both models, the key point is that individuals or units can influence other individuals or units at a distance in various ways and that these influences affect the organization's effectiveness. Thus, leadership can be horizontal and indirect as well as top-down and direct.

Summary

To summarize, the key ideas for the extensions of indirect leadership are the following:

- Transformational leadership can be bottom-up and indirect.
- Indirect upward influence can be understood in terms of both the reverse cascading and reverse bypass models of leadership.
- Transformational leadership can be horizontal and indirect.
- Indirect horizontal influence can be understood in terms of both the horizontal cascading and horizontal bypass models of leadership.

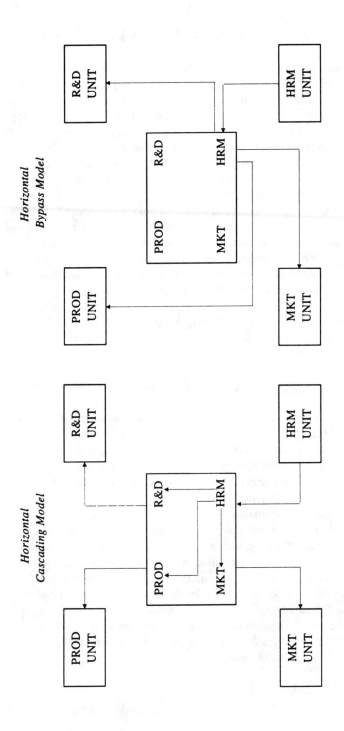

Figure 3.4 Two General Models of "Indirect" Horizontal Influence

NOTE: PROD = production; R&D = research and development; MKT = marketing and sales; HRM = human resource management.

Facets of Indirect Transformational Leadership

Regardless of which model of indirect leadership—cascading or bypass—is of interest, through the use of the Four I's, transformational leadership behaviors can influence and develop others at a distance whether they are superiors, direct reports, or colleagues. Such development would manifest itself in increased influence (top-down, bottom-up, or horizontal) on the transformational leader of focus. Therefore, transformational leadership and its influences can be both direct and indirect, whether top-down, bottom-up, or horizontal. The same transformational leadership behaviors used to develop immediate followers, transform them into leaders, and foster performance beyond their expectations also can be used to develop others at a distance regardless of their position relative to a focal leader. The key is to use this philosophy of and approach to leadership within the context of a cascading or bypass model of indirect leadership. The philosophy, dimensions, and specific behaviors and actions of transformational leadership have been elaborated elsewhere. At this point, therefore, the purpose is simply to briefly mention three key leadership facets that incorporate various aspects of the Four I's that leaders can use to indirectly transform others who are at a distance.

Culture

The first key facet is organizational *culture*, or, more specifically, the role of the transformational leader as the "giver" and "definer" of culture.[11] Through the use of organizational stories, rites and rituals, symbols, slogans, logos, and other cultural elements, the leader provides others at a distance with a picture of the organization. As the definers and givers of culture, leaders set the tone, atmosphere, and philosophy for the organization and its subunits. In this role, there are numerous examples of the leader as the source of cues about reality, expectations, and information for others at levels removed from him or her.

Thus the Four I's can be used in many ways to transmit the organizational or unit culture to others at a distance, setting the vision within an appropriate context. Moreover, the leader of focus does not need to be in a superior position to accomplish this purpose. For example, a junior officer's view of the unit or act of bravery can inspire peer officers and senior officers at a distance to identify with the culture of the unit and lead the unit to greatness in the field.

Communication

The second key facet is organizational *communication* and, in particular, the role of the transformational leader as the communicator of the vision and the inspirer of others to share in that vision. Clearly, the use of language and the management of meaning through symbols, slogans, and the like are critical in this process.[12] Numerous examples of inspiring communication exist in the form of pep talks, campaign-like "political" speeches, more symbolic slogans, or the very actions or behaviors that a leader uses. All of these can influence others at a distance. Although highly charged emotional appeals can be quite effective, so are simple actions such as being a highly visible leader with an open-door policy who also "manages by walking around" and shakes the hands and knows or learns the names of others at various levels. These behaviors provide the leader with the reputation of not being aloof and of being accessible, available, and a "people person."

This set of behaviors is particularly important for higher-level leaders to display so that followers at a distance know that they have top management's support and commitment for their actions and development. But in the cases of upward and horizontal influence, when leaders do not have the added benefit of rank or position, the effective use of communication is equally critical. Again, the Four I's are useful in various ways to communicate with others at levels removed from leaders to confirm, support, and share the vision.

Empowerment

The third key facet is organizational *empowerment* and, specifically, sharing and distributing power through delegation.[13] Essentially, the challenge for transformational leaders is to instill a sense of power in others by changing their internal beliefs about themselves. This can be accomplished with others at a distance by providing positive, emotional support during stressful or anxious times and experiences, words of encouragement and positive persuasion, observable models of effective behavior, and opportunities for successful task accomplishment. Through these behaviors, leaders become the ultimate developers of others, turning tasks over to them, allowing them to take ownership and responsibility for their jobs, and providing them with choices, opportunities, and feedback. In fact, it can be argued that it is "immoral" not to develop others or to not allow them to develop to their fullest potential because of the resulting tremendous waste of human talent. An environment that encourages and rewards constant and new learning and growth in others who are at a distance must be fostered by leaders at all levels.

Again, empowerment is not limited to a top-down approach or to its direct effects alone. Allowing people to write their own job descriptions, self-managed work teams, participation in decision making, and delegation of significant, meaningful, and challenging tasks are ways in which to develop others both nearby and at a distance. Ultimately, the most successful transformational leaders, regardless of organizational level, are those who have made their followers, colleagues, and even superiors nearby or more distant leaders in their own right. Thus, using the Four I's, leaders can empower others at a distance, creating many new leaders to fulfill the vision.

Conclusion

In summary, we have described transformational leadership at a distance by focusing on two models of indirect leadership: cascading and bypass. We also have identified three key facets of such indirect leadership: culture, communication, and empowerment. Although the effects of transformational leadership on immediate followers are well known, with the exception of world class leaders and highly visible CEOs, limited information is available about the indirect leadership influences of leaders at lower organizational levels. Likewise, the indirect effects of leaders on superiors (that is, indirect upward influences) as well as those on colleagues and peers (that is, indirect horizontal influences) are often ignored. Nevertheless, we have integrated and extended these ideas. In short, transformational leaders at all organizational levels are developers of others—followers, superiors, and colleagues—who are nearby and directly influenced as well as those at a distance who are indirectly affected by transformational leaders.

Employees are increasingly working in teams in which the full range of leadership can be applied optimally and with good effect. Part of the basis for team development using the full range of leadership is represented in the influence patterns described in this and subsequent chapters.

Notes

1. For details, see Bass, B. M. (1985). *Leadership and performance beyond expectations.* New York: Free Press; Bass, B. M., & Avolio, B. J. (1990). *The multifactor*

leadership questionnaire. Palo Alto: Consulting Psychologists Press; Avolio, B. J., Waldman, D. A., & Yammarino, F. J. (1991). Leading in the 1990s: Toward understanding the Four I's of transformational leadership. *Journal of European Industrial Training, 15,* 9-16.

2. These ideas are developed more fully in Kotter, J. P. (1990). What leaders really do. *Harvard Business Review* (May-June), pp. 103-111; Zaleznik, A. (1977). Managers and leaders: Are they different? *Harvard Business Review* (May-June); Zaleznik, A. (1990). The leadership gap. *Academy of Management Executives, 4,* 7-22.

3. An extensive review is provided by Bass, B. M. (1990). *Bass and Stogdill's handbook of leadership.* New York: Free Press.

4. Nichols, J. (1987). Leadership in organizations: Meta, macro and micro. *European Management Journal, 6*(1), 16-25.

5. Bass (1990).

6. For details about dyads, groups, and their effects in organizations, see Dansereau, F., Alutto, J. A., & Yammarino, F. J. (1984). *Theory-testing in organizational behavior: The varient approach.* Englewood Cliffs, NJ: Prentice Hall.

7. This model is suggested or described by Bass (1990); Bass, B. M., Waldman, D. A., Avolio, B. J., & Bebb, M. (1987). Transformational leaders: The falling dominoes effect. *Group and Organization Studies, 12,* 73-87; Burns, J. M. (1987). *Leadership.* New York: Harper & Row.

8. This model is developed and described by Dumas, M. (1977). *An empirical approach to the study of leadership in organizations.* Unpublished doctoral dissertation, State University of New York at Buffalo; Dansereau et al. (1984).

9. Bass (1990).

10. For details, see Kipnis, D., Schmidt, S. M., & Wilkinson, I. (1980). Intraorganizational influence tactics: Explanations in getting one's way. *Journal of Applied Psychology, 65,* 440-452; Kipnis, D., Schmidt, S. M., Swaffin-Smith, C., & Wilkinson, I. (1984). Patterns of managerial influence: Shotgun managers, tacticians, and bystanders. *Organizational Dynamics, 12*(3), 58-67; Schmidt, S. M., & Kipnis, D. (1984). Managers' pursuit of individual and organizational goals. *Human Relations, 37,* 781-794.

11. See, for example, Schein, E. H. (1990). Organizational culture. *American Psychologist, 48,* 109-119.

12. See, for example, Conger, J. A. (1991). Inspiring others: The language of leadership. *Academy of Management Executive, 5,* 31-45.

13. See, for example, Conger, J. A. (1989). Leadership: The art of empowering others. *Academy of Management Executives, 3,* 17-24.

4

Transformational Leadership in Teams

DAVID C. ATWATER

BERNARD M. BASS

Center for Leadership Studies,
School of Management, SUNY Binghamton

EXECUTIVE SUMMARY

This chapter presents a set of principles about how teams—and small groups in general—develop and function effectively. These are principles that have been validated in research on small groups and teams over the past 40 years. Awareness of this information can guide the team leader who aims to transform a group composed of members who often differ in education, experience, attitudes, and beliefs into an effective, cooperative, and high-performing team. The format for this chapter will be to present selected research findings and principles derived from these findings, which team leaders might find useful to know. Examples also will clarify or illustrate applications of the principles to the full range of leadership. Chapter 5 then follows with a more detailed application—using research-and-development teams—of multifunctional teams and the transformational-transactional model.

Impact of the Organizational Context

Small work groups operate within a larger organizational context. The surgical team works within a hospital, which in turn operates within the larger health care community. Although external to the team, many aspects of this context nonetheless affect its functioning and effectiveness. Knowledge of the contextual factors that typically affect teams will be useful to team leaders in helping them understand and overcome organizational obstacles that hinder effective team performance. Among the most important aspects of the organizational context that affect team functioning within the organization are (a) its culture, (b) the clarity of the mission assigned to the team, (c) the reinforcers provided for successful performance, (d) the availability of resources, (e) the physical environment, (f) the avenues for communications, (g) the social environment, and (h) significant outsiders.

Organizational Culture

Central Hospital has a reputation for high-quality patient care and is the hospital preferred by outside physicians. Cost containment is a major concern in this hospital and must be figured in the context of the hospital's reputation. This reputation is part of the hospital's culture. It is not surprising that an organization's culture—the beliefs, values, and norms shared by an organization's members—affect the functioning of teams within them, as well as groups in general.

Individual members bring the organization's values to their group and model the group's norms and values on those of the parent organization, particularly if the groups are newly formed and lack clear purpose. "Organizational culture probably figures most prominently in the effectiveness of those work teams [that] are least clearly defined as work groups."[1] The culture can help identify the purpose and reinforce the alignment around a central mission or vision. Teams, particularly those that are not clearly developed or defined, tend to rely on the organizational culture to establish and clarify the values and norms that will guide the team's actions. As these teams develop over time, they should develop their own sense of mission or purpose to be shared by all team members and aligned with the overall organization.

The team is benefited to the degree that the organization's cultural values and norms support accomplishing the team's tasks or goals. But if accomplishing the team's goals will be impeded by the current organizational culture, the effective leader works to establish different norms. For example, team leaders at Central Hospital will have to direct the focus of their teams on how costs can be contained without impairing patient care. In the same way, a team established to develop and implement a new quality customer-service program for a company with a poor reputation will have to ensure that existing organizational values about attitudes toward customer service do not influence the team as it attempts to develop new values and procedures. Here the leader may need to "intellectually stimulate" followers to help them redefine values about the importance of customers and then clarify the mission.

Mission Clarity

Any team established by an organization is or should be established for a purpose. The purpose may be vaguely defined. It may take a transformational leader to envision a sharper focus. However, as observed elsewhere, "Team effectiveness may depend on having a clearly defined mission or purpose within the organization."[2] If the team does not have a clear and accurate understanding of its task and purpose, then the leader must take steps to clarify them.

The team leader in Central Hospital must ensure not only that his or her team has a clear understanding of its purpose and how each member is linked to that purpose, but also that other groups interacting with the team know the team's mission and that it is endorsed by the hospital's leaders. Thus it has been noted, "Communications of a team's mission throughout the organization, especially, may help teams whose work is closely linked to or synchronized with that of other units."[3] The leader should ensure that the mission of his or her team is clearly understood by all units that will interact with, depend on, or be affected by the team's actions.

Mission clarity is enhanced by a team leader's ability and willingness to be inspirational by envisioning and articulating the desired future state (in contrast to the status quo) or by sharing in the development of the vision of the future with his or her team. It also helps if the members view their team leader as having *idealized influence*. This represents the trust, respect, and faith that the leader is moving the team in the right direction, even when it appears to be going against certain organizational norms.

Rewards and Recognition

The leader must recognize that the manner in which the organization rewards team members can have differing effects on the team's and individual's subsequent performances. Organizations should provide team leaders ways to recommend or dispense some type of reward to members of successful teams, whether it be monetary, public recognition, commendation, praise, celebration, or preferential treatment. Researchers report that "team performance may hinge on desirable consequences to individual members contingent on the whole team's performance. . . ."[4] Team leaders may need to point out how each team member may benefit in different ways if the team succeeds in helping the hospital reduce costs. For instance, if streamlining paper flow reduces costs, then nursing heads and lab directors may benefit by having fewer forms to complete; administrative heads and chief accountants may benefit by having fewer forms to review. Establishing these agreements and enforcing them may require contingent reward leadership from the team leader.

Resource Availability

Knowing what new resources are needed above and beyond those available within the existing organizational structure and ensuring their availability is essential for efficient completion of the task. Once a multifunctional team has been assigned a task, the organization must provide the team and its leader with the resources necessary to accomplish the task. These may include monetary support, personnel, equipment, access to people, and documents or technology. Furthermore, "the supervisor and the group members need to determine what resources will be required, and whether these resources are available."[5] The team may decide it needs an outside consultant with experience in cost containment in other hospitals. The team leader will need to seek approval to hire the consultant.

In addition to the practical aspect of having sufficient resources, adequate resources also affect how members perceive the importance of their tasks.[6] Team members are more likely to believe in what they are doing if the organization has invested the necessary resources to accomplish the task. Clearly, there is much room here for transformational and active transactional leaders who understand what resources are needed and strive to ensure that they are made available. (The leader's good relations with superiors and staff who allocate the resources thus are important.) If the team is simply told to rely on existing resources from its own constituent departments, then conflict may result when resources are taken away from ongoing projects in these departments. The overall mission or vision for the team with respect to existing projects (clearly articulated by an inspirational leader) must consider these potential points of conflict.

Physical Environment

Physical environments will affect team effectiveness, particularly in how they foster or impede team processes such as communications and the exchange of ideas and information. Crowding, lighting, temperature, noise, and so on have been shown to interfere with performance in many different kinds of work activities.[7] Other, more complex aspects of the environment also will affect the effectiveness of team functioning. For example, it has been suggested that intermember "communications and cohesion may depend on the extent to which informal, face-to-face interaction is fostered by proximity of workstations and gathering places."[8] Also, "where tasks call for external coordination, exchanges can be aided by reception and conference rooms. In cases in which group processes are easily disrupted, effectiveness may be aided by enclosed working areas."[9] The team leader will need to ensure that the team has good areas in which to work.

In dealing with certain types of problems, obtaining opinions and ideas from one-to-one meetings with individual members may have advantages over meetings with the assembled group. For example, for problems that depend on creative or innovative input, group meetings may inhibit the flow of ideas; for problems that require integrative judgments, the assembled group generally will be superior to decisions made by individuals. (Nevertheless, such groups may suffer from hidden agendas, overpoliteness, and unwarranted support of members for one anothers' positions, as well as destructive conflicts.) It is incumbent on the team leader to recognize these potential problems with communication by being actively involved in the process. As an *individually considerate* leader, he or she must ensure that the appropriate message gets to all members while also considering what each individual needs to know and what information is redundant or inconsequential to performance.

External Communications

Communications media available to the team will differentially affect the quality and quantity of those communications and also will affect a variety of other team processes. Technological changes in the physical environment provide new ways for group members to communicate. Clear evidence has been provided that "electronic communications [electronic mail, bulletin boards, and conferencing] . . . affect work groups by reducing overall communication, equalizing participation levels, weakening status systems, [and] emphasizing informational rather than normative influence."[10]

The transformational leader can use various communications media (face-to-face, telephone, electronic mail, etc.) to ensure that all participants, including those who are reticent to speak out in public, are able to provide the leader with their useful knowledge, opinions, and ideas. Individualized consideration becomes a key leadership style not only in providing colleagues with a forum for acquiring information they need to do their jobs, but also in securing information from them that is critical for team performance.

Social Environments

Teams do not operate in isolation from the influence of other individuals and groups. Thus, a "single person can belong to many different groups. This produces interdependence among these groups, because experiences in one group can affect that person's behavior in all others."[11] In fact, team participants usually are members of several groups and are influenced by the norms and behaviors of each group collectively. Team leaders need to be aware of members' affiliation with other groups and with how it affects their autonomy, interests, opinions, and the roles they are asked to fulfill.

Some team members can focus on the merits of the problem at hand; other will concentrate on the implications of what is being discussed for their own unit's power, resources, and prestige. Team leaders should be particularly aware of members who belong to other groups whose purposes conflict with those of the team. In these cases, linking or aligning the team's purpose to other group's goals probably will significantly affect the team's success. For example, the team leader can point to the extent ideas for cost containment can contribute to more efficient budgeting by Central Hospital's administration.

Outsiders

Team leaders need to consider those who belong to other groups that may provide additional resources or useful information. "Small groups are often influenced by people who are not actually members, such as prospective or ex-members, friends and relatives, customers or clients, and enemies."[12] Outside consultants also can influence the team.

Leaders should be alert for evidence of influence by nonmembers and take steps to make that influence known to team members so that it may be evaluated openly. Often the most important influence on a team comes from outsiders who champion the team's causes because of the effect they see on their own groups if the team is successful. An outside champion of the team's mission often can communicate in an inspirational way the importance of the team's success to the overall mission of the organization. "The success of this project fundamentally represents the future of our organization. We all must support and contribute to its success." At Central Hospital, the team may have such a champion in the hospital president, who often mentions its work at board meetings.

Task Characteristics

Teams can be assigned a variety of tasks. Policy formulation, administrative problem solving, conflict resolution, and project planning are a few of the generic team assignments. The team's task may involve advising, discovering and presenting facts, providing recommended courses of action, or actual decision making. Characteristics of the assigned task can influence how the team should be structured and how it will function.

Task Demands

We can classify task demands in three basic ways: as additive, conjunctive, or disjunctive.[13] *Additive tasks* are those in which individual contributions of members are added together; for example, the sales of each salesperson are added to give the departmental sales figure. *Conjunctive tasks* require that each member carry out the entire assignment in parallel with other members; for example, the console of an assembly is prepared at the same time as its parts are put together. *Disjunctive tasks* require a team choice among alternatives: for example, whether to work overtime. Tasks also can be categorized as divisible or unitary. *Divisible tasks*, such as performing surgical operations, permit the work to be divided among members; *unitary tasks* such as putting a golf ball cannot be broken into separate functions. Tasks such as playing basketball, which require group members to work closely together, are said to be interdependent and to require cooperation between and among members. Divisible and conjunctive tasks are usually interdependent. With tasks of these types, "the group is more likely to be effective under a system of shared rewards, in a physical setting [that] facilitates communication, and under a management system [that] does not make the costs of communication too great."[14]

The transformational leader who is ready to transcend individual members' self-interests recognizes those tasks that require interdependence among members and takes steps to facilitate cooperative behaviors among them. Alignment of the members around a central purpose is a key factor in the overall functioning of the team that is faced with interdependent tasks.

The transformational leader takes care to ensure that all team members are aware of the importance of cooperative behavior for the team's success. He or she also ensures that individual team members' needs are met and that those who are cooperative are appropriately recognized and rewarded. Rewards for team performance should not detract from the level of rewards previously received by individuals. Specifically, by working with this team, members should not feel that they are being treated unfairly or inequitably, are losing ground or status, or are benefiting less than they would by working independently. Transformational leaders must often point out the reasons why individual team members must make short-term sacrifices for the team's overall long-term success.

Clarity Versus Ambiguity of Task

Earlier, we addressed the issue of mission clarity in terms of the desirability of obtaining a clear statement of the task from the organization. In some cases, the team will face tasks that are ambiguous and cannot be delineated more specifically. A team attempting to solve a problem where its cause and solution are unknown or uncertain would be facing a task with a great deal of ambiguity. In such a case, the largest task of the transformational leader and the team becomes that of problem finding. Problem solving here concentrates on trying to define the task that is to be addressed. To assist in this effort, the intellectually stimulating leader moves the group to envision the desired future state of affairs when the problem is solved.

If the task is ambiguous, then the intellectually stimulating leader uses problem-solving strategies to effectively define the task objectives that are to be met. Ambiguous or complex tasks place more demands on the leader, the team, and the group process than do simpler tasks. The team leader in such a situation must continue to focus on trying to reduce task ambiguity and increase the clarity of team objectives; otherwise, the team's efforts will be fragmented, and member motivation and commitment will suffer. The team leader will use intellectual stimulation to operationalize the problem or mission and to generate strategies to achieve it, taking into consideration individual members' needs and capabilities.

An example of a difficult and ambiguous task is illustrated by IBM's difficulties in capturing a larger share of the personal computer (PC) market. IBM management apparently has been unsure why this has been so or how to go about changing it.[15] A team leader given the task of addressing this issue for IBM might face a great deal of ambiguity in determining the true nature of the problem and exactly what the team was expected to fix. Many complex questions must be addressed: How much of the PC market should the company expect? Why did it fail to capture the desired market share? How can IBM increase its share? What are current alternatives for increasing share profitability? Until the leader and the team can determine answers to some of these questions, the leader will have great difficulty in focusing the team's efforts. *Problem definition* thus is a critical step in solving the problem, as well as in understanding the assumptions that individual team members have about the nature of the problem and how it may be solved.

Characteristics of Individual Members

Team members differ from one another in what they bring to the team assumptions, capabilities, and levels of interest; what they can contribute; and how they function on the team. For the most part, personal capabilities will not be altered significantly during the life cycle of most teams. However, the way that individual team members perceive the problem and how they can contribute to its solution may be significantly altered by the leader's use of *individualized consideration* (to determine needs and strengths), *intellectual stimulation* (to address the problem creatively), and *inspirational motivation* (to revise expectations of team members that the problem *can* be solved). Thus the leader must have some idea of the differing strengths and weaknesses of team members and understand how these characteristics may affect the team's functioning. In addition, the leader must recognize that each individual member's contribution will be influenced by the leader's characteristics and leadership style as well as by the task's characteristics.

These individual characteristics can be examined in three clusters:

1. biographical and demographic characteristics such as age, sex, health, marital status, and job experiences;
2. intellectual or cognitive abilities such as knowledge, intelligence, and abilities; and
3. personality or noncognitive characteristics such as interests, motivation, and values.

We will review these clusters of characteristics separately, keeping in mind that the behavior and performance of each individual are the result of a complex interaction of these separate qualities.

Biographical Characteristics

Biographical characteristics often influence team members' performance in complex or unexpected ways. These characteristics include but are not limited to such variables as age, sex, race, religious affiliation, geographic region of birth and upbringing, current and previous jobs, and education level. Although a member's past cannot be altered, the team leader should recognize that individual team members' biographical characteristics can influence their perceptions of problems and acceptable solutions. In other words, the leader identifies key individual differences that may directly or indirectly affect the team's functioning.

For example, team members from blue-collar families may have different attitudes toward seniority than do members from white-collar families. Or team members who are older and close to retirement may view organizational issues such as reorganization differently than do younger workers.

Some characteristics may be of significance to the team's functioning, but their impact is not always clear or easily understood. We would ordinarily expect that groups composed of better-educated and higher-skilled members would do better on a wider variety of problem-solving tasks. Yet converse instances do occur in which a team of less-talented individuals produces a higher-quality product than a team of more talented individuals, because the latter, for example, might be so self-interested that they cannot make the necessary sacrifices for the good of the group.[16]

Team leaders who are transformational are individually considerate and recognize biographical differences in team members. Although they understand that such characteristics usually are not modifiable or under the control of the individual, the involved team leader is aware of such factors and tries to consider them when dealing with team members on any specific project. He or she would appreciate the need to give special instructions to members who have just joined the organization and avoid boring old-timers by recounting already familiar information.

For example, if the task involved downsizing during an economic slowdown, then ages, career histories, employment levels, marital statuses, and number of dependents would affect team members differently, depending on their empathy and identification with employees in jeopardy. The team leader should work over time to establish a team culture in which differences are understood and respected whenever possible and capitalized on for team development. The leader may try to show how different backgrounds and experiences can lead to more creative alternatives if the team is willing to entertain and understand those differences. The individually considerate leader assesses each case task by task, expressing a general willingness to encourage or at least entertain differences of opinion.

Cognitive Abilities of Individuals

Cognitive abilities are the intellectual characteristics of the individual and include the knowledge, skills, and abilities (KSAs) that an individual is born with and acquires through education or experience. Accomplishing the team's task requires members who possess KSAs that are relevant to the task. These are the resources that members bring to the task. Clearly, other things being equal, the more of these task-relevant resources available to the team, the greater its potential effectiveness. "When the overall ability levels of groups are different, groups with the largest proportion of individuals with relevant strong abilities most often perform better."[17] Two classes of KSAs are of particular consequence in teams: (a) general levels of these attributes and (b) those relevant to the specific task. Team production and effectiveness will be influenced by both general and task-specific abilities. For example, those military crews that contain more high-ability soldiers obviously do better than those composed of members of lesser ability.[18] In general, teams composed of members with higher abilities will outperform teams composed of members of lower abilities. Exceptions to this occur when teams of members of lesser abilities pursue better-than-average team strategies, overlearn a task, and are exceptionally motivated to take on the challenges confronting the team. Knute Rockne, the famous Notre Dame football coach, propelled his teams of physically lighter, mediocre players into national champions by overtraining them in new, innovative plays that featured coordination, speed, and deception.

In addition to general abilities, task-relevant KSAs also contribute to task accomplishment. Specific KSAs such as knowledge of organizational procedures, statistical process control training, or relevant technical knowledge can be particularly important in successful team functioning. The team leader who understands the team's task and has spent the time to learn about the skills of team members will more effectively allocate tasks to those team members who are most able to perform them. Transformational leaders understand the task well enough to know what KSAs are needed and take steps to ensure that the team possesses members with the highest levels of the requisite individual skills. Focus on the continuous development of individual skills (that is, individualized consideration) also is critical to team performance, particularly with teams working at the boundaries of innovation.

The leader may not be able to select the team members, although he or she still must address the question of what skills are needed to accomplish the task. Armed with this information and with knowledge of all team members' KSAs, he or she can approach the organization to try to obtain members with the needed skill resources. For this, good relations with higher-ups are often essential.

The team leader may encounter instances where the most intelligent team members apparently are not contributing to task completion. This may happen when these bright members perceive the task as unimportant, insoluble, and lacking in challenge and stimulation. In such cases the transformational leader might attempt to present the task to team members in a light that captures their interest. Arranging the team so that more capable members support less capable ones also may produce higher performance. It also helps to inspire and align those capable members around the team's mission, thus gaining their support and commitment. Research has shown that individual's perceptions of the task's merit are as important as more objective measures of its value.[19] Team members of any given abilities will perform at higher levels if they perceive the task as important or challenging.

Transformational team leaders' most important role may be in inspiring the team by making the task a more meaningful challenge and convincing members of the task's importance.

Noncognitive Traits of Individuals

Noncognitive traits include individual member personality, interests, attitudes, and values. These traits affect performance, motivation, commitment, involvement, and loyalty—and thus team performance. Research has shown that committed individuals are more likely to accept the group's goals and values, experience positive affective ties to other group members, exert effort on behalf of the group, and attempt to meet the group's expectations.[20] The transformational team leader increases member interests in the group (beyond individual self-interests). Favorable attitudes toward and values shared with the group increase member motivation, commitment, involvement, and loyalty to the group and thus benefit the team and task accomplishment.

Individual commitment to the organization typically increases with years of employment with the organization and meaningful involvement in its activities. Thus the transformational team leader can foster commitment by encouraging participation in such activities as group planning and decision making, as well as by involving the member in other team activities.

Greater member commitment also has been shown to reduce absenteeism and turnover.[21] In some teams, the absence and tardiness of certain members may indicate a lack of strong commitment to the team's mission, the leader, and other team members. Diagnosing the reasons behind such lack of commitment and addressing them in a constructive way is a key responsibility of the transformational leader.

Characteristics of the Team

Composed of individuals, the team, once assembled and functioning as a cohesive unit, develops characteristics that are more than just the sum of the individuals' qualities. Like a sports team composed of players with unique abilities, the team may assume a personality with qualities that are characteristic of it rather than any specific individual. Illustrative are teams with "winning attitudes" or those that lack camaraderie. The transformational leader can do much to inspire a "winning attitude" and camaraderie.

Qualities of the team that may affect its functioning and that should be considered by the team leader include the stage of team and individual member development, the team's structure or composition, the team's norms, and its prestige or attractiveness.

Developmental Stages

Small work groups are typically described as passing through a four-stage learning process (forming, storming, norming, and performing) as they go from group formation to maturation.[22] First is the forming of the group, the *development of mutual acceptance*, in which members learn to accept one another and develop mutual confidence and respect. The second stage, storming, involves the *development of open discussion of conflicts* instead of reserved politeness, as the group focuses on examining differences in ideas on problem solving and on developing ways in which it will reach decisions and agreements. In the third stage, norming, the group is considered to be mature enough to set standards for its members and itself. Efforts begin to be *cooperative and productive*. In the fourth stage, performing, the group is fully matured and *operates effectively in accordance with established norms*, making the best uses of available human and material resources. In this stage, group membership is valued, and the group is interdependent, flexible, and able to effectively meet higher-order challenges. The cycle may begin anew with *re-forming* as the team takes on new members or new assignments.

With his or her attention to development, the transformational team leader is cognizant of the stage of team development and how to effectively move the team from a lower to a higher level of development. In addition, with his or her attention to the need for readiness, he or she behaves in a way that is consistent with the team's developmental stage: "The effectiveness of a leader's style depends on the group's developmental level."[23] The individually considerate team leader will pace her leadership to fit the team's perceived stage. She or he will avoid getting too far behind or ahead of the group. Thus during the group's early formative stages, such a leader facilitates the development of communication and trust. During early stages of team development, the transformational leader will be more individually considerate to ensure that all members who wish to be involved and want to participate in the communication development process can do so. Later the leader may become more intellectually stimulating to encourage the expression of creative problem solving and to get beyond boundaries and norms that the team itself created but which are no longer relevant.

During the formative stages, the transformational leader works to build a team culture and facilitates the development of effective norms that govern the team's work habits: "The initial patterns of behavior in a group often solidify into norms."[24] And so the team leader facilitates the creation and establishment of team norms that will tend to endure. Norms may arise from the organizational or environmental context, or the group may develop unique norms in response to events that occur within it. The transformational team leader influences the development of norms to facilitate team functioning. Transformational leaders encourage creation of new methods and procedures to more effectively achieve group goals. Given the importance and persistence of the team's culture and norms, an effective leader will use MBE-A to monitor norm development and take corrective action to ensure that productive norms suitable for the task are encouraged. The effective team leader may take advantage of the standards the team has created for such contingent rewards as praise and recognition for individual members or the team as a whole. Conversely, the leader may intellectually stimulate a shift in attention to avoid stagnation and rigid behavior patterns that are based on overly constrained norms. Understanding the norms that are brought to the team by individual team members and those that need to be created are essential tasks for the team leader.

Group Size

Group size has been shown to affect group functioning in a number of ways. For example, as groups enlarge, communications become increasingly complex, resulting in larger numbers of group members feeling that they have not had adequate opportunity to express their views. In general, "People who belong to larger groups are less satisfied with group membership, participate less often in group activities, and are less likely to cooperate with one another."[25] Good advice for team leaders would be to be *individually considerate* and task-oriented in limiting their groups to the smallest size possible consistent with accomplishing the group's goals and completing its tasks.

Although it is impossible to specify the optimal number of group members without knowing the task, the evidence shows that 5 or 6 are best for discussion groups and many similar kinds of situations.[26] Other studies suggest that groups of 8 to 10 may be optimal for tasks that require less one-to-one discussion.[27] Groups of 5 to 10 seem to provide a workable but sufficiently diverse combination of views and skills while still allowing full participation by all members. Deviating from this number could be acceptable if indicated by the nature of the task. A complex task, for example, that requires many unique skills may require a larger number of individuals to encompass all required KSAs. Or a task that will affect numerous units within the organization may require representatives from each affected unit. Conversely, smaller groups also may be indicated for tasks that require simple judgments that would be hindered by redundant information from more than two or three members. The team leader who is faced with an unwieldy large group is likely to resort to MBE, taking corrective action when necessary. But it would be better to be intellectually stimulating and to split the task and the team into subunits, essentially reconfiguring the problem or mission in order to arrive at more suitably sized working groups. Individual leaders for each subgroup could then preside over groups of more optimal size, or the subgroups could be self-managed.

In addition to complicating communications and interaction, larger groups create other problems. More misbehavior that requires corrective action by the leader occurs in larger groups, perhaps because of the greater anonymity they provide members.[28] Coordination problems and motivational losses in large groups often prevent them from being as productive as expected.[29] A leader must truly be inspirational to motivate the larger group because members see less instrumentality between what they contribute and what the team is able to accomplish. Contingent rewarding is made more difficult for the leader in larger groups. In large groups, the leader must take steps to ensure that each member's role clarity, participation, and contributions are made salient.

If anonymity, lack of recognition, or lack of participation foster misbehavior (e.g., disruptions or loafing), then the leader should actively solicit input from nonparticipating members and clearly identify contributions or input from less-active members. Improving communications with all team members will increase role clarity and involvement and tend to reduce disruptive behavior.

The costs associated with the greater communications problem in larger teams can be offset by improved communications technologies. Transactional leaders can make use of electronic mail or group decision support systems before a meeting to facilitate the team's communications processes. Agendas can be created and circulated in advance based on the leader's interactions with each member, thus ensuring that all members' views and interests will be represented.

Programmed Versus Nonprogrammed Decisions

Transactional leadership may be appropriate for programmed decisions, and transformational leadership may be appropriate for nonprogrammed decisions.

The team may be faced with the need to make programmed decisions. These are routine or repetitive choices. Such team decisions are made according to previously formulated rules, perhaps imposed by the convening authority. Typically, these decisions concern problems that involve little uncertainty, provide little leeway for team input, and do not address issues of great significance to the organization. Ordinary decision making or choosing from among alternatives is an essential function of problem solving. However, often a team is authorized only to make recommendations or list alternatives rather than make an actual choice. Even in such a case, however, the team will make numerous decisions during the process of formulating recommendations or alternatives. By stressing the maintenance of a systematic approach, the intellectually stimulating team leader can play an important role in guiding the team through the programmed decision-making process.

Contrasted to these *programmed* decisions are *nonprogrammed* decisions that are required in novel or uncertain situations of major consequence and which require decision makers' judgment and creativity. Such decisions pose great challenges for a team and its leader.

Clearly, more transformational leadership is needed in dealing with nonprogrammed decisions. On the other hand, for programmed, routine decisions, transactional leadership may suffice.

Individual Versus Group Decisions

Considerable research has addressed the differences and similarities of individual and group decision making. Some evidence suggests that individuals and groups use different processes to reach decisions, and that for some tasks individual or group decision making is superior or has certain advantages. Typically, groups are superior when the task is complex, the group contains members with diverse but relevant skills, communications are open, and members trust one another. For simple tasks, in which each added member is redundant and likely to impede rather than expedite discussion, groups perform only as well as the best person in the group and only if the group is willing to accept that person's answer. For simple tasks, the group may take longer to arrive at a decision.[30] Thus some situations are more suitable for individual decision making, others for group decision making. Intellectual stimulation is needed to properly diagnose the problem to determine how the decision is to be made and by whom. For example, the decision for a company to embark on a new quality-improvement program may be made by the CEO after suitable consultation with outsiders and insiders at various levels in the organization. The task of designing and developing an implementation plan for such a program would clearly be suitable for one or more multifunctional teams, as will be discussed in the next chapter. The design and implementation process will require diverse, in-depth knowledge of the organization (design, procurement, manufacturing, etc.) as well as knowledge of a variety of quality-improvement programs. Successful implementation also will require acceptance by the rank-and-file employees, so shared decision making as well as shared vision would be important to the implementation process.

The team leader must judge when it would be more efficient to ask each member to work alone first before pooling all members' contributions and when it would be more efficient to begin with a team discussion of the problem so that members would have common understandings, purposes, and time frames. The team leader must understand both group and individual decision processes so that he or she may use the most effective approach in dealing with different kinds of problems. For example, when using intellectually stimulating brainstorming, it is more efficient for each member to first work alone to generate ideas. Then the members' lists can be pooled to eliminate duplications. For considering the solution to a problem that requires multifunctional expertise in which no member can give the answer, the team must work with much individualized consideration to define the problem, diagnose its causes, generate alternatives (which might begin individually and then be pooled), evaluate the alternatives, and then make the final choice. After obtaining authorization, implementation may require coordination of individual initiatives and team follow-up. Suitable individual and team recognition needs to be provided (through contingent rewards) as progress is made.

Attributes and Behaviors of the Leader

In this section we will discuss several team leader attributes that affect team functioning.

Sources of Leader Authority

Appointed and elected leaders derive legitimacy from different sources, which will have differing effects on leader-follower relations. Appointed leaders can be more transactional, and elected leaders, more transformational. When a higher-up or an organization forms a team, the convening authority ordinarily appoints the team leader and provides him or her with recognition, authority, and specific responsibilities. Sometimes the team may be allowed to elect a leader from among its members. (Emergent leaders also may arise during the life of the group, but that is not the subject of this section.) Leaders who are appointed derive authority and power from their position in the organization. They can more readily practice considerable managing by exception if they choose. Elected leaders may derive their power from their idealized influence, intellectual stimulation, or individualized consideration, all of which appeal to the team's members. All things being equal, elected leaders can be more transformational, and appointed leaders can be more transactional. Appointed and elected leaders begin their jobs from power bases that will have consequences for their relations with team members.[31]

Certainly, both appointed and elected leaders may be transactional as well as transformational, depending on their personal predilections and training. They may be successful or unsuccessful, depending on their ability to function effectively with the team and meet members' important needs. However, at least during the formative stages of team development, the elected leader may enjoy certain advantages because he or she possesses, to the majority of team members, certain important characteristics such as expertise, popularity, or esteem that bring initial respect and which the group sees as positive and beneficial to leader-follower relations. This advantage will not remain for long, however, if the elected leader is unable to function effectively in the role. In fact, the group's strong expectations for an elected leader may intensify the group's dissatisfaction should the leader fail. An appointed leader who is effective should be able to overcome any resistance to being appointed rather than elected. The appointed leader will not be successful in the long run if he or she relies heavily on the formal authority derived from the appointment to manage-by-exception rather than use the authority to be more proactive and transformational wherever possible. Although there are likely to be differences in initial dealings with team members as a function of the source of authority, the leader's ultimate success will be determined by his or her leadership qualities.

It is important for any leader of a newly formed team to recognize that team members have shared expectations about their leader's characteristics and behavior and that their perceptions of leader actions are influenced by these beliefs.[32] Followers in any group have expectations or implicit beliefs about behaviors and traits that they consider appropriate for their leader based on past experiences with him or her.

The leader of a newly formed team is advised to be individually considerate and to understand the team's expectations of him or her. This does not mean that he or she must meet every expectation. In some situations, the leader may choose to avoid meeting certain expectations if he or she feels them to be unwise, and to alter expectations when they are dysfunctional or inappropriate. The team leader who is unaware or insensitive to member and team expectations may unknowingly impede his or her ability to develop an effective team. If, for example, the team expects the leader to be a strong advocate when representing team viewpoints to other groups but the leader fails to do so, then his or her effectiveness may be diminished even though the leader is known to have the requisite knowledge to perform other functions well. There is also danger that if the leader fails to meet important expectations in one area, then team members may falsely conclude that the leader will fail to meet expectations in other areas.

Few individuals display a single style at all times. Instead, most individual leaders exhibit different amounts of each style: directive or participative, task-oriented or relations-oriented, transformational or transactional. Some patterns are generally more effective than others.[33] But different situations may call for the emphasis of one style rather than another. Thus effective team leaders are cognizant of the need to adjust the style they use as they confront different circumstances, individuals, and problems. Effective team leaders need to be able to recognize that a style they infrequently use, such as management-by-exception, may be called for, and that they must modify their full range of leadership styles to meet demands that vary by situation, task, or team. For example, if the group is spending excessive time in discussing options, then the individually considerate leader who usually is participative may need to become more *directive* to move the team more rapidly toward a decision. Finding him- or herself with no control of rewards and with a team facing a complex problem, the leader who is ordinarily contingently rewarding may remain influential by becoming more intellectually stimulating or inspirational. Deciding that a different leadership style is needed and knowing how to display such a style should reflect a real demand of the task or team. It should be authentic and not a matter of manipulation. Leaders who strive for such authenticity can benefit from mentoring, coaching, and training that explores and practices alternate leadership techniques in varying circumstances. Information gleaned from the writings of reputable researchers also may be of value. For example:[34]

- Directiveness can be beneficial when task demands are vague and time is critical.
- Individualized consideration and supportiveness will help offset team members' dissatisfaction with frustrating tasks.
- Inspirational motivation and an orientation toward tasks encourage followers and colleagues to set higher performance standards and increase their confidence in meeting challenges.
- Participative styles are suitable when team members possess the skills to do the job and when their satisfaction, commitment, involvement, and loyalty are sought.
- Contingent rewarding is most effective in tasks where there is a clear link between the performance required and the rewards for achieving such performance.
- Transformational leadership will be most salutary in crisis conditions and when tasks are ambiguous, although it will have varying degrees of impact in more stable conditions. In fact, such leaders may cause crises by suggesting change to disrupt the status quo.

Personal Characteristics of Effective Team Leaders

Although we may generalize here, bear in mind that attributing team effectiveness to a leader's particular personal characteristics is difficult without referring to the organization, task, team members, and so on. Nevertheless, all other things being equal, the team leader is likely to be more effective if he or she possesses some of the following KSAs:

1. knowledge of the group process,
2. ability to think and react decisively,
3. ability to articulate a position clearly and succinctly,

4. knowledge and competence in the subject area,
5. sensitivity to group trends and needs,
6. self-restraint and respect for others,
7. ability to vocalize group sentiments,
8. ability to clarify objectives again and again,[35] and
9. persistence in achieving difficult objectives.

Many of these personal attributes are those that are central to transformational leadership. All of these appear relevant to the effective team leader even though there are systematic differences between the team and traditional hierarchical supervisor-subordinate arrangements.[36] Team members may be less motivated by their formal roles and job definitions and more committed to the goals of the team. The team leader is likely to have less specific knowledge in some areas than particular members. "Thus, project leadership involves more coordination and communication facilitation activities as well as earning of incremental influence by the project leader."[37] Successful leaders of teams must rely on their motivational and influence skills to a greater degree than leaders in more traditional supervisory roles.

Because the team leader may not possess expert knowledge in all areas essential to task accomplishment, and because of the importance of motivating team members in terms of project goals rather than traditional roles, the successful team leader must develop personal relations with team members that can become the means for the influence needed to motivate team members.

Interactions of Teams and Individuals

To this point we have examined characteristics of the task, individual team members, the team, and the leader as if they were isolated parts of a larger structure. Obviously these elements do not operate in isolation. In this and the following section we will discuss interactions between some of these separate parts. Although team performance logically depends on the performance of individual members, this dependence is modified by the interaction process (a) between and among members and (b) between members and team characteristics. We will note that these interactive processes can have either positive or negative effects on the team's productivity and effectiveness.

Individual Roles and the Team

A role is the shared expectation of how an individual team member should behave. Every member fills at least one role on the team. Thus each member's perception of expected behaviors and the team's actual expectations of the individual will influence how the member behaves. Roles assigned to or assumed by members can lead to several types of conflicts. Common problems occur when "[a] person . . . lack[s] the knowledge, ability or motivation to play a role effectively, or discover[s] that it is inconsistent with roles he or she already plays."[38]

The leader who knows his or her team members will not place them in roles for which they are ill equipped. The individually considerate leader takes the time to learn about his or her team members; he or she obtains a good idea of members' KSAs and personal situations and thus can be more effective in guiding them into suitable roles. Team members also can be encouraged to voice concerns about filling certain roles and thus be reassured of their abilities.

Role conflicts are still inevitable. When they arise, the team leader should attempt to minimize them. Yet even a diligent leader may not be aware of all the roles that a team member fills. Sometimes the roles required to complete a task will create conflict for some team members. For example, a member may come from a supervisory position with attendant perquisites to a team that is designing a "flat" organization that will eliminate differences between rank-and-file workers and their supervisors. Clearly such a task will conflict with the member's personal privilege and compromise his or her contribution to the team's task.

In addition to conflicts caused by an individual's incompatible roles, a member also may experience role conflict as his or her role on the team changes; such role change might result from structural changes for the team as a function of time or with modifications in the team's goals.[39] Members' team roles may not be static and may produce conflict as they change. The team leader needs to remain aware that role transitions will occur and be cognizant of the possible problems associated with such changes. Discussing pending changes and soliciting member's views will help to raise issues that may cause conflict. Discussion may lead to innovative solutions to role conflicts, which, if they persist, will be detrimental to the team, increasing tensions and decreasing productivity.[40]

Tension resulting from role conflict is likely to have negative consequences for team effectiveness. Role conflict and the attendant tension may also be detrimental to the team's functioning, creativity, problem solving, and cohesiveness. (The effects of team conflict will be discussed again in this chapter.)

The Impact of the Leader's Status and Esteem on the Team

Status also is related to issues of roles and role enactments. *Status* is the relative importance of a member's position and rank on a team and elsewhere. Members' status increases with their influence on the team. It affects their esteem in the eyes of other members—that is, their perceived value as individuals. The team leader should recognize that some of his or her own status results from the role of leader. Esteem can be enhanced or diminished by the leader's actions or by the actions of the larger surrounding organization in its dealings with the leader. The effects of status and esteem can be particularly meaningful for the team leader because of the relations among status, esteem, and influence. "One of the best established findings in the study of group dynamics is that higher status (and esteemed) persons tend to be more influential than lower status (and esteemed) persons."[41] Other findings show that people with higher status (and esteem) have more opportunities to exert influence, and they attempt to influence others more often.[42] Highly esteemed leaders and members have idealized influence.

Ordinarily the team leader initially enjoys a relatively high status as a result of his or her appointment or election to the position of leader. (Although sometimes the position is obtained by default because no one wants it!) The leader who demonstrates particular skill in either important technical functions or leadership itself can enhance his or her esteem. In addition, research has shown that certain rather simple behaviors—maintaining eye contact, speaking in a firm voice with few hesitations, being physically intrusive—are characteristic of high-status, esteemed individuals. Aside from considering factors that affect the leader's own status, the leader may want to increase the status (and influence) of selected team members if it will help to accomplish a team's task. For example, special job titles, subcommittee assignments, better equipment, or other perquisites may improve a team member's status. In the same way, praise and recognition may enhance a team member's esteem (and influence).

Team Cohesiveness

Another characteristic of the group-individual interaction involves *group cohesiveness*, or the attraction of members to one another and to the group as a whole. Cohesiveness acts on members to remain in the group. Generally, it has positive consequences when the team's goals match or complement the organization's goals. Cohesiveness also can have negative consequences when the team's goals oppose the parent organization's goals. For instance, members may be attracted to the team by the opportunity to sabotage a new organizational development.

Highly cohesive teams also can have both positive and negative effects on team members in other ways. Highly cohesive teams accept the group's norms and help one another work toward group goals.[43] But, as will be noted in subsequent paragraphs, cohesiveness may generate inflexible norms that are detrimental to the team's creativity.

In groups lacking in cohesiveness, members typically do not like one another and have difficulty forming workable partnerships. On the other hand, reasonably high cohesiveness will help hold the team together: Members will be attached to the team and want to remain active on it.

Cohesiveness is also beneficial in resisting attempts to disrupt the team. Cohesiveness can begin to develop even before a team is formed. The transformational leader will strive to enhance a team's cohesiveness, assuming that its goals and norms are aligned with those of the larger organization.

Certain factors are known to facilitate the development of cohesive teams. For example, a strong external threat or competition will tend to draw team members together. Transformational leaders often highlight pending crises to energize or rally the team into action. Spending more time together also tends to improve cohesiveness, particularly if members have common or similar interests. Success on previous tasks increases cohesiveness as it makes the group more appealing to individual members. "[L]eaders can often strengthen group cohesion by encouraging feelings of warmth and acceptance among followers, or simply by serving as targets for projective identification."[44] The effective team leader makes use of transformational leadership and contingent reward to increase team cohesion.

The effective team leader displays inspirational motivation by striving to make membership attractive; he or she does this by pointing out the importance of an assignment, the positive qualities of other members, and the ways in which members can complement one another's strengths. The leader points to the challenge involved and the recognition that success will bring. Contingent rewards such as commendations and bonuses may provide tangible reinforcements for cooperation.

As noted earlier, high cohesiveness also has potential drawbacks. Highly cohesive teams may redefine their goals so as to perpetuate the group's security and their own satisfying interpersonal relations with one another rather than attend to their common purpose, the original reason for being assembled. Members may refrain from introducing valid but disturbing information or from disagreeing in order to preserve group harmony or avoid violating group norms. This phenomenon, which is known as *group think*, can have serious negative consequences for the group's decision-making process: Critical information may be lost, and new or creative ideas may be withheld. The team leader must balance the level of cohesion with the needs of the task while also considering the nature of individuals who make up the team. The team leader must monitor team cohesiveness to ensure that cohesive pressures are not leading to uncritical conformity and suppression of new or constructive ideas.

To help counter group think, the leader may by example raise issues or points that counter or question both the group's customary thinking and the leader's own original thinking. For instance, the leader may point out how his or her thinking changed over time as more information became available. Through his or her actions, the leader can highlight the importance of questioning old assumptions. She or he may attend in a positive manner to members who voice ideas that deviate from the group's usual approach. By creating an accepting environment that actively encourages unusual or provocative ideas, the leader can reduce the conformist pressure that may develop, while still maintaining a cohesive team. Bringing new members or guests with different points of view also may help the highly cohesive group avoid loss of objectivity and spontaneity.

Other Negative Group Processes

In addition to the negative aspects of strong cohesiveness, other destructive processes regularly occur in groups. One such process is reduced individual motivation, which may result from certain types of group social interactions. These motivational losses are collectively labeled *individual versus team dilemmas* because they represent individual behaviors that may serve the individual but be destructive for the team. Research has demonstrated three individual versus team dilemmas that can appear in teams and reduce the self-interested member's motivation to work toward the team's goals (unless a transformational leader can move the individual to go beyond his or her self-interests for the good of the group):[45]

1. *Social loafing* may occur when individual contributions to an overall project are hard to identify. This can lead to reduced effort by some members in larger groups. Corrective and constructive trans-

actions between members and leader may be needed, along with a transformational effort by the leader to reenergize a team member's commitment.

2. *Free riding* may occur when it is evident that another group member will perform or provide the necessary work so that one's own contribution is unnecessary. Adjustments in work loads are needed.

3. *Exploitation* is likely to be felt by the team member who perceives that he or she is being taken advantage of and is doing the "lion's share" of the work while other members loaf. Again, adjustments in work loads are necessary.

Loafing and free-riding members may lack a feeling of empowerment to take initiatives. Such empowerment can be provided by a transformational leader.

One classic example of a social dilemma is that of the soldier in a foxhole who decides to remain hidden while others engage the enemy. If all soldiers engaged in this behavior, the results would be disastrous for an army. Similar, though less-disastrous, examples may be seen in most work groups. Leaders who note that able team members are not contributing to team's efforts should examine the situations for evidence of these phenomena. These social problems seem to be more common when group members do not know one another, when role and status structures are ill-defined, when the group is expected to be short-lived, or when past leadership has been purely transactional.[46] (With such transactional leadership, rewards are based solely on what one does or does not do. Integration or coordination of efforts results in no additional rewards and may, in fact, diminish earlier reward levels because of lower individual achievement.) If such social dilemmas are observed, then research offers several countermeasures.[47] Actions that make a member's lack of contribution noticeable are often effective in eliminating these motivational losses. Communication between members that encourages cooperative behavior also should discourage loafing and free riding. Social disapproval by the group also can be effective in curtailing these effects.[48] Beyond this, the transformational leader tries to move members to transcend their self-interests for the good of the group and the organization. This requires continual attention by the leader to remind members of the importance of their collective efforts. Participation by the members can be seen as an opportunity for their personal and career growth. The intellectual challenge can be emphasized. An increased sense of individual empowerment may be advisable (although the loafing member or free rider may feel more empowered to loaf and free ride even more).

Individual-Leader Interactions

Earlier, we discussed characteristics of the leader. Here we focus on additional approaches for leaders interacting with diverse team members. A knowledgeable leader understands that actions will have consequences—effects of some kind—and that these consequences can be quite different, depending on the situation and individuals involved.

Recognizing Individual Differences

The team leader recognizes that each individual's abilities and differences are the product of a unique combination of heredity and experience. Although treating all team members the same may might seem to be an efficient use of a leader's time, such an approach will fall short of maximizing each member's contribution to a task. The team leader must keep in mind that "individual differences in task performance are dependent on individual differences in task-relevant specific and general abilities."[49] This idea can be extended to include differences in needs such as affiliation or achievement orientation.

For the team leader, the importance of individual differences goes well beyond recognizing that team members possess different skills and abilities. The concept of individual differences also implies that people are not necessarily motivated and reinforced, or irritated and dissatisfied, by the same things. Having a complete understanding of all unique aspects of each team member is an impossible task that we do not advocate. Rather it is the recognition and acceptance on the part of the leader of the concept of individual differences, with all of its implications, that is important. Leaders should make as few assumptions about members as possible; instead, they should try to treat and understand them as unique individuals and, whenever feasible, test their assumptions. This individuation then becomes a norm for all interactions among team members and their leader.

Individualized Consideration

Individualized consideration combines an appreciation of individuation with interest in the development of the team and its members. It flows from the team leader's understanding and appreciation of individual differences. It represents the leader's attempt to treat each member uniquely and to understand and share each team member's concerns and developmental needs. Transformational leaders do more than just recognize individual differences. They demonstrate specific considerations for each team member. Furthermore, they elevate the needs of the individual as they attempt to increase their followers' confidence in taking on more responsibility.[50] This helps considerably in maximizing team potential. Individualized consideration is one of the hallmarks of transformational leadership and a valuable way of thinking and performing for the leader who wants to maximize each team member's contribution. To be individually considerate, the leader must devote some time to getting to know each team member. This may appear a time-consuming and complex task, but it can be accomplished easily by actively listening to followers and by being sensitive to expressions of their needs. Individually considerate leaders delegate challenging tasks with sufficient follow-up. They provide opportunities that support growth and development, risk taking, and innovation based on individual needs and capabilities. Transformational leaders support their individualized consideration to improve relations with their followers in other ways:

1. They act as role models (idealized influence). They motivate their followers to want to emulate the leader's actions.

2. They communicate timely information to followers and provide continuous follow-up and feedback (inspirational motivation and contingent reward).

3. They align individual member needs to the team's and the organization's goals (inspirational motivation).

Vertical Dyad Linkages

In the process of interacting with individual team members, leaders develop different types of relations with each member. This process has been described and studied in research as vertical dyad linkages, which has been explained by *leader-member exchange theory*.[51] The quality of relations with each member can be different. If the relation is positive, then the leader works to support and include the member in the group's development and decision making. If the quality is negative, then the leader is more likely to ignore or exclude the member. In turn, the member with positive relations with the leader is more likely to be committed, involved, and loyal. Thus, leaders implicitly create *in-groups* and *out-groups* based on such qualities as personal characteristics that are compatible with the leader or superior competence. In-group members tend to be rated higher, have lower turnover, and report greater satisfaction.[52]

The leader should understand that this process occurs and that it can begin early in a team's life. The leader should recognize that assigning some team members to one or another group will result in differential treatment on a host of factors, some of which will unfairly penalize or reward members. In other words, once classified and assigned to a group, a member may be viewed in a stereotypical fashion and rewarded or punished on the basis of his or her assigned group membership rather than on the basis of actual performance. Thus, the development of leader-member relations that result in assignment of some members to favored in-groups is likely to create conflicts and reduce the contributions of members in the nonfavored group.

The knowledgeable team leader will recognize the tendency to form closer relations with team members who are similar in personality, values, or interests or with those who are more competent. Realistically, it is probably impossible not to have different feelings toward different team members. However, the team leader who is individually considerate will strive to ensure that all team members feel like as if they are in-group members, regardless of how they may differ from the leader. In a similar vein, the effective leader will help prevent team members from forming both in- and out-groups because of their destructive consequences as team members become alienated from the overall group's central mission.

Allocation of Rewards, Commendations, and Recognition

The team leader will sometimes have direct control over rewards that are available to team members; more often he or she can provide recommendations to the organization about rewards for team members. These rewards can take the form of pay, benefits, awards, perquisites, or incentives. Although the intent of rewards to team members is typically to recognize superior performance and maintain or increase motivation, the team leader should recognize that the methods used to allocate rewards can have differential effects on individual and team performance. In fact, "allocations of rewards . . . can often affect status, conflict, and leadership in groups."[53] There is convincing evidence that reward allocations based on an equity rule (i.e., rewards are proportional to effort and output) promote increased performance, while an equality rule (i.e., all members receive the same reward) benefits group relations.[54] Thus rewards, commendations, and recognition can be used to reinforce different team outcomes.

The wise use of equity versus equality allocation rules in a team must consider the nature of the team's task. An equality rule will tend to promote harmonious group relations if the team is working on a complex task with all members attempting to make meaningful contributions. But if one or two members are doing the lion's share of work, then an equal distribution of rewards may be unfair and decrease the motivation of more active and more competent members. The team leader who wants to promote or improve group relations may want to structure tasks so that equity rewards are appropriate. The leader must also recognize that the value and magnitude of rewards must be considered worth attaining. This goes back to the leader's understanding of the needs and aspirations of individual team members and appropriately linking those needs to desired rewards. Also, the distribution of rewards should be timely. On shorter projects, rewards and commendations should coincide with the end of the project. For projects of several years' duration, periodic reviews and recognition should be considered.

Managing Team Conflict

All teams need to deal with conflict either within the team or between the team and an outside agent by eliminating, reducing, or resolving it. In learning to handle conflict, the leader and the team should differentiate between conflicts that are destructive and constructive.[55] *Destructive conflicts* result in participants feeling dissatisfied with the outcome and believing that they are worse off as a result of the attempted resolution. Highly disruptive conflicts may interfere with group functioning and process and ultimately will result in poor group decisions. Conflicts within the group are more likely to be disruptive to group functioning and effectiveness in comparison to conflicts between the group and any external entity. In fact, external or intergroup conflict has been shown to increase cohesiveness, task orientation, group loyalty, and acceptance of leaders.[56] External threats tend to unify the group, but intergroup conflicts also give rise to such negative consequences as stereotyping, closed-mindedness, miscommunication, and distorted perception.

Generally, intragroup conflicts, or those within a group, adversely affect the group's functioning. Thus role conflicts within the team create tension and reduce productivity.[57]

Sources of Intragroup Conflicts

Conflicts within a team can arise from a variety of sources. Among the most common causes are:[58]

- poor communications;
- disagreements over the way to do a job;

- different beliefs or assumptions about how to operate as a team;
- incompatible personalities, values, or motives;
- unfair reward allocation;
- disagreements over rules or policies;
- abilities to deal with change;
- inappropriate leadership styles; and
- competition between and among members.

Of these, the greatest source is misunderstandings that arise from poor communication.[59] Such conflicts should be relatively easy to resolve once the misunderstanding is identified and resolved. The transformational team leader who has fostered trust and an open, accepting climate within the team should experience fewer conflicts based on lack of communication. In some cases, conflicts that appear to be based on communication may reveal other problem sources once the communication issues are clarified. However, until the communication aspect has been eliminated, the group will have difficulty coming to grips with other underlying issues.

Intragroup conflict can be constructive: "[C]onflict sometimes fosters innovation and thereby enhances individual and group welfare."[60] Intragroup conflict can be deliberately introduced by the team leader to yield positive effects. For instance, a "devil's advocate" can be appointed to articulate a conflicting point of view that will help to improve the group's final decision.

The team leader who understands the nature of conflict will recognize that conflict may provide opportunity to improve group functioning. Potential benefits include:

- raising hidden problems,
- facilitating innovation and change, and
- increased group loyalty and motivation.

These benefits accrue only if the source of conflict is understood, handled skillfully, and resolved constructively.

Conflict Resolution

A laissez-faire leader ignores or minimizes conflict. An authoritarian leader is likely to force a solution by overpowering the opposition. A persuasive leader may try to talk the opposition into agreement. Democratic leaders may use majority vote to decide, but this may only suppress the minority opposition without resolving the conflict. However, true conflict resolution occurs when the reasons for the conflict are eliminated without lingering antagonisms or unresolved issues. It is one thing to reduce conflict; it is best to resolve it. Reduction techniques that ignore the issues or play down differences are not recommended. Compromise is sometimes appealing and even necessary, but it usually leaves lingering problems that may resurface later. Conflict resolution that eliminates the causes of disagreement leads to win-win solutions in which both parties are satisfied with the solution and more likely to be committed to it. Such solutions can be found when the real issues are openly confronted and effective problem-solving techniques are used to seek mutually agreeable answers.

Accommodation and compromise may be sought to reduce conflict. In some cases, the team leader may require the services of a third party to resolve a dispute. The team needs to be able to judge when mediation or arbitration are the only conflict-reduction or conflict-resolution methods. If, for example, the conflict is between the leader and other team members, then a neutral person may be able to introduce a useful, objective element. In other cases, it is the team leader who needs to assume the role of mediator or arbitrator between two team members in conflict. Unfortunately, such mediation or arbitration is likely to result in reduced rather than resolved conflict.

For the transformational leader to achieve a true consensual resolution of conflict, an integration of the parties' positions can be found through the following steps:

1. Create a positive environment for problem identification and resolution.

2. Search for superordinate goals that transcend the differing objectives of the opposing parties.

3. Define the problem. (Conflicts often focus on differences in the definition of the problem or in the assumptions underlying a problem's definition.)

4. Identify relevant facts and opinions. Have the conflicting parties openly state their positions.

5. Determine the desired results.

6. Propose different solutions with superordinate goals in mind.

7. Reach an agreement that benefits both parties.

8. Implement the solution.

9. Evaluate the solution.[61]

At each step, ask each party to restate the other's position. Conflict often can be cleared up as discrepancies emerge in what one party said and another heard. This approach may be time-consuming, but true conflict resolution in the long run will not only save time that might be spent addressing the problem again, but also help the leader create a cooperative environment based on constructive norms for dealing with future conflicts—and possibly reduce unnecessary conflicts.

Principles for guiding the leaders of teams have been drawn from available research about effective leadership in small groups. These principles deal with the effects of the team's organizational culture; the nature of the team's task; the characteristics of individual members, the team, and the leader; and the interactions among these factors that contribute to the team's successful performance. Much of what we know about transformational leadership suggests that the team leader who is transformational and practices contingent reward will be more effective than a team leader who tries to manage by exception and corrective transactions or who takes a laissez-faire stance with a team. Thus the application of the full-range model to team development and effectiveness is very direct.

Teams may comprise members from different departments and functional areas of the organization. We now turn to examining how the full range of leadership is applied in such multifunctional teams.

Notes

1. Sundstrom E., Muse, D. P., & Futrell, D. (1990). Work teams: Applications and effectiveness. *American Psychologist, 45*(2), 123.

2. Shea, G. P., & Guzzo, R. A. (1987). Group effectiveness: What really matters? *Sloan Management Review, 3*, 25-31 (cited in Sundstrom et al., 1990, p. 123).

3. Shea & Guzzo (1987) in Sundstrom et al. (1990), p. 123.

4. Sundstrom et al. (1990), p. 123.

5. Shea & Guzzo (1987) in Sundstrom et al. (1990), p. 123.

6. Shea & Guzzo (1987) in Sundstrom et al. (1990), p. 124.

7. Oldham, G., & Rotchford, N. L. (1983). Relations between office characteristics and employee reactions: A study of the physical environment. *Administrative Sciences Quarterly, 28*, 546-556.

8. Sundstrom et al. (1990), p. 124.

9. Sundstrom et al. (1990), p. 124.

10. Levine, J. M., & Moreland, R. L. (1990). Progress in small group research. *Annual Review of Psychology, 41*, 585-634.

11. Levine & Moreland (1990), p. 590.

12. Levine & Moreland (1990), p. 590.

13. Steiner, I. D. (1972). *Group process and productivity.* New York: Academic Press. Cited in Seaman, D. F. (1981). *Working effectively with task-oriented groups.* New York: McGraw-Hill.

14. Jewel, L. N., & Reitz, H. J. (1981). *Group effectiveness in organizations* (p. 113). Glenview, IL: Scott, Foresman.

15. Markoff, J. (1989, December 10). A prescription for a troubled IBM. *New York Times,* Sec. 3, p. 4.

16. Friedlander, F. (1966). Performance interactional dimensions of organizational work groups. *Journal of Applied Psychology, 50,* 257-265.

17. Laughlin, P. R., & Bitz, D. S. (1975). Individual versus dyadic performance on a disjunctive task as a function of initial ability level. *Journal of Personality and Social Psychology, 31,* 487-896.

18. Tziner, A., & Eden, D. (1985). Effects of crew composition on crew performance: Does the whole equal the sum of its parts? *Journal of Applied Behavioral Sciences, 70,* 85-93; cited in Levine & Moreland (1990), p. 594.

19. Salancik, G., & Pfeffer, S. (1978). A social information processing approach to job attitudes and task design. *Administrative Sciences Quarterly, 25,* 224-253; cited in Levine & Moreland (1990), p. 616.

20. Steers, R. M. (1991). *Introduction to organizational behavior* (4th ed., p. 79). New York: HarperCollins.

21. Mowday, R. T., Porter, L. W., & Steers, R. M. (1982). *Employee-organizational linkages—The psychology of commitment, absenteeism, and turnover.* New York: Academic Press. Cited in Moreland, G., & Griffin, R. W. (1989). *Organizational behavior* (p. 93). Boston: Houghton-Mifflin.

22. Tuckman, B. W., & Jensen, M. A. (1977). Stages of group development revisited. *Group and Organization Studies, 2,* 419-427.

23. Greene, C. N., & Schriesheim, C. A. (1980). Leader-group interactions: A longitudinal field investigation. *Journal of Applied Psychology, 65,* 50-59. Cited in Levine & Moreland (1990), p. 591.

24. Feldman, D. C. (1984). The development and enforcement of group norms. *Academy of Management Review, 9,* 47-53. Cited in Levine & Moreland (1990), p. 601.

25. Kerr, N. L., (1989). Illusions of efficacy: The effects of group size on perceived efficacy in social dilemmas. *Journal of Experimental Social Psychology, 25,* 287-313. Cited in Levine & Moreland (1990), p. 593.

26. Bass, B. M., & Ryterbrand, E. C. (1979). *Organizational psychology.* Boston: Allyn & Bacon.

27. Steiner (1972).

28. Latane, B. (1981). The psychology of social impact. *American Psychologist, 36,* 343-356. Cited in Levine & Moreland (1990), p. 593.

29. Albanese, R., & Van Fleet, D. D. (1985). Rational behavior in groups: The free-riding effect. *Academy of Management Review, 10,* 244-255. Cited in Levine & Moreland (1990), p. 593.

30. Baron, R. A., & Greenberg, J. (1990). *Behavior in organizations: Understanding the human side of work* (p. 499). Boston: Allyn & Bacon.

31. Ben-Yorv, O., Hollander, E. P., Carnevale, P. J. (1983). Leader legitimacy, leader-follower interactions, and followers' ratings of the leader. *Journal of Social Psychology, 121,* 111-115. Cited in Levine & Moreland (1990).

32. Lord, R. G. (1985). An information processing approach to social perceptions, leadership and behavioral measurement in organizations. In L. Cummings & B. Staw (Eds.), *Research in organizational behavior* (Vol. 5, pp. 87-128). Greenwich, CT: JAI.

33. Bass, B. M., & Avolio, B. J. (1990). The implications for transactional and transformational leadership for individual, team, and organizational development. In *Research in organizational change and development* (Vol. 4, pp. 231-272). Greenwich: JAI.

34. House, R. J., & Mitchell, T. R. (1974). Path-goal theory of leadership. *Journal of Contemporary Business, 3*(4), 85.

35. Seaman (1981).

36. Uhl-bien, M., & Graen, G. B. (1992). Self-management and team-making in cross-functional work teams: Discovering the key to becoming an integrated team. *Journal of High Technology Management, 3*(2), 225-242.

37. Uhl-bien & Graen (1992), p. 6.

38. Levine & Moreland (1990), p. 602.

39. Moreland, R. L., & Levine, J. M. (1984). Role transitions in small groups. In V. L. Allen & C. van de Vlient (Eds.), *Role transitions: Explorations and explanations* (pp. 181-195). New York: Plenum.

40. Jackson, S. E., & Schuler, R. S. (1985). A meta-analysis and conceptual critique of research on role ambiguity and role conflict in work settings. *Organizational Behavior, 36,* 16-78. Cited in Levine & Moreland (1990), p. 602.

41. Baron & Greenberg (1990), p. 273.

42. Gray, T. D., Griffith, W. I., von Broembsen, M. H., & Sullivan, M. J. (1982). Group differentiation: Temporal effects of reinforcement. *Social Psychology Quarterly, 45,* 44-49. Cited in Levine & Moreland (1990), p. 600.

43. O'Reilly, C. A., & Caldwell, D. F. (1985). The impact of normative social influence and cohesiveness on task perceptions and attitudes: A social-information processing approach. *Journal of Occupational Psychology, 58,* 193-206. Cited in Levine & Moreland (1990), p. 604.

44. Piper, W. E., Marrache, M., LaCroix, R., Richardson, A. M., & Jones, B. D. (1983). Cohesion as a basic bond in groups. *Human Relations, 36,* 93-108. Cited in Levine & Moreland (1990), p. 604.

45. Kerr, N. L. (1983). Motivation losses in small groups: A social dilemma analysis. *Journal of Personality and Social Psychology, 45*(4), 819-828.

46. Levine & Moreland (1990), p. 607.

47. Olson, M. (1965). *The logic of collective action: Public good and the theory of groups.* Cambridge, MA: Harvard University Press. Cited in Kerr (1983), p. 819.

48. Messick, D. M., Wilke, H., Brewer, M. B., Krammer, R. M., Zemke, P. E., & Lui, L. (1984). Individual adaptions and structural change as solutions to social dilemmas. *Journal of Personality and Social Psychology, 44,* 294-309. Cited in Kerr (1983), p. 827.

49. Bass, B. M. (1980). Team productivity and individual member competence. *Small Group Behavior, 11*(4), 431-504.

50. Bass & Avolio (1990), p. 243.

51. Graen, G., & Cashman, J. F. (1975). A role making model of leadership in formal organizations: A developmental approach. In J. G. Hunt & L. I. Larson (Eds.), *Leadership frontiers* (pp. 143-165). Kent, OH: Kent State University Press.

52. Graen & Cashman (1975).

53. Levine & Moreland (1990), p. 617.

54. Stake, J. E., (1983). Factors in reward distribution: Allocator motive, gender, and the Protestant ethic endorsement. *Journal of Personality and Social Psychology, 44*(2), 410-418.

55. Deutsch, M. (1969). Conflicts: Productive and destructive. *Journal of Social Issues, 25,* 11.

56. Sherif, M. (1971). Subordinate goals in the reduction of intergroup conflict. In B. Hinton & H. Reitz (Eds.), *Groups and organizations* (pp. 392-401). Belmont, CA: Wadsworth.

57. Jackson & Schuler (1985). Cited in Levine & Moreland (1990), p. 602.

58. Miller, D. S., & Catt, S. E. (1989). *Human relations: A contemporary approach* (pp. 266-267). Homewood, IL: Irwin.

59. Study finds most workers unhappy in their firms. (1982, December 13). *Chicago Tribune*, pp. 1-2.

60. Levine & Moreland (1990), p. 605.

61. Miller & Catt (1989), p. 273.

5

Transformational Leadership in Multifunctional Teams

DAVID A. WALDMAN
Concordia University, Montréal, Québec

EXECUTIVE SUMMARY

As seen in the preceding chapter, transformational leadership can enhance the effectiveness of teams. This chapter examines how transformationally led multifunctional teams (MFTs) of members from different functions in the organization develop cooperation between different functional areas of the larger organization to speed the cycles of product and process innovation and renewal. Traditionally, most organizations have used a sequential model of innovation. Different groups of members from the same functional area engage in a set of tasks at each different phase of innovation. If communications are inadequate between each succeeding group, then much rework occurs whenever a group involved in a later phase finds the product of a group in an earlier phase lacking in feasibility. The end result is slower innovation and an inability to meet customer requirements. To counter these problems, organizations are increasingly making use of MFTs that engage in more than one phase of innovation, sometimes carrying the new product forward from inception to market.

For MFTs of members with dissimilar backgrounds typically brought together for a limited amount of time to solve or address problems or tasks of significance to the organization, the roles of their leaders are crucial. The leaders' tasks are complicated by the fact that they may not be able to rely on personal attributes and leadership styles that served them in other, more traditional leadership positions. MFT leaders may not have typical rewards and reinforcers at their disposal, such as pay and promotion, to be able to practice contingent reward. The MFT leader frequently deals with individuals having critical skills and expertise in areas that are unfamiliar to the leader. In these situations, the influence skills of the leaders are particularly important in developing effective MFTs and guiding them toward successful completion of their tasks.

In reviewing MFT leadership, the role of upper-level management in setting priorities, providing resources, and allowing for autonomy in an MFT's day-to-day operations will be examined. Then the liaison role played by the MFT leader in working with leaders from various functional areas will be considered. The roles of the MFT leader as team leader also will be examined. These roles include: (a) assuming a generalist orientation, (b) dynamically staffing the MFT, (c) encouraging team members to form linkages with customers, (d) establishing a group-based evaluation and reward system, (e) anticipating and tolerating mistakes, (f) removing impediments to team performance, and (g) maintaining the team's vision. Such MFT leadership can make considerable use of the full range of leadership model, particularly the Four I's of transformational leadership, whether applied to total quality-improvement efforts or to innovation and product development.

Introduction

Fran was asked to serve as leader of a team from the production and marketing staffs to see how customer orders could be filled more quickly. She discovered early on that she had to deal with production staff members who saw marketing people always in a rush to satisfy special customer orders no matter how much it disturbed the assembling processes. In the same way, marketing people saw the production staff as stuffy, conservative, and traditional. Although the members were there to work as a team, they had different points of view, depending on the part of the organization in which they worked.

Today's organizations are faced with turbulent and continuously changing business environments. In the 1990s and beyond, the marketplace is and will continue to be characterized by a constant state of flux, with quickly changing customer demands and competition coupled with rapidly evolving technologies. To meet the demands of such an environment, quick product-renewal cycles are required at minimal cost and without sacrificing quality. MFTs are perfect for addressing these challenges.

The Nature of MFTs

MFTs also have been called cross-functional teams, multidisciplinary teams, and cross-disciplinary teams. Whatever their name, such teams are groups of individuals from different functional, technical, or professional backgrounds. One interest in this chapter is examining those MFTs that jointly plan and implement new products or processes. We will also look at actual operating MFTs.

Consider, for example, the MFT led by Nancy Lento, who found herself assigned to lead a team of head nurses, administrative staff members, laboratory directors, and a chief accountant in a special cost-containment project. What she would discover is that as the team pursued its objective, she would need to keep in mind the characteristics of her firm, the nature of the task, each individual member and his or her predilections, and the interactions between and among individual members, the team as a whole, and individual members and herself. Conflicts would have to be managed. General opportunities would occur for transactional and transformational leadership within her multifunctional team. Such opportunities are considered throughout this chapter. These will point to the principles Nancy Lento could use.

The individual MFT members could be actual workers who periodically meet or communicate but separately perform tasks (perhaps with other workers in their respective functional areas) related to the project. For example, an MFT in an automobile corporation might have the task of redesigning and producing the body of a current model. The individual team members could come from marketing, engineering, production, quality control, and accounting. Depending on the nature of the task, time constraints, and resources, meetings between MFT individuals might occur on a regular basis. Specific tasks may be performed together or separately, within one facility or across geographically dispersed facilities.

MFTs could be composed of managers from various functional areas rather than staff professionals or line workers. As such, the teams would essentially be decision-making as opposed to implementing entities. The ad hoc decision-making team of this nature should not be confused with the permanent executive team that makes up the top level of most organizations because the latter is an ongoing group that meets to determine the organization's strategic direction in a variety of business areas. Rather, an MFT is a temporary entity focused on a particular problem such as developing a new product or process. An MFT ordinarily exists only as long as it takes to complete its task or innovation project. However, there is growing use of MFTs that meet on an ongoing basis to monitor or engage in a product-renewal cycle. Therefore, MFTs may eventually become a permanent part of organizational structures. Currently, however, they are more often formed on a temporary basis.

MFTs should not be equated with quality circles. A quality circle is typically a voluntary group of employees from a common work area who come together to solve specific task-related problems. Although quality-circle members may represent more than one functional area, a quality circle is generally not as diverse as an MFT. Moreover, an MFT

is often not voluntary and more commonly represents a formal assignment by management. Finally, MFTs are typically associated with
larger-scale projects than are quality circles.

The Need for MFTs for Innovation

The increasing need for MFTs to effect innovation can best be
understood by first considering the innovation process and how organizations have traditionally attempted to proceed with innovation and
new-product development. In most organizations, innovation and product development (or product renewal) have typically occurred in a
five-phase sequence.[1] Phase 1 begins with idea generation and development. Phase 2 takes the initial idea generation and conducts applied
research to determine both technological and market feasibility. Phase
3 brings the development of a prototype product and continued feasibility
studies. This phase essentially marks the beginning of product "development" and the end of "research." Phase 4 is marked by an intense prepara-
tion for mass production and an emphasis on reconciling process technologies. Phase 5 concludes the innovation cycle by proceeding with mass
production and introduction of the new product into the marketplace.

Thus, the five phases of innovation are:

1. idea generation,
2. technical feasibility,
3. prototype development,
4. production set-up, and
5. production and distribution.

Two issues are noteworthy in reference to the innovation process.
First, few organizations have the structure, resources, or need to engage
fully in all five phases. This is especially true with regard to phases 1
and 2, which involve basic and applied research efforts, respectively.
Many firms and agencies acquire knowledge gained from research done
at institutes, in universities, or through consortiums with other organizations. Information is gathered from technical libraries and library
services, attendance at professional meetings, trade shows, and visits
paid to relevant sites. A company also may not be in an industry with
an initial need for as much technical information, so it may not have to
invest as much effort in phases 1 and 2. These phases probably would
be less important in furniture manufacturing than in biogenetics.

Second, where different groups are responsible for each phase, the
innovation process in organizations is typically likened to a relay race.

Phase 1 is the responsibility of a management or technical group; phase 2, a research group of scientists; phase 3, a team of materials engineers; phase 4, a team of production engineers; and phase 5, manufacturing and marketing teams. Phase 1 is completed before phase 2 begins; phase 2 is completed before phase 3 begins; and so forth. Problems can readily come about with sequential innovation processes. For example, because the people involved in the innovation tend to differ across phases, "ownership" of the project may be diffused, and communication may suffer as one innovation group "hands the baton" to the next. Indeed, as that next group begins its work, it may find the previous group's work to be incomplete or lacking the requirements or constraints of the following group. Communication between groups often can break down. The first group may inadequately specify what it accomplished. This problem has the potential for accentuation at later phases. For example, a deficiency found in the basic technology in phase 4 could cause a project to revert all the way back to phase 1. In sum, ownership and communication problems associated with sequential innovation processes can lead to lengthy product-development or renewal cycles. Such long cycles can, in turn, lead to increased costs in bringing the product to market, a poorer quality product, and a loss of market share as customers quickly turn to competitors who can satisfy their requirements.

For example, research scientists operating in phases 1 or 2 discover how to make a new ceramic material for catalytic converters in automobiles. This material would be much more efficient than the currently used material. Development engineers working in phase 3 are then expected to incorporate this new material into a prototype catalytic converter. After the prototype has been produced, test results show major problems in trying to incorporate the new material into an actual converter system. If the two groups had been working in parallel or at least in overlapping phases or as an MFT, then the chances would have been greater that potential problems with this new ceramic material would have been identified and corrected much more quickly. Indeed, involving the development engineers earlier in the process might have completely eliminated this problem.

To deal more creatively with the sequencing problem, a large international conglomerate in the electronics industry, as part of his organization's total quality management (TQM) effort, arranged for development and design engineers to work alongside line employees to help in the rapid assessment and implementation of those innovative ideas that could improve the production process's overall quality. What would have been considered in the past radical changes in process would have been altered by the organization's bureaucracy;

now they were being implemented quickly and efficiently and with minimal red tape.

Part of the problem is that organizing innovation in a sequential manner lends itself to a generally homogeneous composition of project team members. For example, scientists working on basic research projects tend to be the only ones involved in the first and second phases, development engineers in the third phase, manufacturing engineers in the fourth phase, and line workers and supervisors in the last phase. An MFT structure has been popularly heralded as a means for reducing development or renewal cycles.[2] The rudiments of MFTs were seen 30 years ago in a proposal to help several members of the idea-generation team by increasing members of the technical feasibility team, placing several members from the technical feasibility team on the prototype-development team, and so on. This provided a way to improve communications between phases, maintained a continuing team culture, and increased ownership and commitment in later phases of the activity, particularly in production.[3]

Figure 5.1 depicts the innovation process using MFTs as occurring with overlapping phases. The overlap of phases serves as a stimulus for people from different functional areas to be involved in each phase of innovation. To some extent, selected MFT members can work together on a project from phases 1 through 5. This type of structure would provide the opportunity for continued feedback and a "looping back" to an early phase as needed. Also, from a motivational perspective, seeing a project through from early idea generation and research to the eventual production of a commercially successful product can be a highly rewarding experience for project team members who thus hopefully develop a greater sense of ownership in the product over these various phases. It also instills an enhanced sense of ownership on the part of project members, especially as compared to the innovation model in which only small segments of the larger project are completed by different teams at respective phases. This latter situation can lead to members of one team treating the next team poorly. If any conflicts are already present, then we must rely quite heavily on how each team treats the one responsible for the next phase. This approach also can lead to bottlenecks that put increasing pressure on the teams waiting to take on their phases of the project. Delays more readily occur when a homogeneously staffed group operating in a particular phase passes the project along to another homogeneous group in the next phase. These delays result from a lack of early communication between people in different functional areas and a lack of understanding of requirements at later points in the process. MFTs alleviate such problems by stimulating

Phase 1: Idea generation and initial testing
Phase 2: Applied research to determine product feasibility
Phase 3: Product development
Phase 4: Technological process development
Phase 5: Mass production and introduction to the marketplace

Figure 5.1   A Nonsequential Model of Product Development

immediate communication and troubleshooting potential problems. Redundancies in effort across different phases, start-up time from one
phase to the next, and conflicts in schedules if product transfer is
delayed in one phase can be reduced using an MFT structure. In sum,
MFTs can accelerate and make the innovation process more efficient
by reducing or eliminating these specific problems—often as a consequence of effective leadership.

The Leadership Challenges of MFTs

The increasing use of MFTs provides several leadership challenges
for organizations. For example, recent experience with MFTs at Honda
suggests that the MFT process can generate divisiveness or procrasti-
nation among group members; if left unchecked by the MFT leader,
these can lead to costly delays.[4] Company officials have taken steps to
increase individual-level responsibility, including the assuming of ever
greater responsibility levels by MFT project leaders.

Several questions about effective MFT leadership must be addressed.
What, if any, leadership direction should be provided to an MFT by
upper-level management? Each team member may report to both an
MFT and a functional leader, so what is the general role of an MFT
leader vis-à-vis functional area leaders? What are the specific behavioral roles of an MFT leader in relation to team members? To what
extent should such a leader engage in transactional or transformational
and participative or directive forms of leadership?

Upper-Level Management and MFT Leadership

Currently, MFTs are often formed to engage in projects that have immense potential for dramatic change and transformation in an organization. An MFT may create new technologies, patents, products, and services that could have major effects on how both insiders and outsiders view the organization and what it has to offer the marketplace. Generally, these potential impacts require the involvement of leadership and the commitment of upper-level management in a manner similar to the effort required for a comprehensive TQM effort. What form should such involvement take?

To a large extent, much of the leadership displayed by upper-level management is expected to be at the higher end of the full range of leadership, that is, transformational. Top management first must recognize the need to form an MFT. This is the initial stage of awareness depicted in Figure 7.2 in Chapter 7. It must then provide developmental guidance by establishing commonly agreed upon goals. Alignment of MFT goals with an organization's central purposes will help to give the MFT credibility and importance. Such goals should be highly challenging yet attainable. Working together with the MFT project leader, a shared vision should be established for the members about what the MFT will attempt to achieve and its timetable for completion. Thus, at the outset, upper management exerts direct leadership by providing guidance and "moral support." It allocates money and resources, thus representing a more transactional focus. This orientation must also be limited to the leaders establishing the global direction for the team, setting challenging goals and directives. This represents the transformational dimension of top management's leadership. Subsequently, upper management's leadership becomes indirect. It seldom should intervene in day-to-day MFT activities, allowing the MFT freedom to set its own direction. But it needs to remain in contact at a distance, displaying continuing interest, providing encouragement, and reviewing reports of progress. Upper management also should be prepared for new discoveries by the MFT that may result in altering its objectives and modifying its mission. In sum, upper management should serve in the role of venture capitalist and project champion.[5]

This kind of autonomy was evident in the initial development of personal computers at IBM. A small group of engineers obtained the go-ahead and resources to work on the machine in a converted warehouse in what was then considered to be remote Boca Raton, Florida. Except for occasional progress reviews, IBM headquarters allowed the Boca Raton group autonomy in its operation. Indeed, the group took what were previously considered highly unconventional steps for a company such as IBM, which had a highly centralized decision-making structure. These included selecting outside suppliers for its microprocessor and software package.[6] These speeded up developments but also made cloning by competitors easy, illustrating that what makes for MFT efficiency may ultimately prove costly to the organization. Senior management must continue to pay attention to its MFT development teams ensuring that what is being developed will reach the final consumer with adequate payoff to the firm.

The MFT Leader in Relation to Functional and Divisional Leaders

An MFT usually is embedded in an existing hierarchical organization. As such, the MFT operates as a *collateral organization,*[7] or one that operates parallel to the primary organizational hierarchy. It can be used to quickly and flexibly deal with complex tasks or problems such as those accompanying innovation. The existing hierarchical structure may not be able to deal very quickly or effectively with issues of innovation because of problems with communication, norms, and information exchange. Properties of a collateral organization include the following:

1. new combinations of people (e.g., MFT teams);
2. new or more open channels of communication that can move readily across organizational and hierarchical boundaries;
3. the possibility of different operating norms as compared to the formal organization;
4. a rapid and complete exchange of information, assuming that trust levels are high and members enter without hidden agendas; and
5. norms that encourage a questioning and analysis of goals, assumptions, methods, and alternatives.[8]

Within the framework of a collateral organization, an MFT team is often formed when top, middle, or even lower levels of management (depending on the type of organizational structure) determine that such a need exists. Such determinations can be made in response to a need to change a reactive leadership style or to take advantage of, proactively and transformationally, future opportunities.

The management decision to form an MFT is followed by the assignment of a team leader, who then proceeds to recruit members from some combination of different functional and technical areas. Moreover, members may come from different divisions when the organization is structured according to product, customer, or geographical divisions. Thus, MFTs tend to exist within a matrix structure whereby a team member typically has dual reporting relationships: to the team leader as well to a functional or divisional leader in his or her "home" area. A cost accountant may report to the MFT leader and to the finance director. Further complicating the matter is the possibility that a team member may serve on more than one MFT simultaneously.

The matrix-type structure associated with MFTs increases the potential for conflict between the MFT leader and leaders of the functional areas from which members are drawn. For instance, for the team leader, any functional behavior may place conflicting demands on an individual, leading to competition for the individual's time, role conflict, or role overload. A nursing-unit head assigned to a hospital MFT to improve equipment usage may find it difficult to carry on all of her required duties as assigned by both her department head and the MFT leader. To prevent disruptive conflict, it becomes necessary to delineate the respective areas of influence for MFT and functional leaders.[9]

In general, projects are most successful when the MFT leader maintains influence in the project over organizational and customer decision making; conversely, functional leaders should maintain a high level of influence over technical details of the work completed by a project's team members. In other words, the MFT leader should be responsible for coordinating the internal activities of team members, representing the team and its needs to upper management, monitoring the innovations of competitors, and forming close connections with customers (internal and external) to meet their requirements.

Functional leaders should communicate with both MFT leaders and members in the process of maintaining control over technical details. As outlined below, broader technical control will be maintained by the MFT leader who then attempts to put together the various technical details across the different areas represented by the team. In exercising this broader technical control, the prudent MFT leader will attempt to maintain close advisory communication with the functional leaders of the departments represented on the project. Finally, transactional control of such personnel decisions as performance appraisal, salaries, and promotions should be shared between MFT and functional leaders.[10]

Because of the importance of influence skills for the effective MFT leader, knowledge of the Four I's of transformational leadership becomes particularly relevant for the team leader, whether appointed, elected, or emergent. Each transformational leadership factor will improve the MFT leader's ability to influence the functioning of his or her team.

Examples will suffice to illustrate the importance of each of the Four I's for the effective MFT leader.

Individualized Consideration

The MFT leader is dealing with people from different functional areas and backgrounds and must show sensitivity to these differences. The effective MFT leader must avoid glossing over the different constraints faced by the members, their different career ladders, the different bosses to whom they report, and their different needs. The MFT leader will need to show that he or she cares about the dual loyalties that members must maintain. Whenever possible, he or she should delegate opportunities to individual members and subgroups and make it possible for the different members to represent the MFT well to their own functional areas or even risk representing the MFT in meetings with higher authority.

Intellectual Stimulation

Not being an expert in all areas represented by the members of the MFT, the effective leader should serve as a catalyst for creative activity. He or she should move the members to question their assumptions and to problem solve in stages beginning with trying to reach agreement on the group's mission and major tasks. The MFT leader should clarify, summarize, and test for consensus.

Inspirational Motivation

As much as possible, the inspirational MFT leader should promote understanding of the MFT's mission and importance. He or she should lay out what needs to be done in language that all members find readily understandable. The leader should remain optimistic about likely outcomes and boost the team's confidence in success.

Idealized Influence

The person selected (or elected) to lead the MFT should have a reputation for integrity, capability, and success. In turn, the effective leader should provide a role model for working well with others of different opinions; in short, the leader should be someone whom other members will want to emulate.

MFT leaders will need to be sensitive to the demands placed on individual members from their non-MFT assignments and the quality of their relations with their functional manager. This will require that they exhibit the first element of transformational leadership—individualized consideration—for team members, as well as for the functional manager, who also may have needs that must be met, if not also developed. Intellectual stimulation may be necessary when seemingly unresolvable problems of conflicting time place demands on an individual team member. Often the team will need to break new ground, requiring that basic assumptions be tested and alternative viewpoints, procedures, and perspectives be developed. To accomplish these, team leaders will need to be intellectually stimulating within their respective teams, as well as with other teams and departments. Finally, representing the MFT in meetings with other groups and upper-level management requires inspirational motivation to keep key individuals interested in a project's development. A clear sense of purpose and direction must be developed and articulated by the leader. As suggested by Steven Jobs, the leader of the MFT will then need to become the "Keeper of the Vision."[11] All of this requires that the MFT leader know the capabilities of each team member. The leader also spends considerable time building a culture of cooperation and alignment to tie one individual's responsibilities to another's; this is done more at the operator level than the team player level. This is not to say that MFT leaders can ignore the need to be transactional as they cope with the necessary technical and personal controls and personnel practices. Obviously, the more they can be constructive and active in these matters, the more likely the project will move forward.

The Roles of the MFT Leader

Although MFTs are often designed to be largely autonomous, MFT leaders should not be viewed as lacking authority for their activities or direction. Upper management helps to set the initial direction, shares the vision, and empowers the MFT and its leader to carry out their responsibilities. In addition, MFTs generally will be assigned formal leaders who have certain guidelines to follow and resources to support their efforts.

MFT leaders can best be viewed as walking a tightrope: They need to use their authority to balance the need for control and meeting timetables with the need to stimulate creativity and spontaneity. The best way to accomplish this balance is to move members to higher levels of self-control so that qualified MFT members are empowered to control their own responsibilities—to lead their own components of the project in coordination with other members whose coordination efforts are assisted by the leader. This parallels the arguments in Chapter 2 about the self-defining leader. To accomplish these developments, the effective MFT leader will stimulate team-oriented behavior that often takes a subtle and behind-the-scenes flavor. Specific behavioral roles of MFT leaders include the following:

1. the careful staffing of an MFT,
2. taking on a coordinator or facilitator orientation,
3. encouraging team members to form links with one another and the team's customers,
4. establishing a group-based evaluation and incentive system,
5. anticipating and tolerating mistakes,
6. removing impediments to team performance, and
7. aligning team members' individual goals with the team's ultimate goal.

Careful Staffing

Staffing should bring together team members of sufficient diversity in technical background to effectively complete the group's mission. Care also should be taken to screen team members' personalities to ensure that potential conflict in the group will be based on issues of importance rather than on personality differences. A similar attempt might be made to balance senior with junior team members and those with more conservative approaches with those with more radical approaches to problem solving. Throughout the project, it is the MFT leader's responsibility to monitor shifts in group dynamics and add or drop team members when necessary. It is also the MFT leader's responsibility to maintain an effective culture and problem-solving orientation. In this regard, all of the Four I's of transformational leadership will be needed to maximize both performance and development. Simply focusing on transactional leadership will not suffice.

Generalist Orientation

MFT technical diversity increases the likelihood of conflict among members because of differences in assumptions, perspectives, values, and experiences. Although group decision making may take longer under such circumstances, the result is likely to be greater creativity.[12] MFT leaders must be prepared to deal effectively with such conflicts to maximize the creativity of the group, continuously linking the resolution of conflict to greater achievements. Conflict so construed results in an organization that is willing to entertain and learn from conflict. The conflicts can thus be viewed as constructive and initiations of intellectual stimulation.

To facilitate positive conflict resolution, it is important for the MFT leader to take a global perspective by understanding the needs and values of other groups. It would be good to be able to say, for example, "Our MFT leader is from engineering, but she understands and is concerned about the need for our manufacturing to be timely." The MFT leader should be able to move adeptly across functional turf boundaries and networks, effectively appreciating the individual needs and perspectives of the diverse groups from which team members are drawn. To some extent, this involves a high-level ability to conceptually incorporate technical information from different specialized areas in the decision-making process. Certainly, the MFT leader cannot be a technical expert in all areas of the team. Moreover, any attempt by the leader to do so would probably result in suspicion or resentment on the part of team members. In sum, the MFT leader must be a technical generalist and, perhaps even more important, not show favoritism toward any one functional group. These demands require that the leader demonstrate all Four I's of transformational leadership in varying degrees, particularly individualized consideration, and the thrust and determination that goes along with inspirational motivation and idealized influence.

Customer Linkages

The MFT leader should encourage and help provide opportunities for team members to form links with customers. Such actions on the part of team members will provide growth by producing a broader understanding of the group's mission. For example, an engineer working on his own might be tempted to take the easy way out in meeting design requirements. A different approach might be for the engineer to accompany a marketing team member to field meetings with customers. This would provide the engineer with a broader perspective and desire to more fully meet customer needs. Stated another way, customers might intellectually stimulate the engineer to question existing assumptions, methods, and procedures more carefully. In one sense, the customers intellectually stimulate the engineer to go beyond his or her normal framework of thinking to include the customers' needs, desires, and perspectives. This is the type of essential culture that will likely support the MFT's success. It is a culture that the MFT leader can be instrumental in supporting.

Team-Based Evaluation and Rewards

To ensure that the MFT actually operates as a team rather than as just a collection of individuals, the leader should take steps to encourage each team member to be involved in the collective mission. One way to proceed is for the leader to establish a group-based evaluation-and-reward system. Most workplaces rely on individual performance appraisals and associated reward systems. However, these systems tend to be heavily evaluative and somewhat arbitrary and inconsistent, leading to dissatisfied employees and managers.[13] Moreover, individually oriented systems do little to focus on team-level cooperation, effort, and performance or on work-system problems that can damage the collective effort.[14] Finally, reward systems often concentrate attention on outcomes achieved rather than on developing potential. In the long run, both must be attended to by the MFT leader.

An alternative strategy to those typically seen in organizations is providing a balance to appraisal and reward processes by including a focus on both individuals and the team. Thus instead of the traditional approach of periodically meeting with and evaluating individual team members, group meetings could be held frequently to monitor and find ways of improving system-based factors that may be causing problems for the group as a whole. Such an effort is intellectually stimulating: the traditional focus on the individual moves to the team. Intellectual stimulation also stretches the boundaries by examining the problem using a higher level of analysis. It should follow that recognition and reward procedures also would focus primarily on group rather than individual accomplishments, including some weighting that emphasizes the importance of development. This, however, should not preclude providing individual members with recognition for their accomplishments in the context of the team effort. Individually considerate meetings of each member with the MFT leader may be held that primarily address developmental issues and special problems that team members may be having.

Anticipating and Tolerating Mistakes

Traditional management often involves managing by exception by setting up control procedures so that mistakes or deviations from what is expected will be quickly identified, with disciplinary action taken to prevent repeated mistakes. Unfortunately, this type of behavior will prevent group members from thinking creatively and taking the risks that are necessary in innovation processes. Thus it is essential for MFT leaders to anticipate and tolerate mistakes, rather than simply react to them as is characterized by leaders who passively manage by exception. The underlying philosophy is that a small success rate will inherently be preceded by many mistakes and misdirections in innovation. The leader must be patient and encourage team members to take the type of risks that often lead to small mistakes while avoiding the larger mistakes that do serious damage to the team effort.[15]

Whenever possible, the MFT leader should convert what could be passive or even active management by exception into a more productive, constructive contingent reward situation by removing performance impediments early.

Removing Performance Impediments

Another key role for the MFT leader is removing impediments that may retard a team's performance. A key aspect of this role is what may be termed "running interference" with upper-level management. In other words, the MFT leader needs to ensure that upper-level managers do not slip (with regard to their role described above) by pressuring or attempting to personally redirect team members. This is not to say that team members should have no contact with upper management. Allowing such contact at key times can help to motivate team members by providing recognition and a sense of importance. However, at other times the MFT leader must serve as a shield or buffer between team members and upper management, who may be overly eager to see progress on the part of an MFT. Part of this buffering process is securing resources and, when necessary, championing team members. Another part is simply making sure that team members are free from administrative paperwork and procedures required by upper management. Removing these impediments allows team members to proceed with the central mission of their project, and such action has been linked to the "champion" role that is associated with transformational leaders of highly successful R&D units,[16] or those that have achieved higher rates of productive innovation over time.

Maintaining the Vision

One role of the MFT leader is inspirational leadership, which helps to maintain the team's vision and spirit on a daily basis. Because of technical setbacks and shifting customer requirements, team members may be easily discouraged and lose sight of where the group is heading and the potential importance of its mission. The MFT leader should maintain a broad view and periodically attempt to enhance members' optimism for the future, raising their expectations of what they can achieve. Steven Jobs carried out this activity in his self-proclaimed role of keeper of the vision as he personally became the MFT leader at his fledgling Next Corporation in the latter part of the 1980s. Despite periodic setbacks and occasional controversy in the team, Jobs attempted to keep members focused on their common group goals and values. He championed the cause and inspired his team.

In sum, the internal role of a MFT leader is to bring a diverse group of people together, manage that diversity in an intellectually stimulating way, motivate the team to want to work together for the good of the overall team, and serve as a buffer between the team and upper management. The following quote summarizes this role and comes from an MFT leader in an organization that typically assigns employees to participate simultaneously in more than one MFT:

> At the outset, I must try to get people to want to work for me on a team. For the part-timers [or those who work on more than one MFT at a time], it's like having a choice of restaurants to go to when you come to work in the morning in that they are all working on different projects. I get them to want to spend a lot of time on my project by giving them responsibility, building their self-worth, and giving them ownership. Ownership can be achieved by allowing them to meet and present to upper management and customers.[17]

Summarizing the Four I's and Their Relevance to MFTs

Many parallels can be drawn between effective MFT leadership and the full range of leadership, particularly its upper end of transformational leadership. Individualized consideration is shown by the MFT leader in several ways. First, the leader can be adept in dealing with individuals with diverse backgrounds, values, and perspectives. Empathy is shown to individuals who are struggling with difficult problems. The leader also avoids playing favorites with individuals from particular functional areas, thus maintaining a clear sense of equity. Second, the leader allows individuals to make mistakes in the hope that they will learn from their mistakes and increase future chances of success. The leader emphasizes the learning potential in mistakes. Third, the leader transforms individual appraisal processes away from single-person evaluations, using evaluation for both individual and team development.

Intellectual stimulation is also intertwined in the MFT leader's role in dealing with individual team members, the team as a whole, and outside functional leaders. For example, in team problem-solving sessions, it is often necessary to help the team get at the heart of complex problems by offering linkages between vastly different technical areas and concepts. The leader also may be instrumental in getting the team to reexamine assumptions that may inhibit creativity and innovation, assumptions tied to various functional specialties that make up the team.

Inspirational leadership is directly enacted by maintaining the team's vision of its objectives. By repeatedly reminding the team of where it is heading, its incremental successes, and the importance of its mission, the MFT leader is able to maintain optimism despite setbacks and lingering doubts. A collective enthusiasm and effort is fostered by shifting appraisal processes toward the team as a whole. "Going to bat" and championing the team's mission are other ways in which a leader can inspire, in addition to getting what will be the ideal future or desired state for the team.

Idealized influence enhances the success of MFT leadership. The leader sets examples for followers and exhibits integrity. The generalist orientation and an appreciation of each member's point of view help to build members' trust. The effective MFT leader does not "hog the limelight." Team members are personally allowed to present progress findings to upper management, thereby providing them with visibility and recognition for their accomplishments. The MFT leader's strength is demonstrated to team members when the leader is successful in buffering them from upper management, in the persistence shown toward completing the mission, and the confidence that the team's mission will be attained.

Finally, transactional leadership needs to be used judiciously. Transactional behavior, particularly after-the-fact corrective transactions, often does more harm than good. As mentioned earlier, management-by-exception leadership is likely to lead to the avoidance of risk and associated mistakes on the part of team members. Unfortunately, this also reduces creativity and innovation.

Professionals, technical experts, and committed staff or line employees chosen to work on an MFT are typically self-motivated. Thus, although they are likely to have individual career needs, they are likely to have little need for a leader who emphasizes material rewards for performance within the group. The extensive use of contingent reinforcement is perhaps best relegated to other leadership settings or to certain circumstances when the MFT leader is attempting to garner resources (e.g., from upper management) that would benefit the overall team. Nevertheless, contingent rewarding remains important for the MFT leader. Thus the leader must continue to clarify and refine agreements among members and to coordinate many of the interdependent actions that occur within an MFT. Moreover, there will be times when the MFT leader will meet to negotiate with functional managers or other MFT leaders for an individual's time or resources to achieve the project's aim. The effective use of such transactional leadership with functional managers or other MFT leaders is likely to enhance the project's success. As suggested in Chapter 1, the full range of leadership entails appreciating both transactional and transformational leadership.

In conclusion, the purpose of this chapter has been to extend the examination of the role of the MFT leader in research development, innovation, and other common contexts. By nature, the MFT comprises a diverse collection of individuals, usually highly trained technical employees, who bring to the team strong beliefs and assumptions. These differences in perspective must evolve into new ideas and approaches rather than being allowed to derail the team from carrying out its search for innovative solutions. The MFT leader's efforts to innovate must be coordinated with those of leaders and groups from the various functional areas represented by team members. The MFT leader and team almost inevitably face pressures from upper management to hurry the group's effort along. Dealing with these complications becomes the challenge for MFT leaders. To succeed, such a leader requires more transformational leadership and less transactional leadership. He or she also can benefit greatly from the lessons learned from research on the dynamics of leadership and small groups as discussed in this and the preceding chapters.

Notes

1. For a more complete discussion of the typical sequential innovation process, see Musselwhite, W. C. (1990). Time-based innovation: The new competitive advantage. *Training and Development Journal, 44*(1), 53-56.

2. An expanded explanation of the need for nonsequentially phased innovation processes is provided by Takeuchi, H., & Nonaka, I. (1986). The new product development game. *Harvard Business Review, 64*(1), 137-146.

3. See Fische, G. G. (1961). Line-staff is obsolete. *Harvard Business Review, 39*, 67-79.

4. See Chandler, C., & Ingrassia, P. (1991, April 11). Just as U.S. firms try Japanese management, Honda is centralizing. *Wall Street Journal*, pp. 1, 6.

5. Takeuchi & Nonaka (1986).

6. Takeuchi & Nonaka (1986).

7. A more complete discussion of collateral organization can be found in Zand, D. E. (1974). Collateral organization: A new change strategy. *Journal of Applied Behavioral Science, 10*, 63-89.

8. Zand (1974).

9. For a more complete discussion of research findings on areas of influence for both MFT project leaders and functional leaders, see Katz, R., & Allen, T. J. (1985). Project performance and the locus of influence in the R&D matrix. *Academy of Management Journal, 28*, 67-87.

10. Katz & Allen (1985).

11. Job's lot. (1992, December 12). *The Economist,* pp. 74-75.

12. For more details about the effects of heterogeneous team composition, see Goodman, P. S., Ravlin, E. C., & Argote, L. (1986). Current thinking about groups: Setting the stage for new ideas. In P. S. Goodman & Associates, *Designing effective work groups* (pp. 15-16). San Francisco: Jossey-Bass.

13. An expanded explanation of group- or system-based performance-appraisal systems can be found in Waldman, D. A., & Kenett, R. S. (1990). Improve performance by appraisal. *HR Magazine, 35*(7), 66-69.

14. W. Edwards Deming has been instrumental in questioning the value of traditional, individually oriented performance systems. For more details, see Walton, M. (1986). *The Deming management method.* New York: Putnam.

15. For a more complete consideration of the need to allow for mistakes in MFTs, see Peters, T. J. (1989). *Thriving on chaos.* New York: Random House.

16. An expanded discussion of champions of innovation is supplied in Howell, J. M., & Higgins, C. (1990). Champions of technological innovations. *Administrative Science Quarterly, 35*, 317-341.

17. Job's lot. (1992).

6

Transformational Leadership and Team and Organizational Decision Making

BERNARD M. BASS

Center for Leadership Studies,
School of Management, SUNY Binghamton

EXECUTIVE SUMMARY

This chapter merges the model of the Four I's of transformational leadership—individualized consideration, intellectual stimulation, inspirational leadership, and idealized influence—with a model of how team and organizational decisions are made. With this merger we then can suggest how the leadership involved in each of the Four I's can enhance the effectiveness of the various steps in the process of organizational decision making (ODM) as well as the forward and backward connections between the steps.

A Nonlinear Model of Organizational Decision Making

Until approximately 1950, the orderly, forward-moving, causal course of organizational decision making as conceived by Western philosophy was unchallenged.[1] In this model, organizational decision makers were expected to be alert to problems that require solutions and decisions. The decision makers were responsible for actively scanning the external and internal environments of their organization for such problems. The external environment included the organization's market and suppliers, as well as society. The internal environment included the processes of personnel, production, and service. As a problem became apparent, it was brought into sharper focus. Affected parties would be noted. Once the problem was identified and judged to be important, interest in the problem and possible remedies followed from a diagnosis of the problem and the unmet goals involved. This was followed by a logical search for solutions (including doing nothing), from which one alternative was chosen based on a comparison of the expected effects of the available choices. Finally, authorization and commitment was sought to implement the solution.[2]

For example, sales of a firm's trucks might fall unexpectedly despite a steady truck market. Management could be alerted to the problem either by actively monitoring truck sales or by facing an obvious situation that required a reaction. A diagnosis would be made of the reasons for the sales decline, which might include lack of repeat sales because of customer dissatisfaction, lack of product reliability, and too much required servicing. Solutions would be sought for enhancing product quality under selected constraints in price and performance. A new inspection system might seem to be a good solution to the problem. The new inspection system would then be tested and approved. Implementation would follow, often with reevaluation of the solution's adequacy, continued monitoring of customers, and market follow-up.

Although such an information-seeking and decision-making process would seem logical, observation and experiment found quite a different story about how such organizational decisions are made.[3] In the early 1980s, this writer reviewed the available concepts and research on the subject and designed a model (see Figure 6.1) that better fits descriptions of how organizational decisions are actually made.[4]

As the figure shows, the decision process may begin at any phase. It may move backward or forward from one phase to another, and certain phases might be skipped altogether. Feedback from an advanced phase in the decision-making process can stimulate a much earlier phase. When an MFT is involved in the decision process, often the absence or presence of a member may substantially alter whether the process is progressive or regressive. Similarly, the quality of record keeping and attention to such detail, as well as the time between phases, also will determine how much "going over old ground" will be required to reach authorization and implementation.

In the case of the declining sales of trucks, we have already presented the logical forward stepping of Figure 6.1 as arrows a, b, c, d, and e. For a more realistic picture of how decisions are really made, we must add arrows a', b', c', d', d'', d''', e', and f moving backward from later to earlier phases.

For example, consider linkage a', which signifies that problem discovery and diagnosis call for more detailed scanning information. More scanning is required. Decision makers remain dissatisfied with the explanations for the decline in sales of the truck. They initiate an

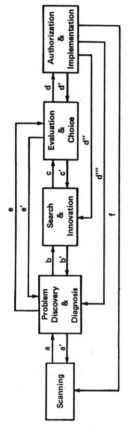

a Scanning detects a possible opportunity, threat, variance, or disturbance.

a′ Diagnosis calls for more detailed information.

b Discovery and diagnosis determine the direction and location of search.

b′ Search and innovation lead to redefinitions of the problem, changes in level of aspiration, and displacement of the ideal.

c Search and innovation provide what is to be evaluated and chosen.

c′ Evaluations and choices foreclose on what will be sought. Search is conducted to justify what already has been chosen as a solution.

d Evaluation and choice must be authorized before being implemented.

d′ Rejected authorization or failed implementation forces reevaluation, redesign (d″), or redefinition (d‴).

e Problem diagnosis determines the evaluation and choice. Search is eliminated. Problem solutions are given by the diagnosis.

e′ Evaluation and choice lead to modifications in the diagnosis. What we want to do leads to the articulation of problems.

f Implementation experience changes scanning focus.

Figure 6.1 Potential Causal Linkages in Organizational Decisions

SOURCE: Adapted from Bass, B. M. (1983). *Organizational decision making* (p. 175). Homewood, IL: Irwin.

examination of recent experience with related products. They also gather information about sales by their different competitors. They may even question the assumptions underlying the problem. They question what is figure and what is ground, thus invoking intellectual stimulation at the very outset. Consider linkage b', which describes how searching and innovative ideas produce a redefinition of the problem. One solution reached may be to improve the quality of the truck chassis by a radical redesign in process, using alternative materials, incorporating new design specifications, and so forth. The question must be redefined from "Why have sales declined?" to "What is wrong with the quality of the trucks?" In the extreme, the question of whether trucks should even be built by the organization may be posed.

The c' backward linkage is most common to the process of organizational decision making. Evaluations and choice of solution are made prematurely. There is a foreclosure on what information will be sought. Such information will be used to justify the solution rather than to choose one solution from an array of alternatives.[5] One favorite solution is chosen early on, often that favored by the top-ranking executive involved, and then a search is made for information that justifies that choice. A favorite solution may be to provide a long-life guarantee to the truck transmission. Then efforts would be directed to show how such guarantees would enhance sales of trucks that had such guarantees. Or decision makers may become convinced quickly that a rebate policy coupled with an enhanced advertising campaign will revive sales. They close the doors on further search or innovation. They often close the door on gaining commitment and involvement in the new plan by not involving the right people in the decision-making process.

As feedback loop e' in Figure 6.1 shows, choice and evaluation may affect the diagnosis of what needs to be done. For instance, the marketing manager's solution is to provide better training for salespeople. He or she then diagnoses the problem as a lack of follow-up selling. Or the engineering manager calls for redesigning the truck and then justifies it with a diagnosis of poor product design.

Rejected authorization or failure in implementation forces someone back to the drawing board (or to computer-assisted design programs) (d' in the figure), to redefining the problem (d") or to search for more solutions (d'''). For example, higher authority remains unconvinced about the chosen solution to do more selling by following up with former customers who did not elect to trade their old trucks for new models. Or salespeople rebel at having to spend time with older customers who have rejected the product. These outcomes force the decision maker to reconsider other alternatives, to review the diagnosis, or even to look for other problem conditions in the market place. A tremendous amount of energy and time may go into these recycling processes, which may or may not have added value. More important, through proper diagnosis and use of intellectual stimulation, many of these steps in the process could have been dealt with at the outset, thus reducing the cycle time for decision making.

Not shown in the model are other events and developments that further impede the assumed orderliness of the organization's decision process: interruptions (the chief engineer is called away for an emergency in production), scheduling delays (meetings are canceled), timing delays (the data on foreign imports take longer than expected to obtain), speed-ups (higher authorities with greater amounts of discretionary power are brought into the decision process), compressions (the owner or president suddenly decides to sell the truck division), and failures (the bank refuses to make a crucial loan at the anticipated interest rate).[6]

In sum, organizational decision making does not ordinarily occur in the neat linear order that complete rationality dictates. Instead, it is erratic, cyclical, and political. Its process can potentially be reversed, with certain phases even skipped. The process is likely to be more effective if decision makers are ready, willing, and able to move backward as well as forward in their efforts. The failure to put enough emphasis on the backward linkages can account for the demise of many a high-flying firm.

For example, for many years the *Saturday Evening Post* was one of the most popular magazines in the United States. It pursued the logical progression when its profitability began to decline: That is, it concluded from its diagnosis and evaluation of alternatives that increasing its subscriber list would provide economy of scale, reduce costs, and increase revenue. Subscriptions were increased through various promotional campaigns. Yet losses still forced the *Post* out of business. The magazine's decision makers had failed to look back on its main sources of profit as well as its main sources of cost. Profit accrued as a consequence of its advertising revenues; costs increased as its subscriber list grew.

In the same way, a tapioca-pudding company found that its sales tripled when it placed spot advertisements on television. It then did what seemed most logical: It doubled its advertising. When the anticipated effect on sales failed to materialize, the company doubled the advertising again—and sales declined even more. Finally, the firm's management returned to the diagnosis and collected data on customer behavior, which showed that television ads promoted new customers who made initial purchases that tripled sales volume. This required the firm to contract out its production to meet demand. But management also discovered that product quality was seriously jeopardized by outside production. Customers were attracted by the ads to make a first purchase but refused to purchase the product again because of its poor quality. In fact, despite the television advertising, the pudding's reputation with the public was ruined by the poor quality of much of what had been placed on store shelves.

Phases, Linkages, Leadership, and Organizations for Effective Decision Making

The phases and cause-and-effect linkages between the phases of our ODM model are likely to be observed in differing amounts and with varying significance. When broken down into their component phases, different team and organizational decision processes will display more of some phases and linkages between phases than will others. Effective decisions will be described by patterns of such phases and linkages that are different from the patterns observed in ineffective decisions. Effective decision processes will spend amounts of time on each phase of the decision process that are consistent with the realistic needs of the problem involved. Ineffective decisions will be seen when some phases are given too much time and others too little. For example, to satisfy the whims of a senior executive, some decision makers will become ineffective by devoting too much time justifying a favorite solution to a problem rather than searching for new alternatives. Their linkage pattern will likewise be ineffective as they skip from diagnoses directly to justification of the favorite solution. They are overly controlled by their own organization.

If the senior operating decisions of the organization remain supported by naive advocacy and senior management is ineffective, then the organization will deteriorate and decay. More balance is clearly needed between the wholesale generation of ideas and the focusing on the other phases of the decision-making process dealing with the "real-time" problems confronting the organization.

Organizational Cultures

Organizational cultures have been typed according to how much they are transformational or transactional. We are likely to see systematic differences among them in their patterns of organizational decision making. Thus, the *garbage can* culture is one that lacks transformational as well as transactional leadership.[7] The garbage can organizational culture is in organizational anarchy. Preferences are ill-defined, inconsistent, unclear, uncertain, or problematic. Learning and precedents are a matter of trial and error. Participation in the decision process is fluid; the mix of decision makers changes capriciously and arbitrarily. The problems to be examined depend on who shows up for a decision-making meeting. Discussion is likely to skip around helter-skelter, with little closure on any phase of the process. Linkages among phases of decision making are particularly weak.

On the other hand, the *purely transformational* culture is likely to reveal openness to wide and narrow scanning, resulting in strong forward linkages to intensive diagnosis and wide search for alternatives. At the same time there will be an avoidance of premature closure indicative of a willingness to step backward as necessary. Because trust and empowerment are high, there will be a readiness to move back and forth among the decision-process phases. Confidence will be strong that authorization and implementation can be achieved. Nevertheless, such organizations are likely to be surfeited with innovations and good ideas but remain short on coordination and cost controls. The *purely transactional* culture lacking transformational leadership will be a consummate bureaucracy in which almost all member behaviors are regulated by rules or negotiations. Here much decision making is "lawyerly," emphasizing precedents and rulebooks to reach decisions.

The *high-contrast* culture reveals a great deal of both transformational and transactional leadership, which is exemplified by a highly effective military organization—which also is likely to have considerable internal conflict. Organizations that lie between these four cultural extremes—garbage can, purely transformational, purely transactional, and high-contrast—are seen to be moderate in one direction or another, coasting or pedestrian in their activities and performance.

Contiguity

Some degree of contiguity in time or place of decision making and decision makers is mandatory for easy process flow. Organizations and teams with effective decision making take advantage of contiguity by making it easier for certain executives to be closer together in time and space. They discourage artificial barriers to communication associated with differences in status and group identification by the way they organize meetings, office space, travel, and so on. For example, in many Honda Corporation sites, the managers and workers are located on the same floor in open areas. Status symbols are minimized to enhance the level and frequency of interaction between management and workers. A statement by Honda's president is representative of the company's attitude toward interaction and participative decision making: "I decided to step down when employees agreed with me 70% of the time."

A second example of the importance of contiguity can be seen in the self-managed team that clearly is advantaged by the extent that all relevant decision makers are together, share similar status and current experience, and are in close communication with one another.

Characteristics of Effective Linking

Organizational and team decisions are likely to be most effective if characterized by stronger forward linkages (a, b, c, d) with bursts of accompanying backward linkages (such as c', b', and a') and some stronger backward linkages (particularly d''' and f). To be avoided in organizational decision making are many weak and missing linkages and erratic movements back and forth among the steps as occur in anarchic organizations. Thus an effective decision process would be illustrated when scanning detects a lot of discontent in the organization about a new contract that the organization has become obligated to service. Before taking any rash actions, management completes a series of interviews and telephone calls to obtain an idea about the pervasiveness of the discontent and details about its causes. A task force is convened to develop ways to deal with the plan. In its deliberations, the task force asks for more details before proceeding. Early on, some members are convinced that the budget will need to be renegotiated with the client, but an early rush to judgment is avoided. Several alternatives are proposed. The choice is to convene a series of meetings between relevant client members and organizational members who are directly involved in the servicing. Diagnosis of needs using individualized consideration is pursued. This choice is accepted in principle by the head of the service division, although she wants to see a proposed schedule and costs before authorizing the chosen solution. She also suggests that the task force survey a representative group of service people to determine how willing they are to implement the proposal. Final approval and implementation then follows, along with a plan to monitor the proposal's success.

Rational Problem Solving

The typical rational programs of problem solving emphasize such elements as orderly staging of the process. At an early stage, a phase

such as diagnosis must be completed before solutions can be sought.[8]
Such idealized problem solving can be conceived in the model as
maintaining strong, direct, forward linkages from problem to search to
evaluation (a to b to c). This rational problem-solving orientation forms
the preliminary logical basis for intellectual stimulation.

Long- Versus Short-Term Decisions

The process will be substantially different if the problem at hand is
developing a new corporate vision for the next millennium or solving
a nagging short-term technical problem. In the former there will be greater
emphasis, time, and resources placed on scanning, diagnosis, and searching or innovation. For instance, seeking out benchmarks for comparison
may dominate the early phases of scanning and even diagnosis, while the
short-term problem would require a more abbreviated search.

Crosscultural Differences

Crosscultural differences are likely to surface. The Cartesian-trained
French manager is likely to be more comfortable with the just-described
rational problem solving than will be the Japanese manager, who has
been less indoctrinated with Western forms of logic. Thus Japanese
managers feel freer to work simultaneously at several phases in the
decision process. For example, in their R&D work, they may be carrying on basic research to establish the causes of a problem while also
testing the market on some early versions of problem solutions. Parallel
processing and concurrent engineering are consistent with their level
of comfort in not pursuing linear (a to b to c) solutions to problems.

The French are likely to put more energy into developing a theory
that explains the causes of the problem before proceeding to consider
methods of solution. Mexicans are likely to put more effort into the
planning stage and less into the execution and implementation of the
plans. This predilection for feeling that the work is done after it has
been planned is well recognized by Mexicans who refer to it as *pro-
jectismo*. More empirically minded North Americans will spend less
time on theory building and more on planning actions to solve the
problem while also detailing elaborate plans for data collection.

Emotional Problem Solving

Romantic, mystical, political, and rationalizing teams and organizations maintain strong backward linkages from evaluation to search to

problem (c′ to b′ to a′). For instance, company image may completely outweigh logical reasons for a decision.[9] Demagogues begin with a chosen plan for salvation and then regress (e′) to invented causes.

Another example of the heart taking precedence over the head in decision making occurs when linkages are skipped. Scanning generates sympathy for a distressing state of affairs such as what occurs to drought victims. Hasty, short-term emergency aid is provided that skips diagnosis and searches to generate long-term solutions. The problem detected in scanning is taken directly into a hasty search and choice without adequate diagnosis. There is premature closure about options.[10]

The contribution of transformational leadership to decision making will be considered by what it can and does accomplish at each phase and each cause-and-effect linkage of the decision-making model, beginning with scanning and its linkages a, a′, and f. We will examine how intellectual stimulation, individualized consideration, or inspirational motivation or transformational leadership in general can contribute to this improvement in team and organizational decision making.

Scanning

Scanning may be too wide and superficial or too narrow (missing the proverbial forest for its trees). It may be haphazard and lack focus.[11] The assumptions upon which it is based (where to look, what to look for, how and when to look) may need to be questioned by the intellectually stimulating leader. Hasty responding may need to be avoided as well as overconfident misreadings of potentially threatening information. Conversely, the inspirational leader may need to convert alarmist reactions by followers into more sober and deliberate considerations. Exhibiting confidence that a careful analysis of assumptions and interpretation of the problem will yield positive results is often needed in chaotic periods to avoid premature closure. Creating alignment around a sense of purpose is crucial. Individualized consideration comes into play where the leader senses and empathizes with followers' concerns to get the problem solved now. Also, such leaders continue to stimulate followers' learning and to develop their problem-solving capacity.

Linkages to Scanning

In developing transformational leadership, with reference to linkage a (between scanning and diagnosis), we stress the extent to which leaders need to look at threats as opportunities.[12] Emphasized also is the need for leaders to be proactive rather than reactive, alert to changing technologies, markets, and their followers' attitudes and needs. Leaders need to be ahead of followers and to stimulate their followers to do the same, thus multiplying inputs.

With reference to the backward linkage a', we can point to the intellectually stimulating leader's questioning assumptions that may generate a second look at scanning information and how it was acquired. With reference to linkage f, transformational leaders, as a consequence of their inner conviction and intuitive sense, may ask for a new check of the environment before authorizing action. They may have to take the risk of going against a popular line of reasoning and information that has resulted in a choice that is on their desk for authorization but is believed by the leaders to be a wrong or inadequate decision. Convincing followers why it may be wrong will require the self-confidence, determination, and intellectual stimulation of the trans-formational leader. Pursuing an unpopular course of action will require inspiration and idealized influence, which correspond to high levels of trust and commitment to the leader.

Specifically, the leader may simply have to make an unpopular choice, believing that choice relates to the group's long-term well-being. "Neutron" Jack Welch of General Electric (GE) completely disrupted the company's standard way of operating by envisioning GE as a world-class leader in high technology. Welch sensed the changes that would occur in the late 1980s and early 1990s based on his scanning of GE's external markets; he determined through diagnosis, search, and innovation the direction that GE should take. Fortunately, he had the commitment and the sense of purpose to convince the naysayers that his vision of GE's future state should be rigorously pursued. Although the risks were high in his strategy to transform and reorganize the company, the organization's payoffs proved to be great.[13]

When called on for their approval, leaders must have the maturity and inner confidence to acknowledge their mistakes and those of their followers and to stand up against popular sentiment if they find flaws in the decision-making process that culminates in a request for authorization—even when the request is their own.

Problem Discovery and Diagnosis

Each of the Four I's has relevance for improving the problem discovery and diagnosis process:

Individually considerate leaders make sure that all parties to the problem are heard.

Intellectually stimulating leaders reformulate with followers, colleagues, or superiors into more familiar and concrete terms what may have begun as an ill-structured, fuzzy problem.

Inspirational leaders increase confidence and raise aspiration levels that the problem can be solved once its causes have been determined. This helps to depict a desirable future state that is worth pursuing, one that the inspirational leader convincingly articulates to followers.

Leaders with idealized influence show their concerns about the problem and the need for its solution. They step into the future, creating a "sense of becoming" in the organization. Those followers who identify with the leader come to share the leader's concern. The problem may be personalized by leaders who have idealized influence. This will increase the readiness of followers to accept the problem as their own. "We are all in this together."

Convinced of the importance of the problem, the inspirational leader will clarify and show its importance in ways that are simple enough for followers to grasp. "We've got to do more with less." Goals may be articulated in expressive, vivid, or simple language. "Just say 'No.' " Expectations will be raised about what might happen if nothing is done about the problem. "If we don't, who will?"

The inspirational leader will repeat and reemphasize the same theme throughout the organization—for example, "We have an obsolescence problem in this firm." The inspirational leader will help define the context in which the problem is embedded. Metaphors and symbols may be introduced. "Think of this problem as a river that has overflowed its banks." "The clasped hands in this logo are to show that cooperation, not competition, is the goal of our merger."

In 1974, Xerox had 86% of the market share. By 1984 the company's market share had dropped to less than 17%! Meeting customer needs became Xerox's major objective as a consequence. Its chairman repeatedly communicated his message about quality: "We are in a race without a finish line."[14]

Linkages to Diagnosis

Individually considerate leaders can contribute to linkages b and b′ between diagnosis and the search for alternatives. Such leaders may foster an unbiased examination of the causes of the problem with attention to individual differences of opinion and experience.

Intellectually stimulating leaders may change the context or discover hidden assumptions to reveal root causes that change the direction of search. Inspirational leaders raise awareness about what is important in the problem and encourage the use of "gut feeling" and intuition in connecting causes with effects. They also exhibit persistence and confidence that the best solution will be found.

Leaders with idealized influence may help to align individual and organizational interests in the problem so that serious attention will be given to the search for alternatives. The trust and respect for the leader who has idealized influence makes it easier for followers to take risks with suggestions and to be more open and forthcoming. A higher quality of information will be available when needed for deliberation in the various phases. Obviously, this sort of trust and respect must be established well ahead of when it is actually required.

With reference to d' (a return from a requested authorization to implement a decision), the individually considerate leader may move to increase ownership of the problem by those who must authorize or implement it by delegating more responsibilities and control. The intellectually stimulating leader may ask challenging questions about where the first diagnosis went wrong. The inspirational leader may work to maintain followers' level of aspirations that would likely have fallen as a consequence of the failure to obtain authorization. "Each failure brings us one step closer to the correct solution." The leader who has idealized influence might air his or her own feelings of regret and then ask followers to join in a new commitment to more exhaustive diagnosis and eventual problem resolution.

Search and Innovation

Ordinarily, the search for alternatives or the creation of a new solution uses an analysis of which means are likely to achieve which ends. The complexity of the diagnosis and its uncertainties may require subdividing and simplifying issues and goals by inspirational or intellectually stimulating leaders before followers can generate meaningful alternatives. If a new solution needs to be created, then its vague initial image must be increasingly sharpened and narrowed in focus. Problems and their potential solutions can be compartmentalized to simplify analysis and chance. In other cases, a combination of alternatives not previously considered may seem appropriate.

Individually considerate leaders can encourage balanced, well-distributed participation by followers in the search or innovation process. Intellectually stimulating leaders, except when making early use of brainstorming, will refuse to uncritically accept readily available but inadequate solutions. Instead they will strive for an optimal rather than a merely satisfactory alternative, encouraging others to do the same.

Inspirational and ideally influential leaders are likely to increase the enabling and empowerment of their followers and their encouragement and commitment to the search for or creation of optimal alternatives. Innovative thinking and acceptance of calculated risks will be encouraged. By envisioning what is needed, such leaders help to direct attention to the elements of consequence that are required for the best solutions.

Linkages to Search and Innovation

With reference to the c and c' linkages to evaluations and choice, premature closure with the one initially most popular alternative needs to be avoided. Given their personal support from followers, leaders with idealized influence can stop the usually popular effort to cut short the process by an immediate choice without seriously comparing the alternatives. Or if a deadlock continues over which alternative to choose, the inspirational or intellectually stimulating leader can convince his or her followers to resume searching or efforts at innovation (linkage c) or to diagnose the problem again (e').

Authorization and Implementation

The persuasive abilities of an articulate, inspirational leader may be needed to obtain authorization or implementation. Here is where the leader may need to champion the optimal solution. The individually considerate leader will sense and respond to the individual needs and concerns of those who are responsible for authorization and implementation. And, as mentioned earlier, returning to earlier phases in the decision process (linkages d', d'', d''', and f) may occur as a consequence of intellectually stimulating leaders who are the responsible authorities questioning deeply rooted opinions and challenging basic assumptions.

General Contributions to Effective Decision Making

Transformational leaders have greater interest in continuous organizational change and improvement, transcending or aligning self-interests for the longer-range good of the organization and its members. This is in contrast to transactional leaders, who are more focused on the satisfaction of self-interests and the maintenance of the organization's status quo. With these differences in mind, we can conclude with observations about the potentially more effective decision-making stance of transformational leaders.

In contrast to transactional leaders, transformational leaders are likely to be:

- more proactive and more alert to incipient problems, anticipating the emergence of problems more frequently and farther in advance;
- more flexible and therefore able to deal with more problems simultaneously;
- quicker to react to emerging problems;
- more willing to be incremental, taking small steps toward solving a problem without having to wait for a guarantee of complete success before taking initiatives;
- more willing to view a problem in a larger context and longer time frame;
- more prone to take failed decisions in stride as learning experiences;
- more likely to view achieving objectives as more important than avoiding the violation of rules and precedents;
- less likely to limit focusing search and innovation solely on variables and alternatives over which they now have control;
- more likely to encourage search and choice that take into account the wider context of the larger organization and outside environment rather than limiting the search to the immediate neighborhood of the problem;
- more likely to seek informally the information for making their decisions rather than as prescribed by organizational rules;
- more likely to change the rules and even the culture as needed over time;
- more likely to practice walk-around management to promote the upward flow of communication and information; and
- more likely to make decisions that favor exploration so as to achieve higher payoffs at higher risks rather than decisions that favor exploitation and achieve lower payoffs at lower risks.

In the Persian Gulf War of 1991, for example, U.S. General Norman Schwartzkopf and his associates illustrated much of the above in the way they were able to develop a high degree of cooperation and coordination instead of the usual interservice rivalries and international squabbling that have frequently characterized allied army commands. Advance planning was superb, but particularly salient were many of Schwartzkopf's personal characteristics, including his:

- propensity to work closely and informally with the commanders of the allied forces;
- his walk-around management;
- his willingness to ignore precedents about the superior forces required for attack; and
- his willingness to take the risks of an "end run" into Iraq itself around the Iraqi forces in Kuwait. Saddam Hussein was "fighting the last war" of highly fortified defenses; Schwartzkopf and his associates were ignoring the earlier successes of costly amphibious landings except as diversions.

To conclude, theory and supporting research strongly suggest that team and organizational decision making are likely to benefit if transformational leadership is involved in the process. For example, scanning can be improved by the intellectually stimulating leader, problem discovery and diagnosis by individualized consideration, and search and innovation by inspirational motivation. Authorization and implementation can be enhanced by all three transformational styles of the full range of leadership, including idealized influence. With all Four I's of transformational leadership, decisions are made based on internal standards of commitment. They are reviewed and revised continuously to accommodate critical changes in the context. As noted earlier, the individual as well as organization are self-defining to the extent that they are both driven by a more global perspective coupled with high moral and ethical standards. We next turn to the particular relevance of continuous quality improvement to the full range of leadership.

Notes

1. Hummel, R. P. (1975). Psychology of charismatic followers. *Psychological Reports, 37,* 759-770. Hummel suggested that charisma was a Judeo-Christian concept applicable to biblical prophets, priests, and kings and subsequent leaders in the West. China and Japan had no such experience. Nevertheless, one can point to Chinese and Japanese leaders who have attributes of the charismatic.

2. Feldman, J. M., & Kanter, H. E. (1965). Organizational decision making. In J. G. March (Ed.), *Handbook of organizations.* Chicago: Rand McNally. The authors point out many human, legal, social, and administrative constraints that severely restrict search and innovation.

3. MacCrimmon, K. R. (1974). Managerial decision making. In J. W. McGuire (Ed.), *Contemporary management.* Englewood Cliffs, NJ: Prentice Hall. Search should be adventurous and "gambling-focused." Conservative focus will be inefficient.

4. Bass, B. M. (1983). *Organizational decision-making.* Homewood, IL: Irwin. The author details each phase of the organizational decision process and their forward and backward cause-and-effect linkages.

5. Alexander, E. R. (1979). The design of alternatives in organizational contexts: A pilot study. *Administrative Science Quarterly, 24,* 382-404. Three cases are examined that show the dynamics and effects of premature closure.

6. Mitzberg, H., Raisinghani, D., & Thoret, A. (1976). The structure of "unstructured" decision process. *Administrative Science Quarterly, 21,* 246-275. The authors studied and categorized the phases in the decision process in 25 organizations and concluded that the idealized orderly process of decision making is a fiction.

7. Cohen, M. D., March, J. G., & Olsen, J. P. (1972). A garbage can model of organizational choice. *Administrative Science Quarterly, 17,* 1-25. For these authors, the outcome of a decision depends on who shows up at the decision-making meeting and what is on their minds at the time.

8. Maier, N. R. F. (1963) *Problem solving discussions and conferences: Leadership methods and skills.* New York: McGraw-Hill. The author argues for the conversion of negotiation into systematic (rather than free), step-by-step problem solving.

9. Stagner, R. (1965). Corporate decision making: An empirical study. *Journal of Applied Psychology, 53,* 1-13.

10. Alexander, E. R. (1979).

11. Arrow, K. J. (1974). *The limits of organizations.* New York: Norton.

12. See modules 12 and 13 on intellectual stimulation and inspirational leadership in Avolio, B. J., & Bass, B. M. (1990).

13. Jack Welch reinvents General Electric—again. (1991, March 30). *The Economist,* pp. 59-60.

14. Hard copy. (1985, November 23). *The Economist,* pp. 78-80.

7

The Alliance of Total Quality and the Full Range of Leadership

BRUCE J. AVOLIO

Center for Leadership Studies,
School of Management, SUNY Binghamton

EXECUTIVE SUMMARY

This chapter will integrate the concepts of total quality management (TQM) and the full range of leadership to offer a more comprehensive model for designing and running optimally effective organizations. This objective is approached from several perspectives. First, we look briefly at some of the key historical trends in these two areas to provide a basis for discussing where each can contribute to the other's development. Moving from historical trends in quality control to current work in TQM and on to the full range of leadership, we will attempt to sharpen how other writers have described TQM and where the full range of leadership can play a central role in the overall success of TQM efforts. Examples are provided throughout to offer potential benchmarks and guidelines for TQM efforts. The final sections of this chapter integrate current work on transformational leadership and TQM. Specific recommendations are made for implementing more effective TQM programs that incorporate the Four I's of transformational leadership.

The author is indebted to Tom Land of Motorola and Ron Kenett formerly of SUNY-Binghamton for providing key insights into the TQM movement and its relationship to leadership.

Introduction

Research in both leadership and total quality management have developed over the last 40 years, largely independent of one another.

Leadership researchers rarely make reference in their empirical papers to quality or total quality, except in instances where one or the other was used as a criterion of performance. Until recently, the link between models of "continuous process improvement" and leadership research and theory were only loosely coupled.

Leadership researchers have traditionally focused on identifying the nature of leadership (e.g., a trait, a behavior, or an attribution), how it can be recognized or measured, how it varies across different situations or contexts, and those of its dimensions that constitute effective rather than ineffective leadership. Except for brief interventions with leaders in training programs, there has been little attention paid to the continuous development of leadership potential across an individual's career or life span. Rarely has time been incorporated in the analysis or development of leadership.

Change of Focus

Only recently have leadership researchers begun to focus on the development of leaders and their followers using a life-span framework.[1] Most of the popular models of leadership over the last 30 years did not attempt to explain leadership in the context of development or over extended periods of time, so the connection to continuous improvement and development that has evolved in the area of total quality has been noticeably absent in the leadership field.

In instances where models of leadership did discuss development, the focus of the model was on lower-order change—changes in degree—and limited in discussions to a rather narrow range of leadership styles (e.g., participative versus directive). *Development*, however, refers to qualitative change: a fundamental shift from one level to another in understanding, beliefs, values, morals, and perspective. As individuals develop, the assumptions they maintain at one level of development no longer apply to the next higher level.

Fundamental change or development described in this manner is critical to understanding how transformational (or self-defining) leaders move followers to higher levels of development and potential. For example, where followers become concerned about the needs of their group instead of focusing on satisfying their own immediate needs and self-interests, then a fundamental shift in perspective has occurred in followers' values and assumptions. Shifting followers to this higher level of development is essential to the operation of effective teams and to improving the overall effectiveness of organizational systems and cultures. Understanding how this change process occurs in followers as a consequence of the leader's influence and own personal development strategy is critical to understanding the concept and perhaps the model of continuous process improvement (CPI).

Leadership Development and TQM

Although leadership researchers and theorists have rarely mentioned the concept of quality, except as an end goal, the emerging TQM field has frequently linked the importance of effective leadership to achieving the goals of total quality and CPI programs.[2] However, the linkages between TQM models, leadership research, and theory have typically been weak. Stronger, even "visionary," leadership frequently is called for by writers and practitioners, as an essential requirement for promoting total quality and continuous improvement efforts. Invariably, however, how strongly leadership has been operationalized or developed has varied across different authorities who write on these topics. Such authorities as Deming or Juran have focused on the importance of strong leadership at the tops of organizations to the success of a total quality-improvement program, placing less emphasis in their writings on what takes place at lower organizational levels.[3] For example, some of the key criteria for the Malcolm Baldrige Award (annual national award for total quality improvement) specify leadership in the following manner: "How the *senior executives* create and sustain a clear and visible quality value system along with supporting management system to guide all activities of the company toward excellence."[4]

The focus at the top is an essential ingredient to the success of any TQM effort, as many writers have suggested. Yet this focus is limited because it does not consider the specific requirements for leadership at middle to lower levels in the organization, which may differ from those applied to top management.

Almost by definition, creating a TQM culture requires that leadership at all levels must be involved in the process of continuous improvement. Furthermore, we believe that a clear specification of how such leadership should be accomplished and the time span in which it must occur is critical to understanding what is required to achieve total quality and optimally effective leadership. Continuous improvement and leadership can each be viewed as interrelated developmental processes that are both time-based and relevant to each other's development. In that regard, leadership and total quality efforts must be developed in concert to maximize individual, team, and organizational effectiveness.

Defining Quality and Its Leadership Counterpart

How quality is defined has direct relevance to the appropriateness or inappropriateness of the full range of leadership styles that could contribute to or detract from achieving total quality. For example, Jackson makes the following distinction between *quality* and *total quality*: The former is conformance to specifications at the lowest cost, while the latter is application of quality to every task in the organization, which ultimately is a "self-learning" process.[5]

Conforming to requirements as indicated in the first definition of quality represented the period of "detection or inspection." For example, immediately after World War II, anything that was produced could be sold. A laissez-faire attitude toward quality was the norm: That is, "Let the consumer beware." Organizations shipped out products without real concern for customer satisfaction.

The Era of Quality Control

The first generation of systematic discussions about quality took place just before and after World War II. These discussions concentrated on the importance of leaders detecting errors and reducing the cost of production. The focus was more narrow than current TQM efforts and now can be characterized as "reactive."[6]

The emphasis on quality control and standardization, however, dates back much farther. Five thousand years ago, the Egyptians developed the "royal cubit" as the prime factor of measurement for building pyramids—structures that would conform to prescribed quality standards of measurement. Over the next 2,000 years, Egyptians, Greeks, and Romans all worked to develop and employ quality standards for trade and commerce. Still, the emphasis was on detection or inspection.

Similarly, early U.S. colonial governments called for export representatives to ensure the quality of products going overseas. In this period, strict apprenticeships were designed to teach individuals standards for acceptable performance. Also during this period, viewers, gauges, inspectors, and reeves were created to examine merchandise to ensure the maintenance of appropriate standards of quality. Again, much of the emphasis was on setting standards and reacting to deviations.

At the Springfield Armory in 1819, there was an elaborate gauging system installed to comply with quality standards—a system that minimized the amount of individual judgment required to evaluate product quality. Throughout the remainder of the 19th century, the development of gauging and control systems became increasingly more refined and sophisticated. Emphasis was placed on post hoc inspection, control, and evaluation of product quality—a pervasive trend that would continue well into the current century.[7]

Not until 1922, when G. S. Radford wrote *The Control of Quality in Manufacturing*, were inspection and quality operationalized as a distinct and independent responsibility of management.[8] The solid scientific basis for quality control, however, did not emerge until 1931 with the publication of *Economic Control of Quality of Manufacturing Product* by W. A. Shewart of Bell Laboratories.[9] Shewart's work at Bell on process control, as well as Dodge and Ronnigs's work on sampling-inspection procedures, provided the foundation for later TQM developments by Juran and Deming.

A heavy imprint on the field was left by these early writings on ensuring quality in production. Initially, responsibility was placed on the individual worker or crafts worker for control and inspection. As the industrial period unfolded in the 1920s, 1930s, and 1940s, organizations formalized their structures, shifting much of their responsibility for inspection and quality assurance to the supervisor or independent inspector.

Much of the change paralleled what Max Weber referred to in his discussion of organizational bureaucracy.[10] As organizations formalized their structures, creating specific functional areas, the roles became increasingly more specific, especially with respect to the responsibility for product quality. The total trust that had been traditionally placed in craftspeople to produce a high-quality product had been completely eroded in manufacturing industries by the early 1960s. Now the responsibility for quality was allocated to many specially trained inspectors. Workers produced products, while others checked the quality of their work. Using the developmental perspective described in Chapter 2, leaders treated followers as if they were at a lower stage of development, a stage where continuous monitoring and immediate feedback were required to control their behavior.[11] Maintaining quality was accomplished through the detection of errors—that is, by managing by exception. At the same time, organizations distanced themselves from their customers, standardizing feedback on product quality, but doing little to use such feedback for products or processes.

Detection and Correction

Throughout the 1940s and 1950s, the leading firms attempted to institute systematic programs to reduce the number of errors by detecting and eliminating them after they occurred. In truth, many of the less enlightened organizations did not concern themselves with quality at all, because the consumer or market brought no demand for quality products. In reflecting on the issue of quality, former General Motors president Robert Stempell said "commercial grade" quality was the automotive industry's target. The inference was that if the customer did not complain, then the company did not take action to improve quality. Quality or lack thereof was what the market would bear.[12]

Summarizing to this point, paralleling the full-range leadership model (see Figure 7.1), early approaches to quality were either characterized by a completely hands-off inactive approach (such as laissez-faire leadership) or one that focused on error detection, monitoring, and correction (labeled as passive and active in the figure). An assumption that often parallels the use of an MBE style is that the individual employee is immature—at a lower level of development—and cannot be trusted. In the literature about quality, this is typically referred to as the era of quality control. Preceding and following World War II, the type of directive and autocratic leadership frequently found in most organizations at the time was generally consistent with the requirements of a rather limited definition of quality: Conformance to standards or else!

Shifting Back to the Craftsperson

Current efforts to achieve total quality stress a return to reliance on the individual worker or teams of workers to ensure quality in all aspects of organizational functioning. Currently, the benchmark organizations at the forefront of total quality efforts seek to offer more responsibility for maintaining and improving quality. However, the responsibility of the individual or team and the definition of quality is much broader than before. This reorientation in strategic direction requires a much higher level of trust, much of which had eroded during the era of detection and correction.

Forestall and Reward

The 1960s and 1970s witnessed a change in emphasis toward motivational techniques to improve quality; this paralleled the human relations movement in organizational theory and leadership. Referring to the model in Figure 7.1, it was the era of transactional leadership: exchanging rewards for quality products. Treating individuals in a more considerate manner and allowing more participation in decision making implied that individuals were now viewed as being more trustworthy than before and thus at a higher level of development.

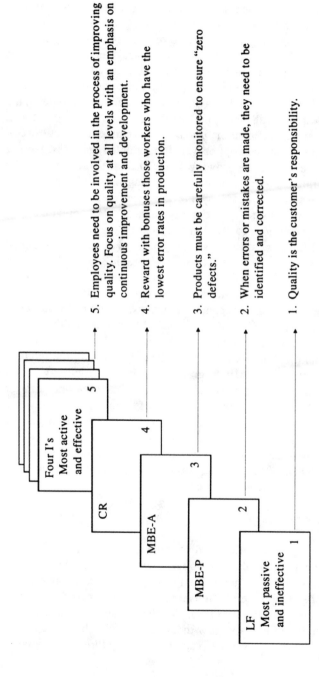

5. Employees need to be involved in the process of improving quality. Focus on quality at all levels with an emphasis on continuous improvement and development.

4. Reward with bonuses those workers who have the lowest error rates in production.

3. Products must be carefully monitored to ensure "zero defects."

2. When errors or mistakes are made, they need to be identified and corrected.

1. Quality is the customer's responsibility.

Four I's
Most active
and effective

5

CR

4

MBE-A

3

MBE-P

2

LF
Most passive
and ineffective

1

Figure 7.1 Historical Parallel Between Quality and Leadership Theory

127

Programs such as the "zero defects" effort were popularized by NASA, which used the slogan, "Developing products right the first time." Many organizations offered recognition programs and rewards in exchange for achieving higher levels of quality. Setting goals and objectives became the norm with the advent of management-by-objectives (MBO) programs. The emphasis in the 1970s and early 1980s continued to shift toward the development of quality management and quality assurance programs. The emphasis on empowerment was still down the road—with the focus still being on techniques and "quick fix" tools, rather than on any significant or fundamental change in the culture of the organization, its leadership, or how it conducted business. During this period, there was also a growing sense of dissatisfaction with the quick fix to organizational problems, including those of low quality. This concern was exacerbated by the advances being made by the Japanese in the area of total quality performance.[13] U.S. organizations were groping for solutions to problems of quality and searching for the "tricks" behind Japanese success, so many of them uncritically grabbed on to the quality-circle concept. The idea was rapidly put into place in many U.S. organizations without much consideration for how it affected overall organizational structure, system, and culture. Problems naturally arose as the team concept was introduced into rigid, autocratically run organizations. This was evidenced by the unhealthy failure rate of quality circles in the United States.

Highly autocratic and directively run firms were using the quality-circle concept, touting a shift to greater levels of participative team management. In reality, workers quickly realized that the only change in the organization was in the development of the quality circle, while little else changed. Unfortunately, in many organizations the circle concept was seen as a Japanese technique that could not be successfully imported into individualistic Western cultures. Ironically, the quality-circle concept had originated in the United States in organizations such as General Electric some 40 years earlier.[14]

Improve the Organization

Clearly missing in the period of forestall and reward was the longer-term view of how the emphasis on quality would change the management and leadership of organizations, the focus on process, the support of top management, and the relationship to their customers (both internal and external). Also missing from the change process was specific attention to the individual and how individuals could and should cope with changes in their respective responsibilities. Moreover, management was simply not ready to listen to what it was doing wrong. The culture of many large organizations hovering at the abyss was to either avoid or punish mistakes when they were observed: what we describe in the full-range model as managing by exception. The long tradition of detection and correction could not simply be shed in an instant with yet another new gimmick or technique. Obviously, this did not present an optimal climate for either the development of workers or continuous process improvement, which are both fundamentally linked to the organization's willingness to make and to learn from mistakes in order to innovate and perform at the highest levels of potential. Unfortunately, it often took an extreme crisis to begin the transition to a whole new way of operation, the type of crisis that often precedes significant developmental change.

A company such as Xerox in the 1970s had to lose almost 70% of its market share before significant and irreversible changes occurred in its way of doing business. Only in the 1980s did Xerox begin to resume leadership in the photocopying business. Similarly, Hewlett Packard achieved a necessary tenfold increase in quality over a 10-year period by radically transforming its organizational culture. Unfortunately, many other organizations reacted too late to reclaim their market positions.[15]

As we examine the 1990s and beyond, the quality revolution characterized by CPI and *Six Sigma*[16] efforts represents a fundamental change from earlier conceptions of quality. The concept of quality is no longer restricted to products or services; instead, it has evolved into a way of thinking and a philosophy that runs parallel to the principles underlying the Four I's of transformational leadership.[17] With the emergence of TQM, there are now strong links to concepts such as commitment, development, acceptance, innovation, envisioning, prevention, culture, empowerment, and values. These concepts derive additional meaning from the emphasis we place on organizations being run by and developing transformational leaders at all levels, not just among senior executives.[18]

Leadership

At least 9 of Deming's 14 principles refer to leadership and its importance to achieving total quality. Crosby, Juran, and other quality gurus also place a great deal of emphasis in their writings on leadership and its effects on quality. Many current quality programs can and perhaps should be embedded in leadership training, or vice versa, because the components of total quality programs in effect are leadership and cultural processes, plus the "right" tools. Unfortunately, most organizations still have not made this connection, even though the criteria for the Malcolm Baldrige award point to leadership, culture, and values playing key roles in achieving total quality. They see the program as a way of stamping out quality problems and not as a transformation in philosophy, values, and, ultimately, a state of being and purpose. Leadership is recognized as being important, but it is not fully developed.

The lack of connection to a total change process associated with many organizational leaders' views of TQM was captured by Ray F. Boedecker, the first director of quality at IBM: "I am an examiner for the Baldrige Award, and most companies we see don't know what they're doing in quality improvement."[19] In a similar vein, at the opening session of a TQM workshop after the presenter completed an hour-long lecture on the merits of working in a total quality company, a participant raised his hand and asked how he would be directly compensated for employing these new techniques. As the discussion continued, it became apparent that the organization had not prepared its employees to view the change to TQM as a complete and fundamentally different way of doing business (see Chapters 1 and 2). Through this simple observation, it became apparent how important it was to shape an alliance between transformational leadership and efforts toward total quality improvement.

TQM and Transformational Leadership

One contradiction that seems to underlie much of the writing on TQM involves the distinction (or lack thereof) between leadership and management. Many authors in the leadership literature have gone to great pains to highlight the distinction between leadership and management, including Burns, Zaleznik, and Kotter.[20,21,22] This distinction is by no means arbitrary and is quite important to moving organizations toward improved CPI levels. Viewed within a developmental framework, leadership changes our perspective by moving us to a higher level of understanding and stage of development. Many top leaders argue that they create chaos to underscore the need for change. After achieving a higher-order change, they work to reestablish order and control. At this higher level, management facilitates the achievement of objectives within that stage of development.

Change Perspectives

Consider a concrete example to see this distinction. Assume that our customers are only people who "buy" our products rather than the "internal" customer that is often cited in the TQM literature. Viewing customers in this manner, management structures the organization to maximize external customer satisfaction. Management is geared toward focusing and directing employees, as well as rewarding them for achieving the highest level of external customer satisfaction, perhaps at any cost. Now we change this perspective and consider both internal and external customers. A fundamental shift in perspective of this sort requires a change in operating assumptions, values, orientation, and perspective that is driven by leadership rather than by management processes. The management of the organization is disrupted by fundamental shifts in perspective or crisis. Management processes involve the stabilization and refinement of procedures, not their disruption, even though leadership and management may stem from the same individual.

TQM and Leadership

The augmentation effect of adding transformational to transactional leadership demonstrates the benefits that both management and leadership can offer to the change and restabilization of organizations as they develop and respond to demands in their respective markets.[23] TQM, therefore, is effective management *plus* effective leadership, which is built over time and reflects a new expression: TQM + L.

Following these arguments, we can view the system referred to by TQM authorities as encompassing the managerial functions that drive an organization toward its objectives. Effective transformational leadership involves the envisioning of goals and the development of an appropriate culture to accomplish those goals. For instance, we can view the establishment of standards and requirements, prioritization of goals, measurement of performance, allocation of resources and rewards, coordination of people, coordination of information and information processing, application of TQM tools, maintenance of discipline, and assessment of progress as distinctly appropriate to CPI management. This distinction becomes very useful for training and development purposes by providing a focus and direct links between total quality management and effective transactional leadership.

Starting at time zero, an organization's management might envision a completely new frontier for the organization. As one industrial president noted, the leader creates a vision that gives meaning to the employee's job.[24] The vision of a new frontier of total quality entails a fundamental reorientation for the organization. The leader is the catalyst, not the controller of change and development. The leader points out the discrepancy between the present and the desired future. Envisioning the future is a key starting point in any transformational process, although it is not as simple as simply creating a desirable vision such as achieving Six Sigma level quality. Other factors are clearly involved that round out the entire process of total change. Leadership actions called for by such total quality authorities as Deming, Crosby, Ishikawa, and Juran include:

- creating a sense of awareness for change,
- building a sense of purpose and direction,
- developing a philosophy and culture to support change,
- establishing the "added value" of continuous improvement,
- building trust and reducing fear,
- understanding individual strengths and differences,
- providing mechanisms for self-development or the achievement of one's full potential, and
- initiating new problem-solving strategies.

The Four I's of Transformational Leadership

The Four I's of transformational leadership introduced in Chapter 1 contain the leadership actions to achieve a successful TQM effort.[25]

Idealized Influence and TQM

Idealized influence represents the building of trust and respect in followers. It provides the basis for accepting radical and fundamental changes in the way one conducts business. Without such trust and commitment to the leader's intentions, motives, and purposes, attempts to change and redirect the organization's mission are likely to be met with extreme resistance, if not subterfuge. This is not at all necessarily the fault of the follower. As Ted Levitt suggests, organizations often block innovation and progressive change: "In most organizations most really new things get accomplished by subterfuge and cunning."[26] Building trust will take time, along with the many other changes that must take place for CPI to take hold. Depending on the culture and size of the organization, one can expect the changeover process to take from three to five years.[27]

Leaders with idealized influence serve as role models with the appropriate behaviors and attitudes that are required for an organization to become a culture based on the assumptions that support CPI. As many of the authorities who promote TQM have lamented, for the change process to ultimately succeed, the leader cannot simply preach total quality at the annual retreat—he or she also must practice it on a daily basis and thus demonstrate a visible commitment to his or her beliefs.

Followers want to emulate leaders who display idealized influence. The payoff for the leader who has built high levels of trust and respect is that associates will now emulate the principles of continuous improvement so that they can be like their leader. Without such trust, the leader often struggles to convince followers of the need to change, particularly where a crisis is not imminent.

Trust and respect are not simply important to the beginnings of the change process. They are key to all facets of what the leader tries to accomplish and how successful he or she will be in the end. Continuous disruptions to the system in pursuit of continuous improvement will work to the degree that there is trust in organizational leadership.

Inspirational Motivation

Inspirational motivation also plays a central role in the development of the vision that establishes a framework or extends the area in which the organization will operate. The frame or lens to be used must be clearly and repeatedly communicated to followers. This aspect of transformational leadership is often associated with creating and maintaining the energy to pursue new directions. Now, however, the change that is expected is continuous in nature, thus the requirement of the leader is one of continuous reinvigoration of others to pursue or modify the vision as organizational needs change. Higher levels of involvement and alignment with the purposes behind the vision are key objectives for the inspirational leader. The persistence to achieve benchmark levels of quality will require much higher levels of energy than may have been provided by leaders and their followers in the past.

The long-term perspective must be continuously kept in sharp focus to override the tendency of short-term pressures to derail the organization and its members. Steven Jobs, reflecting on one of his key roles as a leader, said that a leader should operate as both architect of the future and keeper of the vision. Jobs's description of his leadership role is consistent with leadership as defined in the criteria for the Malcolm Baldrige Award: "How the senior executives create and sustain a clear and visible quality value system along with a supporting management system to guide all activities of the company toward excellence."[28] The combination of idealized influence and inspirational motivation will help to promote change not just at the senior level, but throughout the organizational system, cascading from one level to the next.[29]

A note of caution, however, is in order. Specifically, "the price of enthusiasm is involvement." Managers or leaders must become comfortable in allowing for greater involvement by others in all aspects of their work. As will be described below, they must allow their work to be questioned and improved. Many managers are not prepared to pass this test of follower involvement. However, the current generation of new workers clearly is demanding such involvement.[30]

Intellectual Stimulation

Intellectual stimulation is the third contribution to CPI. In some ways, the idea of continuous improvement itself is intellectually stimulating: One must continually balance the need for freedom to explore with some semblance of order. Indeed, intellectual stimulation can play a central role in the process of continuous improvement.

At a very basic level, questioning assumptions provides the basis for choosing different ways of doing things as needed. For example, in the Hiroshima steel plant, a piston rod formerly took 15 hours to complete because of scratches produced by the manufacturing process. One morning, a shop foreman at the plant observed two men running toward each other at a train station until they collided. When he arrived at work, he relayed his observation to his work group and used it as an analogy for the way the piston and rod were joined in the manufacturing process at the plant—from opposite directions! The collision of the piston and the rod caused scratches that led to a significant increase in the time needed to process the materials. The production process was eventually changed to avoid the collision, which saved countless work hours and a substantial amount of money.[31]

Such examples abound in organizations where leaders encourage followers to take intellectual risks, question assumptions, reverse figure and ground, use analogies and metaphors, and alter the scale of measurement as needed to solve problems. These tools and ways of thinking are fundamentally important to achieving continuous improvement in processes and systems.

In a similar vein, as a result of Deming's influence and work, Ford Motor Company executives undertook to build the Taurus and Sable automobiles by questioning some of their basic assumptions regarding the overall process of building a new car. For instance, one assumption was that Ford avoided long-term contracts. In the past, Ford had signed only one-year contracts with its suppliers. Nevertheless, the company rejected this assumption and signed a five-year contract with A. O.

Smith to build the cars' frames. The message to A. O. Smith was to build a partnership with Ford to develop the new car.

The five-year contract also departed from previous contracts in that price reductions were built in for each year over the five-year span. The assumption underlying the price reduction was that if the Smith organization continuously improved its production process, then the cost to Ford would continuously decrease. In addition to these changes in procedure, Ford also built prototypes of the cars nine months in advance of production to receive and incorporate customer feedback into the design.[32] Rewarding this proactive effort, the Ford Taurus became the best-selling car in the United States in 1992.

Continuous improvement requires leadership that insists on constant, open examination of everything and total receptivity to change. "Nothing characterizes the successful organization so much as its willingness to abandon what has long been successful."[33]

Individualized Consideration

Individualized consideration is at the very core of CPI because it represents how all employees can contribute fully to higher levels of performance if they have fully developed their potential and can participate individually and as team members in using it. Embedded within this concept is the idea that followers learn to take responsibility for their own development, which in effect parallels the type of responsibility we expect them to take for total quality improvement. They move from being outer-controlled to inner-directed.

The involvement of people as just described underscores the need for leaders to appropriately diagnose the values, needs, and capabilities of their followers. It is a leader's responsibility to assess the willingness and ability to change and then pursue strategies to do so. These assessments are critical to providing the appropriate level of challenge to followers to retain high levels of interest, involvement, and trust.

Walter Trosin, chairman of Merck, captured the emphasis we believe should be placed on development in the following comment: "We tend to treat people like adults at Merck, which leads to adult behavior."[34]

Transformational leaders move followers to higher levels of development, responsibility, and commitment or, in Trosin's terms, more adultlike behavior.

CPI is applied to the individual, as well as to what the individual does in his or her organizational roles. Transformational leaders continuously strive to develop followers to higher levels of ability and motivation. As detailed in Chapter 2, they also strive to raise the moral standards of followers from the level of self-interest to consideration of the larger interests of group, organization, and society. This shift is essential to the promotion of total quality, which requires a systematic effort coordinated and implemented by teams of individuals. The constant upward spiral of improvement that characterizes systems devoted to total quality is the same upward spiral that we referred to when discussing continuous individual development.[35]

Remembering that people learn best in different ways and over different time spans is key to the successful development of followers. As with any production process, continuous feedback is critical to the development of followers, as is support and the establishment of benchmark standards such as those exhibited by role models and mentors.

Relevance to Customers and Suppliers

All of what we have been saying about the follower is equally relevant to the relationships that organizations have with customers (internal and external) and suppliers. For instance, organizational understanding of customers' needs and values is critical to success. Taking suppliers' needs into account, involving them in the process of change, and developing their capabilities and skills are relevant to the continuous-improvement process. Thus the boundaries of leadership extend much farther than the impact on immediate followers and include customers, suppliers, relationships with outside agencies, and even competitors.

Integration of Past Practices and Future Possibilities

Curiously, work on TQM and the full range of leadership have evolved quite independent of each other, as evidenced by the fact that the practices and programs of each rarely have taken account of the significant developments and research of the other. Also, most organizations that offer programs in these areas tend to treat the topics independently. For example, Motorola, which is renowned for its Six Sigma quality program, announced that one year's theme would be leadership. Yet in both programs one may find general references made to the importance of the other.

Now it would seem appropriate to apply the concept of parallel processing or concurrent engineering to the need to have both leadership and total quality efforts operating in parallel rather than sequentially. This is not a criticism of either field; it only points to the current stage of development of organizational theory in practice. However, it does suggest that organizations that are looking at TQM programs ought to consider linking leadership development with overall change processes and programs.

A primary goal for this chapter was to bridge the gap between TQM and transformational leadership. Achieving this goal should help to avoid retracing steps that too often occur as parallel behavioral sciences progress toward new horizons. We will now briefly outline how TQM programs and the full range of leadership could be merged. By necessity, this discussion must remain at a general level of analysis given the broad range of organizations to which it must apply.

TQM, Leadership, and Individual and Organizational Development

The Primacy of Awareness

Awareness must come first to develop understanding of the full range of leadership. This starting point is also consistent with many TQM efforts.[36] Often organizations and people "[d]on't know what they don't know."[37] For example, Ford officials were unaware of the design problems in their transmissions until they entered into a contract with Mazda. Ford officials found that the Mazda transmission occupied 27% of the distance between "acceptable" specification limits, whereas the Ford transmission occupied 70% of the allowable range for design specifications. To heighten the awareness of employees, Ford developed a short film that contrasted key differences in process and results.[38]

When Deming first introduced the concepts of statistical quality control (SQC) into the United States, one of the most important principles he tried to convey to organizational leaders was the idea that systems accounted for much of the variance in performance. Causes of poor quality, often attributed to the individual, were more correctly attributed to the system and its leadership. Deming's message focused on getting organizations to concentrate on variability, in addition to mean differences in performance. In a rather simple exercise, using the now classic red-and-white beads experiment, Deming demonstrated that individual variations in performance largely resulted from systemic or what he referred to as "common" causes. Selecting red or white beads out of the hopper in random fashion showed how variable the pattern of selection could be over time and how the design of the system or process can affect results.

By establishing a band within which variability was considered acceptable, rather than a mean, one could move a system to a much higher level of performance. Awareness of the inherent variability in systemic processes led to orienting the organization's awareness of the need to attend to process and input and away from a strict concentration on measuring the quality levels of output. Creating such awareness and the means by which this is accomplished is fundamentally important to successful change efforts. Raising the level of awareness to the system level and away from the individual is itself intellectually stimulating because we reverse the figure (formerly the individual) and the background (formerly the system in which the individual is embedded).[39]

Nobel laureate Herb Simon's comments take on even greater significance in light of such changes in perspective and awareness described above. According to Simon, "An ant, viewed as a behaving system, is quite simple. The apparent complexity of its behavior over time is largely a reflection of the complexity of the environment in which it finds itself."[40] This message, repackaged by Deming for a different purpose, still emphasizes the need to make organizational leaders aware of systems and the impact those systems have on individual, team, and organizational behavior and performance.

Often awareness is stimulated by an impending crisis similar to those that occurred with companies such as Chrysler, Massey Fergusson, International Harvester, Montgomery Wards, Clark Equipment, and Western Union in the 1970s and 1980s. When Pistner took over as CEO of Montgomery Wards, he wrote *A Charter for Survival*. His actions were intended to send a clear and unmistakable message to employees that the troubles at Wards were deeply ingrained and life-threatening. Radical changes had to be made immediately for the company to survive.[41] He got his employees' attention!

In some situations, the crisis is not always beyond the threshold of awareness. As the above instances suggest, the leaders were at the point of raising employee awareness, operating in a management-by-correction mode. "We're in deep trouble and we simply must react!"

We argue that leaders should not only respond effectively to crises, but also create them. In a sense, a vision creates a crisis by highlighting the difference between the current state and the desired future state. The vision is a rational extension of the present into the future, thus emphasizing the discrepancy. The vision often revises the organization's orientation and focus.[42]

At 3M, one might say that the corporation is in a continual state of "bounded" chaos. As part of its vision, the organization's leadership is committed to generating 25% of its net profit based on products each year that did not exist five years previously!

Perhaps simply making people aware of the following contrast is enough to stimulate the energy needed to change: In 1978, 30% of U.S. consumers indicated that the quality of the product was more important than price. In 10 years, that percentage has grown to 80%. In light of the change in customer preferences toward quality, perhaps it is not surprising how much attention is being given to TQM and continuous improvement.[43]

Strategies for running organizations are being radically changed as a consequence of this shift in customer perspective. Nothing is likely to get done without some sort of awareness that a problem exists even if the problem is an opportunity as opposed to a threat. Thus awareness is key to the change process. Such awareness often stems from the leader's vision, which is typically linked to proper diagnosis—the first stage in effective problem solving and decision making. The vision points to the peak we must all climb, but does not provide the necessary guidance on how to ascend the peak or the conditions that would be optimal for the ascent.

The Roles of Leadership

In organizations, the conditions or context relates in large part to the culture of the organization, including the assumptions that guide behavior, implicit rules, values, and symbols that identify what is and is not important to the organization's leadership. Leaders at both the top and subsequent levels must help to define or redefine the goals for the culture, as well as the goals for continuous development and improvement in performance.

Demonstrating the importance of quality can be done symbolically by the leader. For example, Stanley Gault, formerly of Rubbermaid, says, "On quality, I'm a son of a bitch." Gault became legendary at Rubbermaid for his actions, which exemplified the importance he placed on total quality in Rubbermaid's culture. For instance, walking in New York City one day, Gault heard a doorman complaining about the thick lip on a Rubbermaid dust pan. Gault brought the dust pan to his engineers and told them to redesign it! Similarly, he routinely visited several stores a week that carried the Rubbermaid label. He bought up all of the products in the store and if he found even one product with a crooked label, he then went back to lecture his top managers on the importance of producing the highest quality products. "When it comes to encouraging quality, passion at the top counts as much as engineering precision at the bottom."[44]

Once awareness has been achieved and the momentum for change is underway, leaders throughout the organization must work assiduously to bring followers into alignment with the vision and to provide the environment to approach problems from unique and perhaps controversial perspectives. Different units may have a different vision of how they will achieve continuous improvement. Nevertheless, it is important that these visions align with the organization's overarching vision and direction. Needless to say, the greater the diversity among the different units for which a leader is responsible, the more the leader will be required to coordinate activities and, in many instances, tolerate differences in opinions. Intellectually stimulating leaders will promote such tolerance for differences in perspective and approach, allowing for and championing changes in perspective and missions needed to take on more difficult challenges. Of course, the type of coordination that goes hand in hand with this process must be couched in a forward-thinking framework that functions as a means of making sense out of the discrepancies of the moment for the long-term benefits that will accrue to the organization. During this transition period, individuals will need to learn new strategies for working more effectively in their jobs.

The problem of discrepancies and their resolution on a unit-by-unit or organizational basis is not unlike the process individuals go through as they move to higher levels of personal development. Specifically, development has been defined as the resolution of conflicts that result in a broader perspective being achieved, and thus achieving a higher level of learning and development. It is critical, therefore, for the leader to link continually the conflicts and contradictions of the moment to the long-term strategies for the future. This is accomplished by clarifying the vision and reclarifying it as conditions change, inducing followers to do the same by stimulating them to look at their worlds from unique and hopefully broader perspectives. Such perspectives eventually become part of the operating assumptions of the culture and the individual. Development has occurred both at the organizational and individual level.

Much of the success in implementing change and balancing the aforementioned incongruities at any one point in time depends on the leader's use of individualized consideration. A leader must understand the needs and capabilities of his or her associates to know how far to stretch them, to communicate the vision in a way that is understandable and inspiring, and to provide strategies for solving problems that do not go beyond the followers' comprehension level. In essence, the leader must effectively diagnose not only the situation and its needs, but also the needs of followers to determine the appropriate paths for elevating those needs to meet higher levels of performance and development. In many ways the culture of the organization and how colleagues treat one another is symbolic of the type of individualized consideration shown by the leader. With increases in span of control, coupled with reductions in middle-level management positions and the growth of MFTs, the need has never been greater for applying the principles of individualized consideration to the development of individuals, relationships among peers, and teams and organizations. The concept of how one treats the internal and external customer is clearly rooted in the construct of individualized consideration.[45]

Key Facets of TQM + L

We will briefly summarize here and in Figure 7.2 some of the key facets that need to be considered in moving an organization toward continuous improvement.

Starting from the left-hand side of Figure 7.2, the impetus for change often stems from the awareness of a need. Leaders are instrumental in recognizing the needs of the organization either in the current context or by extrapolating to the future. Recognition must then be followed by an articulation of the problem (threat or opportunity) in a manner that is understood and accepted by other organizational members. Successful leaders will highlight key aspects of a more desirable future state, building in the emotion or inspiration necessary to address the challenges confronting the organization. Once the "master template" has been created, the leader must articulate how to change the conventional wisdom of the past to the flexible thinking of the future. Attacking the "tried and true ways" of operating will meet with certain resistance, but keeping the vision and its potential benefits clear should help override early skepticism as change unfolds. Discarding old norms and assumptions will take some time, which will vary for different individuals. However, the more the leader models the new way of operating and gets other key leaders to wholeheartedly accept the new way, the higher the probability for success. The roles in which individuals have operated must change—including the leader at the top. Thus during this period of time, significant activity takes place in role redefinition and learning alternative roles to support change.

During the transition phase to a new orientation and to new roles, there will be a need to provide extensive training and development activities to proceed. Individual managers and employees will need to learn new strategies for addressing problems, as well as new ways of defining what a problem is and is not. Establishing these new roles will take some time: The roles of individuals, groups, and the organization

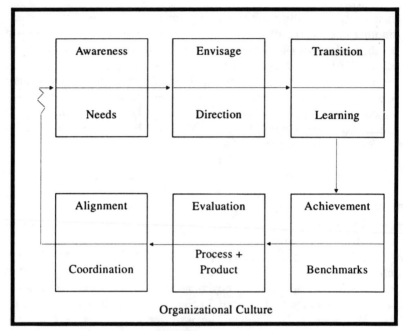

Figure 7.2 Continuous Improvement Loop

often will be in transition, causing some confusion and uncertainty. Furthermore, the change in roles and the reestablishment of new roles will fundamentally alter the organization's culture, again taking some time to unfold properly. Depending on how ingrained the beliefs and assumptions, the stabilization of new roles could take several years. The need for trust between leader and follower is underscored as one moves through the various phases of the change process.

Once the new roles, norms, and assumptions are established, the need to practice, evaluate, and provide feedback becomes critical. The new way of operating must become routine. Evaluation and reevaluation will become an integral part of CPI. The type of change being undertaken requires a sense of purpose, commitment, support, and persistence on the part of all those who are involved, not just the senior managers.

Factors that can affect the transformation to a TQM + L organization include the organization's structure, reward, and resource system; the allocation of responsibilities; methods and criteria for evaluation; investment in training and education; tolerance for conflict; and the attributes of the work force.[46]

As the process of change unfolds, organizational leaders will need to realign followers continually around the central mission or vision. However, over time and as needs change, the vision may need to be revised and updated, which leads to a new level of awareness, thus beginning the cycle shown in Figure 7.2 all over again.

In sum, the change process that has been described in this chapter requires a thorough reevaluation of the way an organization operates, from its leadership paradigm to its reward and evaluation systems. The change will require involvement on the order described by Teddy Roosevelt in his summation of what constitutes effective leadership:

> The credit belongs to the man who is actually in the area, whose face is marred by dust and sweat and blood . . . who knows the great enthusiasms, the great devotions; who spends himself in a worthy cause, who at the best knows in the end the triumph of high achievement, and . . . if he fails at least he fails while daring greatly, so that his place shall never be with those old timid souls who know neither victory nor defeat.[47]

Throughout the remainder of this decade and into the next millennium, the changes that organizations will undergo will be dramatic. During this period, the transition of organizations striving to achieve CPI will require the full attention of transformational leaders and all members of their units and organizations. However, as described by Horine and Bass, the early returns on organizations that have already made this transition underscore the benefits that can be accrued from the merger of TQM and the Four I's of transformational leadership. Horine and Bass reported that the Malcolm Baldridge winners had organizations that were run by leaders who were seen as more transformational than those from comparable organizations in their industry.[48] These results, coupled with the main thesis of this chapter, point to the potential benefits of a "new alliance."

Notes

1. Avolio, B. J., & Gibbons, T. (1988). Developing transformational leaders: A lifespan approach. In J. Conger & R. Kanungo (Eds.), *Charismatic leadership: The elusive factor in organizational effectiveness* (pp. 276-308). San Francisco: Jossey-Bass.

2. Feigenbaum, A. V. (1983). *Total quality control*. New York: McGraw-Hill.

3. Bass, B. M. (1985). *Leadership and performance beyond expectations*. New York: Free Press.

4. U.S. Department of Commerce. (1990). *Application guidelines for Malcolm Baldrige National Quality Award*. Washington, DC: Government Printing Office.

5. Jackson, S. (1990, October). Calling in the gurus. *Director*, pp. 95-101.

6. Garvin, D. A. (1988). *Managing quality*. New York: Free Press.

7. Hughes, J. R. T. (1987). *American economic history* (2nd ed.). Glenview, IL: Scott, Foresman.

8. Radford, G. S. (1922). *The control of quality in manufacturing*. New York: Ronal.

9. Shewhart, W. A. (1931). *Economic control of quality of manufacturing product*. New York: Van Nostrand.

10. Weber, M. (1924). *The theory of social and economic organization* (Trans. by A. M. Henderson & T. Parsons). New York: Free Press.

11. Kuhnert, K. W., & Lewis, P. L. (1987). Transactional and transformational leadership: A constructive developmental analysis, *Academy of Management Review, 12*, 648-657.

12. Castro, J. (1989, November 13). Making it better. *Time*, pp. 78-81.

13. Castro (1989).

14. Mitchell, R. (1984). Rediscovering our roots: A history of quality circle activities in the United States from 1918 to 1948. *IAQC Conference Transactions*, pp. 26-43.

15. Castro (1989).

16. Avolio, B. J., Waldman, D. A., & Yammarino, F. J. (1991). Leading in the 1990s: Towards understanding the four I's of transformational leadership. *Journal of Industrial Training, 154*, 9-16.

17. Bass, B. M., & Avolio, B. J. (1990). *Manual for the Multifactor Leadership Questionnaire*. Palo Alto, CA: Consulting Psychologists Press.

18. Deming, W. E. (1986). *Out of the crisis*. Cambridge: MIT Center for Advanced Engineering Studies.

19. Thomas, R. M. (1990, October). New crisis in quality. *Industry Week*, pp. 11-14.

20. Burns, J. M. (1978). *Leadership*. New York: Harper & Row.

21. Zaleznik, A. (1989). *The managerial mystique*. New York: Harper Collins.

22. Kotter, J. P. (1990). *A force for change: How leadership differs from management*. New York: Free Press.

23. Waldman, D. A., Bass, B. M., & Yammerino, F. J. (1990). Adding to contingent-reward behavior: the augmenting effect of charismatic leadership. *Group and Organization Studies, 15*, 381-394.

24. Nonaka, J. (1988, Spring). Creating order out of chaos: Self-renewal in Japanese firms. *Sloan Management Review*, pp. 57-73.

25. Avolio, Waldman, & Yammarino (1991).

26. Levitt, T. (1990, Spring). The innovating organization. *Harvard Business Review*, p. 7.

27. Schein, E. (1990). Organizational culture. *American Psychologist, 45*, 109-119.

28. U.S. Department of Commerce (1990).

29. Bass, B. M., Waldman, D. A., Avolio, B. J., & Bebb, M. (1987). Transformational leaders: The falling dominoes effect. *Group and Organization Studies, 12*, 73-87.

30. Howard, A., & Bray, E. W. (1988). *Managerial lives in transition*. New York: Guilford.

31. Walton, M. (1986). *The Deming management method*. New York: Putnam.

32. Walton (1986).

33. Levitt (1990).

34. Leonard, B. (1990, December). Trosin discovers the right mix at Merck. *HR Magazine*, pp. 56-58.

35. Kuhnert, K. W., & Lewis, P. L. (1987). Transactional and transformational leadership: A constructive developmental analysis. *Academy of Management Review, 12,* 648-657.

36. U.S. Department of Defense (1969). *DOD directive on total quality management.* Washington, DC: Government Printing Office.

37. Pascarella, P. (1986, September). Personal breakthroughs create new corporate possibilities. *Industry Week,* p. 71.

38. Walton (1986).

39. Avolio, Waldman, & Yammarino (1991).

40. Kotter, J. P. (1988). *The leadership factor.* New York: Free Press.

41. Castro (1989).

42. Walton, R. E. (1986). A vision-led approach to restructuring. *Organizational Dynamics, 14,* 14-16.

43. Leaders of the most admired. (1990, January 29). *Fortune,* pp. 40-54.

44. *Fortune* (1990).

45. Offerman, L. R., & Gowing, M. K. (1990). Organizations of the future: Changes and challenges. *American Psychologist, 45,* 95-108.

46. Horine, J., & Bass, B. M. (1993a). Transformational leadership: The cornerstone of quality. *Report No. 92-3,* Center for Leadership Studies, Binghamton University.

47. Roosevelt, speech delivered April 10, 1989, at the Hamilton Club, Chicago, IL.

48. Horine, J., & Bass, B. M. (1993b). The leadership behavior of Malcolm Baldrige national quality award-winning company chief executives, *Report No. 92-4,* Center for Leadership Studies, Binghamton University.

8

Organizational Transformation

STRATEGIES FOR CHANGE
AND IMPROVEMENT

LEANNE E. ATWATER

DAVID C. ATWATER

Center for Leadership Studies,
School of Management, SUNY Binghamton

EXECUTIVE SUMMARY

This chapter has four purposes: (a) to provide a description of the types of change efforts undertaken by multinational companies; (b) to suggest innovative change and change-evaluation processes; (c) to suggest several possible approaches for determining the degree to which these changes have permeated and are affecting the organization, which is referred to as the *diffusion* of changes into the organization; and (d) to show the relevance of the full range of leadership to organizational change and development efforts.

Change Objectives

In a general sense, any major change process will focus on the company's culture, structure, and human resources (HR) procedures, which require alteration to better meet the organization's strategic goals and objectives. A common target for change in many organizations today is altering the prevailing managerial style from one based on formal top-down authority to a more employee-centered style that is designed to maximize the return on HR capital. This parallels the trends of "de-leveling" an organization and shifting toward self-managed teams. Moving in this direction generally requires the development of human resource strategies for improvement. We can parallel these areas with the full-range model of leadership as follows:

- Improved selection, training, and development of personnel to meet the new organizational requirements for team building, maximize individual potential, and ensure equitable treatment and opportunities for all.
- The use of positive reinforcement to encourage the creation of employee-employee and employee-employer relationships that are long-lasting, satisfying, and mutually beneficial (contingent reward).
- Linking the quality of work performance processes or product generated by the individual or team to recognition by the organization (contingent reward).
- Developing trust and empowering individuals to encourage them to demonstrate their abilities, develop new ones, and seek unanticipated challenge (individualized consideration, idealized influence).
- Improve upward, downward, and lateral communication to ensure that individuals at all organizational levels understand their responsibilities and are aligned around a central purpose, mission, and vision (inspirational motivation).
- Building cooperative relationships with unions that foster the development of agreements and programs that are in the best mutual interests of the corporation and its workers (contingent reward, individualized consideration).

A principal mechanism that can be used to bring about such changes is the adoption of the full-range model of leadership and the institution of a management-development program based on this framework. To the degree that such training is effective, it should support the types of HR changes outlined above by facilitating desired changes in the behaviors and attitudes of those who are trained and charged with leading an organization into the future, including the HR staff. Such training also should improve interactions between colleagues, supervisors, and followers; alter their behavior and attitudes; and be reflected in the policies and procedures that are implemented within the company with its suppliers and customers.

The Promotion of Organizational Change

Understanding organizational change and transformation in a large, complex corporation can be aided by knowledge of the models that have evolved as investigators have studied the change process. Although each organization's experience is undoubtedly unique, enough common elements support the development of a general framework that can be useful in understanding, assessing, and managing the transformation process across a diverse range of organizations. In addition, knowledge of a framework for organizational transformation also may be useful in identifying areas that are likely to be affected by these changes, and it may suggest mechanisms for measuring and evaluating the changes that take place.

The Meaning of Organizational Development

The methods that organizations use to respond to the need for change have been the focus of much research and study in recent years. The body of knowledge that has accumulated can be subsumed under the broad heading of organizational development (OD), especially when defined as follows:

The term *organizational development* implies a normative reeducation strategy that is intended to affect systems of beliefs, values, and attitudes within the organization so that it can adapt better to the accelerated rate of change in technology, in our industrial environment, and in society in general. It also includes formal and informal organizational restructuring, which is frequently initiated, facilitated, and reinforced by the normative and behavioral change.[1]

This definition highlights three principal OD objectives: (a) to change attitudes or values, (b) to modify behavior, and (c) to bring about change in structure, policy, and culture.

As typically used in contemporary management practice, OD has certain distinguishing characteristics that parallel components of the full-range model:[2]

- It is planned and long-term in perspective, thus requiring inspirational leadership. OD is data-based, involving all of the elements of good managerial planning.
- It is problem-oriented and benefits from intellectual stimulation. OD attempts to apply theory and research from several disciplines to identify and solve organizational problems.

- It reflects a systems approach that is similar to that advocated by TQM. OD is a way of linking organizational human resources to such systems and processes as technology, structure, and management (individualized consideration).
- It is action-oriented. It focuses on accomplishments and achieving and exceeding expected results (contingent reward, inspirational motivation).
- It involves change agents and champions of the change process. The process usually requires a change agent who has developed trust and respect to assist the organization in redirecting its efforts. The change may stem from either outside or within the organization (inspirational motivation, idealized influence).
- It involves refining and learning new principles. OD's basic feature is its use of reeducation to bring about change at the individual and systemic levels (individual consideration, intellectual stimulation).

OD interventions can be considered within one of three major classifications based on the depth and the target of the change. The *depth* of the change refers to the extent to which the intervention will penetrate the operations of the formal and informal organization. *Formal components* refer to such observable and rational structural factors as policies, goals, and reporting structures. *Informal components* refer to less obvious components such as power relations, needs, satisfaction, and values. The target of the change can be structural, behavioral, or both.

Figure 8.1 displays a model of the types or ranges of OD interventions and their intended effects.[3] As the figure indicates, interventions can focus on technostructural, human process, or combined aspects. Most companies' OD intervention strategies can be best classified as *multifaceted* because they involve formal and informal, structural and behavioral changes. This is a more optimal change strategy: It acknowledges the multiple forces that affect individual and group performance and offers the greatest chance of improving organizational performance over time. Again, it also parallels Deming's suggestions to change the system or the common cause to improve overall individual performance.

Technostructural interventions include strategies such as structural change (e.g., "de-layering"), job redesign (e.g., self-managed teams), and management by "collective" objectives and mission. The human process interventions include strategies such as team building, interpersonal skills training, and leadership development. Rather than elaborating on each approach, we will summarize the lessons learned from their implementation in traditional OD interventions and their links to the full-range model:

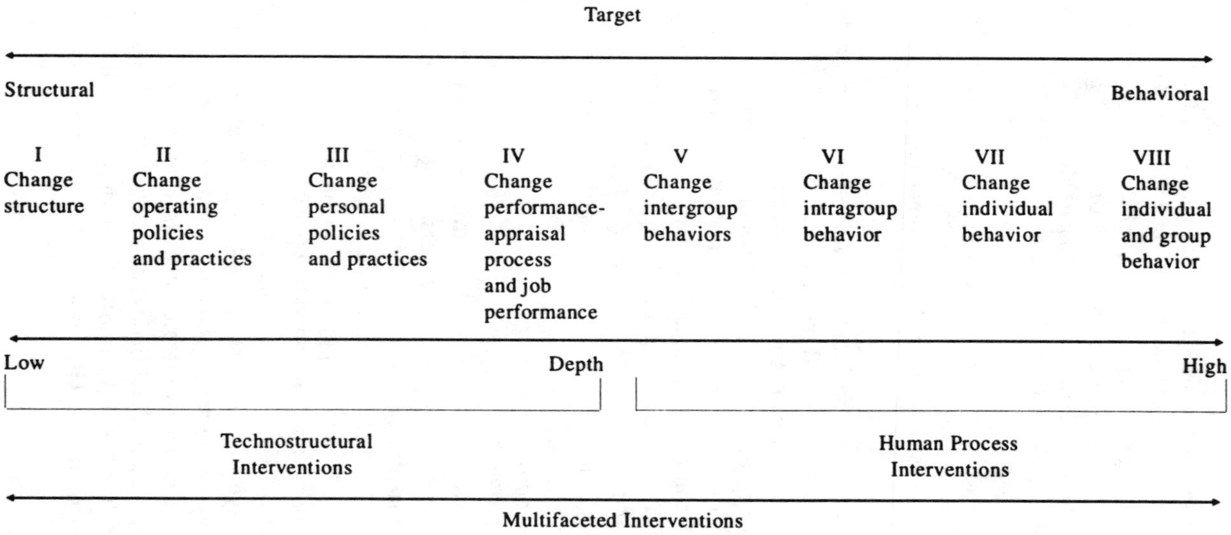

Figure 8.1 Change Intervention

- Management and all those who are involved must have a high and visible commitment to the change effort (inspirational motivation, idealized influence).
- Individuals involved must have information in advance that enables them to know what will happen and why (individualized consideration).
- The change effort must be connected to other facets of the organization, especially the evaluation and reward systems (contingent reward).
- The initial change effort should be directed by top management and assisted by a change agent if necessary (inspirational motivation).
- The change effort should be based on the results of a thorough diagnosis of conditions in the organization (individualized consideration).
- Management must demonstrate commitment to the change process in every step, from diagnosis to implementation and evaluation (the full range of leadership).
- Evaluation should take place at several levels and people should be asked how they feel about the change; comment should come from employees on how best to facilitate the direction of change and evaluate the effects on individual and team motivation and performance (individualized consideration).
- Employees should be educated on the relationship between the change effort and the organization's mission (individualized consideration, intellectual stimulation).

Recent Innovative Suggestions

The more traditional OD strategies just discussed have brought both lessons and improvements, but a good deal also can be gained from considering recent suggestions from organizations that may complement the full-range leadership-training program and model. These proposals may serve as a springboard for creative ideas to be used in organizational change efforts.

1. Stace and Dunphy challenged the universality of OD theory, suggesting that a contingency model is in order. Specifically, they contrast incrementalism (slow, small changes) and radical transformations in organizations.[4]

Incrementalist strategies apply when the organization's methods basically fit its current and predicted environment and only minor adjustments are needed. Incrementalism also works if there is plenty of time to make changes without threatening the organization's viability. Radical transformational strategies are necessary when the organization is markedly out of fit with the demands of its environment or change is needed quickly for survival.

A second factor Stace and Dunphy highlighted is the method of change: participative versus authoritative. They dispute traditional organizational change theorists, suggesting that there are conditions or stages in the implementation of change where full employee involvement in the process is counterproductive. They suggest that when conflicts of interest and win-lose scenarios are severe, full participation in the change process will be difficult, if not impossible. In these cases, directive strategies for change implementation, which can be either transformational or transactional, probably are necessary and ultimately more effective.

2. Poole, Gioia, and Gray suggested that the real challenge to the success of organizational change efforts is in altering organizational members' "meaning systems and frameworks of understanding—their schemas."[5] Changes in schemas represent a shift in the way individuals think, perceive, and eventually act. Management tactics to phase out existing schemas and to introduce new schemas include:

- highlighting or profiling those aspects of the desired change (inspirational leadership) that illustrate management's new schemas [e.g., employees' creative ideas will be recognized and honored (intellectual stimulation)];
- reacting to incidents in ways (management-by-exception, contingent rewards) that indicate what management now deems important (e.g., provide requested resources to effective MFTs);
- redistributing resources to emphasize new ideals [e.g., increase training budgets (contingent reward)];
- hiring new employees whose schemas (ways of thinking) are more consistent with the desired change.

Poole et al. categorized four influence styles used during the transformational change process, which was implemented in a large bank over a 2-year period. The modes of influence were as follows:

Enforcement—legitimate disciplinary measures and organizational rewards to keep behaviors in line with the change process (management-by-exception, contingent rewards).

Instruction—clarifying the desired changes in behavior at meetings and in speeches, and modeling those changes whenever possible (individualized consideration, inspirational motivation, idealized influence).

Manipulation—controlling resources to align followers with the desired change process (management-by-exception, contingent rewards).

Proclamation—specifying behavioral and stylistic changes in writing, with appropriate memoranda, policy statements, handbooks, orientation materials, and so on (individualized consideration).

To their surprise, the authors found that the enforcement mode was most effective in initially changing schemas.

3. Poras posited an implementation strategy called *stream analysis*,[6] which is a graphics-based technique for diagnosing organizational problems, creating action plans, and evaluating and tracking outcomes. Stream analysis can be used to analyze the change process from beginning to end. Poras suggests that the framework for stream analysis consists of four dimensions: organizing arrangements, social factors, technology, and physical setting. Each must be considered in the change process.

4. Taking stream analysis a step farther, Leifer proposed a *dissipative model* of organizational transformation in which regular and significant change is a natural, continual response to changing environmental and internal conditions. In other words, organizational change was seen as the natural state. Managers should view their world from that perspective.[7] Stability is only a resting period between dynamic change brought on by an increasingly complex environment that overtaxes the existing organizational structure and its practices.

The dissipative structure change process has four phases:

- Point of singularity: This is the point at which pressures are such that inherent tendencies toward equilibrium can be overcome. Trigger events (such as the breakup of AT&T or Japanese competition in the U.S. auto industry) can push an organization into transition. Transformational leaders often view these crises as opportune points for change and so inspire followers to pursue a new vision.
- Transformation using radical strategies: When faith in the old system collapses, faith in the corporation's new vision results. Ultimately, success is determined by the quality of the new vision (idealized influence, inspirational motivation).
- Experimentation: This occurs with new forms that are consistent with the new vision but with which the organization has little experience (intellectual stimulation). This phase requires large amounts of energy and resources.
- Resynthesis: New organizational characteristics maintain openness with the environment and allow for the next cycle of transformation to be stabilized. Emphasis or alignment around a new vision and culture often dominates this stage of the change process.

The dissipative model seems increasingly applicable as the pace and intensity of externally induced change increases. The model provides managers with a unique perspective, shifting their focus from one that seeks stability in an ever-changing world to one that recognizes the opportunities for growth and improvement that are available to the organization for adaptation to a changing world.

5. Brown contended that effective organizations recognize that people are the factor that can make a difference in an organization's maintenance of success: "More and more companies as they move into global competitiveness see that the one thing that can make a difference in the world market is people. Raw materials, technologies and systems are available to everybody. The right people can be a unique commodity."[8] Thus in 33 of 50 of the largest U.S. companies, the HR director reports directly to the CEO. HR executives are being given responsibilities to oversee mergers, articulate the organization's vision, and help set leadership agendas. The traditional staff role for the HR manager is becoming a thing of the past in many multinational organizations.

6. Ulrich and Wiersema suggested that an organization can make changes to increase its capabilities.[9] These changes include:

- encouraging transformational leadership (e.g., strategic redirection for Fortune 100 firms was preceded by significant leadership change);
- seeing change as an ongoing process, as suggested by the dissipative model, not as a response to a short-term problem;
- involving key individuals in the change process (e.g., Honeywell managers attend a one-week executive-training program dedicated to teaching middle managers how to manage and influence change.);
- reducing layers, increasing spans of control, and delegating to lower levels (individualized consideration), thereby increasing ability to respond to change (e.g., implementing MFTs);
- implementing performance systems in which employees share risks and benefits (contingent reward);
- continually developing employee competencies through education and training (individualized consideration); and
- sharing information across levels in unique and different ways (intellectual stimulation).

7. Want discussed strategies for entering into the change process with minimal worker and management alienation (when employees actively resist, retire in place, or quit).[10] He suggested the following strategies:

- Recognize that previously successful and even comfortable organizational and leadership qualities may no longer be appropriate and will need to be replaced with an alternative set of critical leadership styles (the full range of leadership).

- Identify aspects of the organization's culture as a stimulus for new and innovative ideas (intellectual stimulation).
- Apply strategies that are appropriate for prevailing change conditions, not just conventional strategies of restructuring or cost control (the full range of leadership).
- Embark on a systematic and ambitious leadership-development process to prepare management for the increasing changes affecting industry (begin with individualized consideration, then move into the full range of leadership).

8. Carlyle discussed the unintended consequences of decentralization.[11] For example, progress in the delayered organization will be measured by the individual's span of responsibilities rather than control over individuals. Engineers will progress by taking on more functions. The need for managing people will not disappear, but it will change form. A new breed of manager will emerge in which leadership will be consultative rather than autocratic or directive (individualized consideration).

Summary of Key Points in the Change Process

Optimal change efforts have both a structural and behavioral focus. Management is committed to the change effort, and changes in behavior are connected to evaluation and reward systems. Schemas or ways of thinking must accompany structural changes. The best styles to use in influencing behavioral change are contingent on the type of change and the attitudes toward change among organization members. In addition, note that strategic redirection in large corporations has been preceded by leadership change. Encouraging transformational leadership, delegation, and employee development ultimately can increase the organization's ability to successfully meet new challenges.

Transformations of Benchmark Companies

Several large companies have recently undergone significant organizational changes: for example, Motorola, General Electric, and Corning Glass Works. An overview of the changes each company has carried out now follows, including a description of some of the tactics, tools, and procedures that were used (with emphasis on those representing the full range of leadership and innovative HR management).

Motorola

A U.S. company, Motorola in the mid 1990s enjoys a reputation as a world-class competitor in electronics. The company is the world leader in the production of cellular telephones and computer modems, the top U.S. producer of semiconductors (and fourth in the world), and a leader in two-way mobile radios and paging devices (including the leading share of the Japanese paging market). In 1988, Motorola was one of the first recipients of the Malcolm Baldrige National Quality Award, the United States' most prestigious award for corporate achievement in total quality.

Motorola's enviable position today starkly contrasts with that in 1979 when it became evident to top management that the Japanese could bury the company with their high-quality products, pushing Motorola into a secondary role in the electronics market. Chairman Robert W. Galvin launched a companywide drive to accelerate new product development and drastically improve product quality.[12] To carry out his demand for a tenfold reduction in defects by 1986, the company began a 2-year examination of virtually every aspect of its manufacturing operations. At the same time, Motorola executives began an extensive program of visiting manufacturing operations around the world in a search for techniques that could be adapted for the company's own use. The company embraced such Japanese tactics as driving relentlessly for market share and constantly honing manufacturing to reduce costs.

Strategies and Tactics

Managers were charged with improving quality and customer service, cutting cycle times and costs, and increasing productivity. We now examine some of the successful strategies and tactics that have made Motorola a world leader in cellular phones, pagers, automotive electronics, and semiconductors.

Training

At the executive-development and manufacturing-force level, Motorola has expended a large amount of time and money to educate, train, retrain, and motivate its workforce. One of the most critical elements in the success of any training program is top management's strong support. At Motorola, top management not only supported the programs, but also initiated them.

Cutting Manufacturing Cycle Times

Motorola managers conduct an energetic program of scouting plants around the world to look for advanced, new, and adoptable production techniques. For example, Motorola's Boynton Beach, Florida, plant followed the Japanese lead by using robots to assemble pagers (although mass-produced, pagers are often tailored for specific buyers with special frequencies, different labels, and so on). At this plant, robots efficiently assemble pagers and, through the use of innovative integrated processing, can be quickly reprogrammed to customize the product. Within 17 minutes after an order has been placed from the field, a bar-code reader will send instructions to assembly-line robots to build a single pager to meet that specific order.[13]

To improve cooperation and interaction between functional areas and across organizational levels, management-training programs have been set up to breach the barriers between design, purchasing, production, distribution, and marketing. These efforts resulted in the company's Bravo pager being designed, developed, and produced in 18 months rather than in the normal 3 to 5 years. And by 1989, only three days were required from receipt of an order to shipping for two-way radios—a substantial improvement to the 18 months required only a year and a half earlier.[14]

Quality Improvements

Despite winning the Baldrige award for quality, Motorola has not rested on its quality laurels. The company has now embarked on a program to eliminate defects throughout the entire company. The program, Six Sigma, aims for zero-defect manufacturing, as well as extending the same concept to shipping, clerical work, and decision making.[15] Educational activities at the company's training and education center, which has been dubbed "Motorola University," provide educational support for this concept. Performance reviews and bonus incentives also are tied to quality criteria. The Six Sigma program is an all-pervasive, continuously improving campaign supported by a $100-million yearly education and training effort in addition to management's total commitment.

Motorola has now instituted a program whereby all suppliers of parts and materials have been asked to implement Six Sigma-like programs if they want to continue doing business with Motorola. The company's intent is to diffuse the program throughout its supplier network.

Productivity Increases

A main element in increasing productivity has been to shrink the organizational structure by removing layers of unnecessary supervision and widening spans of control. The process undertaken to accomplish this was constrained by Motorola's desire not to sacrifice employees in the changeover process.[16] The process involved five steps: (a) data gathering, (b) analysis, (c) discussion, (d) goals negotiation, and (e) implementation and tracking. It also used employee involvement at all steps.[17] A relatively high level of trust was maintained among employees. The process is reported to have saved the company in excess of $4.3 million in the first year of operation.

Customer Service

Several initiatives have been implemented to make Motorola a more customer-driven company:

- developing and evaluating a management system that essentially turns the organization inside out (e.g., the salespeople become surrogates for customers and are moved to the center of the organization),
- increasing sharply the number of visits made to customers by sales and top-level managers, and
- introducing techniques that attempt to help managers and workers think about customers as they perform their jobs.

These and other customer-oriented strategies are discussed below.

Attacking Unfair Trade Practices

Motorola has been an industry leader in lobbying for changes in the rules of international competition when these rules are perceived as unfair to U.S. companies. In 1982 and 1984, Motorola convinced the U.S. Department of Commerce that Japanese companies were illegally dumping pagers and cellular phones. Washington responded by levying tariffs as high as 106% on the Japanese products. Motorola also prodded the commerce department to force the Japanese to allocate promised additional cellular-phone frequencies to allow U.S. companies access to Japanese markets.[18]

New Ventures

A strong belief pervades the company that the product areas that make Motorola healthy today will not be the ones that will make the company healthy in 20 years. To encourage developments in new areas, Motorola has several companies in a new venture program called "New Enterprises." These are described as high-risk ventures.[19] These new subsidiaries are not organized like the parent company: They report directly to the CEO, they do not have short-range financial pressures, and their managers are paid according to company performance. Motorola expects that these subsidiaries will be generating 5% to 10% of Motorola's total revenues within 10 years.

Specific Techniques for Change and Improvement at Motorola

Training and Development

Motorola has had the foresight to realize that nothing less than top-to-bottom employee education and retraining was needed to change how the company was operating if the company were to compete effectively. Motorola developed one of the best and largest corporate-training programs in the United States. The program not only directly improves Motorola, but also increases the self-worth of employees and their commitment to the company. Motorola executives believe that they must continually train all employees.

One indication of the commitment to training has been the decision of a top-echelon policy committee that mandated a minimum budgeting of 1.5% of payroll for training. In recent years, actual expenditures have exceeded this figure. However, the important point is that the committee's action recognizes and ensures that training activities are supported by substantive corporate actions. In a symbolic and substantial way, the company supports a thinking workforce, as shown by the following programs:

Tailored Executive Development. This program focuses on training executives to understand corporate strategy and how to achieve it. Top senior executives as well as lower-level managers attend these courses. The focus of Motorola's executive development program has shifted from honing skills and increasing awareness of the complexities of management to programs that focus on corporate strategy and how to achieve it. The courses, some of which are taught by Motorola senior executives, have two overriding objectives: (a) to increase senior executives' knowledge of future external events and their potential effects on Motorola and (b) to enhance the ability of senior executives to influence Motorola's future in the face of anticipated sweeping change both internally and externally.

Competitive Awareness Program. This program educates 2,500 managers each year. Sixteen hours of training make them more aware of Motorola's competition and of what the company can do about it. The program uses benchmarking to identify procedures that are being done better by competitors.

Workforce Training. Motorola's workforce training program has reportedly become one of the largest and best in the country.[20] Motorola conducts a massive education and training program for its employees (manufacturing through top management), which is conducted primarily at Motorola University. In 1990, the company reported budgeting $60 million annually in direct school costs plus another $60 million in lost work time to education and training efforts. Motorola University's charter is not so much to educate people as to be an agent of change, with an emphasis on retraining workers and redefining jobs. The program also plays an important role in transmitting the company's work culture. In addition to courses in technical and business skills, an emphasis is placed on remedial mathematics (algebra) and improved reading skills (to a minimum seventh-grade level for all employees by 1992 and to the ninth-grade level by 1995).

One final element concerns Motorola's use of competitive advantage to select its training programs. Motorola's large in-house training program, run through its university, must compete with outside vendors, consultants, and universities for business. Managers may send their employees to whichever programs they feel will most benefit them and Motorola. The training programs developed in-house must compete with those developed elsewhere, thus encouraging in-house training to continually improve its courses.

Quality Improvements

Several techniques are used by Motorola to continue its quest for continuously improving quality. The Six Sigma program described earlier is supported by educational programs and by bonus and incentives programs. In addition, the following procedures are also in place at Motorola:

Self-Managed Work Teams. Motorola workers are trained in several skills areas to improve quality. The company shifted responsibility for detecting defects from inspectors at the end of the assembly line to individual production workers. The company also overhauled its compensation system to reward those who learned the variety of skills needed on these teams.

Quality Function Deployment (QFD). QFD is a new and potentially powerful customer diagnostic tool. QFD brings the ideas of the customer into the design and production process. The object is to reduce design time, labor, defects, and costs. Ford and Toyota also use this program. The American Supplier Institute, Inc., a nonprofit organization in Dearborn, Michigan, offers courses in this technique.

The B Versus C Test. This is a technique to evaluate proposed improvements including quality. It involves selecting six locations, implementing policy B at three of them and policy C at the other three. After one year, the locations are ranked on several relevant criteria, and statistical tests are used to assess the results. Even though it is not exceptionally sophisticated experimental design, it is an attempt to objectively evaluate suggested improvement, something which is not often done in any industry.

Customer Service

As already noted, several initiatives have been implemented to make Motorola a more customer-driven company. As surrogates for customers, the salespeople channel customer needs and problems back to the technical people, who thus stay in touch with customer needs. Motorola wants to be confident that it *knows* what its customers want. Along these lines, Motorola pursues the following strategies:

Customer Visits. Sharp increases in the number of visits to customers by sales and top-level managers not only provides another avenue for customer input, but also shows customers that Motorola is seriously interested in resolving their problems. From talking with customers, Motorola learned that product quality is not as big a source of major complaints as billing mistakes, credit, back ordering, and delivery. These complaints were then addressed as Motorola sought total customer satisfaction through all phases of customer contact.

Quality Audit. The quality audit attempts to put the manager in the customer's place. The objective is for management to see how the customer is being treated from the customer's point of view. This is accomplished by having managers buy the product or service with the idea of comparing it to the competition's.

Next Operation as Customer. This technique can be used to improve service and product quality and applies to both internal and external processes. Essentially, it requires every person to view the next user of the product or service on which they are working as a customer. In this sense the next customer may be the next department, person, process, or operation to receive that product or service. The benefits include better knowledge of customer needs, better communications and cooperation, and improved understanding of one another's needs.

Summary and Future Directions

Motorola's move to its current position has been based on a relentless drive to improve product and service quality. To accomplish this Motorola has invested heavily in its human resources—in training and educating both its management and workforce in the techniques of continuous quality improvement. Both the emphasis on quality and training receive strong support from top management, backed by financial resources to fund training and compensate employees who have learned the necessary lessons to continuously improve performance.

Although Motorola's top executives see the company as a world-class competitor, they believe that the key to corporate success in the 1990s will be a willingness to take calculated, long-range major risks with the accompanying anticipated high payoffs. The best companies will be better anticipators of change, willing to commit resources, and capable of recognizing the need for constant improvement. Chairman Galvin sees the quality of leadership as the essential ingredient needed by companies in the years ahead: "Quality leaders are those who can accurately anticipate technological applications for products and processes and can then commit themselves to these opportunities better than their competitors. We view such leaders as transformational."[21]

General Electric

When Jack Welch became CEO of General Electric in 1981 he believed that the company, while essentially successful, had become less dynamic and creative. He thus took dramatic steps to revitalize GE. One of the first was articulating the corporate strategy that would guide the company for the next decade. The following key components of

Welch's initial message formed the basis of GE's tactics and strategies for the decade to come:[22]

- GE's strategic business units (SBUs) would be number one or two in their industry or they would not remain GE businesses.
- GE would remain lean and agile, able to respond to changes in its environment.

During the mid-1980s, the company pursued these strategies as it acquired and sold numerous businesses. By 1988, GE comprised only 14 SBUs, down from 43 in 1981, all of them with commanding shares of their markets. A 1989 *Fortune* article reported that 10 of GE's business units were ranked first in their industry, 2 were ranked second, and 2 were in markets that were too fragmented to rank.[23] Having arrived very nearly at the position envisioned in 1981, GE then became concerned with developing a strategy that would allow the company to remain successful and continue growing. To do this, GE believed that its focus had to shift to the people side of the company. Determined to energize its employees, GE presented the following two additional strategic objectives:[24]

- A companywide drive to identify and eliminate unproductive work.
- Transformation of the attitudes of GE's workforce to encourage creativity and feelings of ownership and self-worth.

The first objective sought to energize employees and improve organizational effectiveness. As Welch has pointed out, it is not realistic or useful to expect employees to become more efficient, flexible, and effective if they also are required to attend to and complete all of the reports, reviews, meetings, forecasts, and so on that were previously required.[25] The second objective attempts to create employees who can deal with the challenges of global diversity and opportunity without the costs and constraints of bureaucratic controls and hierarchial authority, and without managers who are focused on personal power and self-perpetuation.

To reach these goals, GE embarked on several broad programs.

Simplifying the Organization

GE streamlined and reduced the size of its corporate headquarters. Welch regards bureaucracies as counterproductive because they get people to focus inward on the organization rather than outward on the customer and competition.[26]

Increasing Productivity

By improving productivity, the company could better control its destiny. GE measures productivity by dividing real revenues (revenues after removing the effects of price increases) by real costs (costs after discounting for inflation) to yield a measure of efficiency that is called the *level of productivity*. Yearly increases in this measure constitute productivity growth. By 1988, such growth had increased to 4.5% and had a goal of 6%.

Developing a Competitive Workforce

To meet its forecasted challenges, GE sought to instill in its employees the attitudes, knowledge, and skills necessary to function effectively in the company.

Specific Techniques for Change and Improvement at GE

Management Development

The company of the future will have no boundaries, which will facilitate cooperation between functions. Such a company also will be lean, agile, and flexible to serve the changing needs of its customers, and it will be run by people who are *leaders* rather than managers.[27] According to Welch, "Call people managers and they are going to start managing things, getting in the way. The job of a leader is to take the available resources—human and financial—and allocate them rigorously. Not to spread them out like butter on bread. That's what bureaucrats do. It takes courage and tough-mindedness to pick the bets, put the resources behind them, articulate the vision to the employees, and explain why you said yes to this one and no to that one."[28]

Crotonville-on-Hudson

A secluded camp, once attended exclusively by high-level GE executives, has been expanded to receive 5,000 GE managers annually, including everyone hired or promoted to that rank. Welch has used Crotonville as a strategic tool to focus top management on the changes he proposed.[29] The creation of new cultures at GE has taken place, in part, at these retreats.

The Building Blocks Approach

GE's management-training program continually and systematically reinforces organizational vision and values. It provides a vehicle for communicating strategic change and developing the necessary knowledge, skills, and attitudes required to achieve the change. It uses core mandatory training programs that follow a sequential order. GE's program is composed of blocks for:

1. new professional hires,
2. newly appointed managers,
3. 300 to 400 managers who have the potential to move to top positions in GE,
4. 150 executives with high potential, and
5. corporate officers.

Each training program builds on earlier stages to establish and reinforce the key capabilities needed at each level of management. Two procedures that support this training are the GE Corporate Value Statement, and a team exercise called "Work-Out."

GE's Corporate Value Statement. This statement of corporate values was developed with the input of 5,000 GE employees. The statement describes the corporate characteristics of the new company (lean, agile, creative, a collective sense of ownership, and reward), and individual characteristics of the leaders GE wants to be running the revitalized company (faces reality, candid and open, strives for simplicity, demonstrates integrity, encourages individual dignity). This statement is used not only by GE to provide a clear concept of the company's corporate values, but also must be used by each subsidiary company in evaluating its officers. The participative manner in which it was developed helps to ensure that it is seen as a product of GE and its employees rather than as a directive imposed from above.

Work-Out.[30] Work-Out is designed to identify sources of frustration and bureaucratic inefficiency, eliminate unnecessary and unproductive work, and overhaul the evaluation and rewarding of managers. The idea is to get the 14 heads of the main business units to join their salaried workers in groups that must agree on lists of unnecessary meetings, reports, approvals, and tasks—and formally pledge to eliminate them. A typical Work-Out session involves some 50 employees drawn from all levels of a GE company. During the five-day Work-Out, cross-functional teams go through an intense effort to unravel and evaluate the procedures used to do the company's work. All participants focus on ways to reorganize work and maximize return on organization time, team time, and individual time. The session ends with individuals and teams signing written contracts to implement new procedures.

Although Work-Out does impose some structure on participants, it is designed to be flexible enough so that no two GE businesses approach or use it in the same way. No formal evaluation has been reported thus far, but the sessions have identified and modified many of the worst procedures.

Articulating and Communicating a Vision

Welch's orchestrated transformation of GE is testimonial to his ability to develop, articulate, and effectively communicate a vision of what the company should be. He started by enunciating a clear strategic vision for the company and continuously supported attaining that vision through speeches, interviews, executive development and training, specific procedures, and broad corporate actions, such as changes in standard operating procedures. He added to the vision as the corporation changed, but the modifications were not done arbitrarily or quickly.

Throughout Welch's tenure he has consistently avoided allowing the strategic vision to become stagnant and thus reduce the company's flexibility. According to Welch, "Once written, the strategic document can take on a life of its own, and it may not lend itself to flexibility."[31]

Simplifying Operations

To ensure that all of GE's company presidents know the competitive dynamics faced by every SBU, each president was asked to answer five questions about the competitive environment and to do so using one page per question.[32] (The questions concern the global dynamics of their markets and what they and their competitors had done and were planning to do to alter those dynamics.) Using this simplified approach, GE felt certain that all top managers would have a concise document that ensures common and clear understanding of the competitive environment they collectively face.

Summary and Future Directions

Welch's dynamic corporate strategy has transformed a stodgy bureaucracy into one of the most forward-looking corporations in the United States and has retained GE's reputation as a role model of successful management. In keeping with that sentiment, Welch sees the successful corporation of the future as a company without boundaries, whether structural internal barriers or external geographic barriers. To operate successfully in this environment, a flexible company relies on trustworthy, self-confident employees to perceive realities, attend to necessary changes, and act decisively in the company's best interests.[33]

Corning Glass Works

Corning Glass Works in Corning, New York, is a relatively small manufacturer (28,000 U.S. employees) that is known for its high-technology industrial and consumer glass products.[34] It has recently undergone significant strategic changes as it reshaped its product lines while implementing a total quality program. Spurred by the quality-improvement program, numerous organizational changes (de-layering, self-managed teams, and changed culture) have been successfully implemented so that Corning is now a growth company with leading shares in several expanding markets and is considered by some knowledgeable industry analysts as a likely Baldrige award winner in the near future.[35]

Strategies and Tactics

Corning's rebirth began in 1983 when Chairman James Houghton launched a major quality-improvement drive. Corning's profits had been declining as foreign competition, changing markets, and inefficient operations curtailed its growth. Corning's transformation is summarized in six strategies that illustrate its progressive approach to competing in today's market.[36]

Focus on Quality. The goal is complete customer satisfaction. All employees have gone through a two-day training program that emphasizes leadership, customer needs, employee involvement, communications, and quality processes, tools, and measures. Thousands of employee teams have been established to identify and eliminate quality problems.

Forming Alliances. Corning participates in 19 joint alliances and many market and technology alliances. These link free capital, increase market impact, and augment the company's skill base without adding significantly to its employment base.

Sharing Technology. Corning's centralized research department serves all company activities, improving the communication of technological expertise and spreading out the costs of research to all divisions.

Cooperating With Labor. Corning has been able to develop a mutually beneficial partnership with its unions. Teams develop work schedules and have helped design factories. U.S. workers participate in bonus plans based on plant performance.

Promoting Diversity. Corning has taken steps to increase the numbers of women and minority group members in both factories and management. Managers and salaried workers all attend seminars to build sensitivity and support for minorities. The CEO has taken an active and central part in promoting this program.

Improving the Community. Corning takes a very active role in supporting the local community's cultural, educational, and business assets. It has, for example, acquired, rehabilitated, and leased commercial properties to minority tenants.

Specific Techniques for Change and Improvement

Orienting New Employees. Corning's attempts to make employees feel that they are important to the company begins with an exemplary new employee-orientation program. The program involves many hours of providing information so the new employee will understand the company's goals, its vision, and the roles that the employee is expected to fill in the company's future. Spouses are invited to participate in relevant sessions. The program also helps employees get oriented to the community by providing information on housing, schools, and recreation. Corning determined the cost of hiring and training a professional employee to be $30,000 to $40,000—an expense that is wasted if the employee leaves after a year or two. Corning feels that getting employees started in a positive fashion increases the probability that valued employees will remain with the company.

Creating a Culture of Trust. In the process of becoming a total quality-oriented company, Corning made a significant commitment to employee empowerment and self-managed teams. Changing people's attitudes to support these changes was difficult and took more time than expected.[37] Managers had to give up some of their privileges—parking places, separate dining rooms, and so on—and supervisors were threatened by possible losses of power, prestige, and position. Training and education programs have been the vehicle for addressing these concerns. Approximately 6% to 7% of the employees' time on the job is spent in training, a large part of which is devoted to educating employees to the necessity and advantages of implementing the needed culture changes. Some of the specific techniques in place include the following:

- Everyone, from top managers down, is involved in teams. One result of this approach is a flattening of the organizational structure. This tends to weaken the role of formal power structures so that skills such as influence strategies become more important. Training in new skills (networking, empowering, visioning, and accurate self-assessment) also has been incorporated into Corning's training program.
- Everyone has a key to the plant door. Trust plays an important role in Corning's new culture, and keys are symbols of management's trust in its employees.
- Climate surveys are taken regularly, and the results are disseminated, discussed, and acted on.
- Employee suggestions are encouraged. In 1982, employees submitted 400 suggestions; now some 18,000 are submitted annually.[38]

Summary and Future Directions

Corning's quality-improvement program and the attendant company restructuring have made significant changes and improvements in its structure and culture. Although this program began in 1983, it is viewed as ongoing. Some critics contend that workers have had to give up more than they have gained, but Corning is unarguably a more successful company today than in 1983.[39] The progress made thus far, the need for continuous process improvement, and attention to the as-yet-unsolved issues illustrate both the successes and never-ending challenges faced by both large and small companies as they cope with the demands of the changing world market.

Summary

Five general lessons emerge from studying the benchmark companies and connecting those transformations that have occurred to the full-range leadership model:

1. Successful major changes were initiated by transformational top-level managers, usually CEOs, who repeatedly articulated a clear corporate vision.

2. Changes were supported by broad programs that integrated skills training, cultural restructuring, and compensation contingent on achieving the desired changes.

3. Many of the traditional assumptions on which the organizations operated came into question.

4. Transformation was not accomplished quickly; it often took 5 or more years.

5. The effective use and development of the company's human resources was seen as critical to accomplishing the changes.

Reviewing the actions of these benchmark companies, we saw numerous applications of transformational leadership, including the following:

Individual Consideration. All of the companies offered extensive learning opportunities for their employees and actively encouraged training and development of individuals to their full potential.

Intellectual Stimulation. GE's strategic plan encourages worker creativity and self-worth. This is an attempt to develop workers who can and want to function in the company's best interest without the need for bureaucratic authority and control. The Work-Out process in itself represents a good example of intellectual stimulation.

Inspirational Motivation. GE's Corporate Value Statement, which was developed jointly by management and workers, provides a clear vision of what kind of company GE wants to be and of the types of leaders needed to become that company. It also helps to align each individual in the organization around central core values.

Idealized Influence. At Corning, everyone is a member of a team. Because this weakens the role of formal power, skills in influence become more important. Building trust is elevated to a much higher status. Recognizing this, Corning has provided training for leaders in these skills.

In sum, we have shown in this chapter some direct relationships between the full-range model of leadership and changes that occur at the organizational level. We have gone beyond more traditional OD models and strategies in examining change as an agent of the transformational leader. In Chapter 9, we will focus more specifically on the human resource techniques and processes that are involved in the types of transformations described in this chapter.

Notes

1. Winn, A. (1968). The laboratory approach to organizational development: A tentative model of planned changes. Paper presented at annual conference of British Psychological Association, September, Oxford, UK. Cited in J. L. Gibson, J. M. Ivancevich, & J. H. Donnelly (Eds.). (1991). *Organizations: Behavior, structure and process* (p. 640). Homewood, IL: Irwin.

2. Gibson, Ivancevich, & Donnelly (1991), p. 641.

3. Gibson, Ivancevich, & Donnelly (1991), p. 641.

4. Stace, D. A., & Dunphy, D. C. (1988). Transformational and coercive strategies for planned organizational change. *Organization Studies, 9*(3), 317-334.

5. Poole, P. P., Gioia, D. A., & Gray, B. (1989). Influence modes, schema change, and organizational transformation. *Journal of Applied Behavioral Science, 25*(3), 271-289.

6. Poras, J. I. (1987). *Stream analysis*. Reading, MA: Addison-Wesley.

7. Leifer, R. (1989). Understanding organizational transformation using a dissipative model. *Human Relations, 42*(10), 899-916.

8. Brown, D. (1991, March). HR: Survival tool for the 1990's. *Management Review*, pp. 10-14.

9. 10. Ulrich, D., & Wiersema, W. F. (1989). Gaining strategic and organizational capability in a turbulent business environment. *Academy of Management Executives, 3*(2), 115-122.

10. Want, J. H. (1990, November). Managing change in a turbulent climate. *Managing Review*, pp. 22-29.

11. Carlyle, R. (1990, February). The tomorrow organization. *Datamation*, pp. 22-29.

12. Bob Galvin's grand vision. (1989, July). *Business Month*, pp. 107-114.

13. Customers drive a technology-driven company. (1989, November-December). *Business Review*, pp. 107-114.

14. The rival Japan respects. (1989, November 13). *Business Week*, pp. 108-118.

15. Stalking Six Sigma. (1990, January). *Business Month*, pp. 42-46.

16. Motorola is also well known as a "people company" with a reputation for treating employees with dignity and respect.

17. Motorola restructures to improve productivity. (1987, January). *Management Review*, p. 48.

18. The rival Japan respects. (1989, November 13). *Business Week*, p. 110.

19. Customers drive a technology-driven company. (1989, November-December). *Harvard Business Review*, pp. 107-114.

20. Bob Galvin's grand vision. (1989), p. 30.

21. Bob Galvin's grand vision. (1989).

22. Aquilar, F. J., Hammermesh, R. G., & Brainard, C. (1984). General Electric. *Harvard Business School, 9*, 385-395.

23. The mind of Jack Welch. (1989, March 27). *Fortune*, pp. 39-50.

24. Charan, R., & Tichy, N. (1989). Speed, simplicity, self-confidence: An interview with Jack Welch. *Harvard Business Review, 67*(5), 112-120.

25. Charan & Tichy (1989).

26. The mind of Jack Welch. (1989). *Fortune* (March 27), p. 46.

27. Today's leaders look to tomorrow. (1990, March 26). *Fortune*, pp. 30-31.

28. The mind of Jack Welch. (1989). pp. 39-50.

29. Tichy, N. (1989). GE's Crotonville: A staging ground for corporate revolution. *Academy of Management Executives*, pp. 99-106.

30. Charan & Tichy (1989), pp. 116-117.

31. Welch, J. (1983). *Managing change*. Address given in April at Fuqua School of Business, Duke University, Durham, NC.

32. Charan & Tichy (1989), p. 116.

33. Today's leaders look to tomorrow. (1990, March 26). *Fortune*, p. 30.

34. In search of Six Sigma: 99.9997% defect free. (1990, October 1). *Industry Week*, p. 60.

35. In search of Six Sigma (1990), p. 64.

36. Corning's class act. (1991, May 13). *Business Week*, pp. 68-76.

37. Corning's rebirth of the American dream. (1991, January 7). *Industry Week*, pp. 44-47.

38. In search of Six Sigma (1990), p. 64.

39. Corning's class act (1991), p. 72.

9

Corporate Reorganization and Transformations in Human Resource Management

K. GALEN KROECK

Department of Management,
Florida International University

EXECUTIVE SUMMARY

This chapter explores innovations in human resource (HR) practices that are significant to the success of corporate reorganization. Experiences of a variety of companies are described, and some of the most effective ideas that have emerged are detailed. Corporate reshaping and resizing are depicted as components of a dynamic process: Continuity of transition is shown to be superior to static, massive reorganization, representing at the organizational level the contrast between reactive leadership and leadership that strives toward continuous improvement as discussed in Chapter 7.

The importance of corporate culture as it relates to HR practices during reorganization is also a primary focus of this chapter. Certain management actions at a critical period during transformation are shown to determine the direction a company takes toward revitalization. Transformational leadership and an awareness among employees of the essential need for change are emphasized as crucial to successful reorganization.

Strategies are described that transform a company from a control model of HR management to a model of commitment. Methods for enhancing creative contributions and motivating workers are identified. Discussed and contrasted are specific HR philosophies of inducement, investment, and involvement, as well as corresponding compensation policies.

Introduction

Corporate Experiences With Reorganization

Reorganization has become a matter of course for a large number of major companies. Some corporations have restructured entirely to deal with declining markets or in recognition of more profitable ones.[1] Boeing Aircraft shifted to the production of commercial jet aircraft and consumer beverages (Miller Beer and 7-Up). Johnson & Johnson moved into high-tech medical hardware, and U.S. Steel redeployed its assets to the oil industry (Marathon Oil). Pillsbury found that its knowledge of the food industry prepared the company to expand further in the industry by purchasing Burger King fast-food restaurants.

Other strategies have focused on changing the internal structure of the organization. Many U.S. and European conglomerates have recently undergone a reduction in force to cope with the debilitating costs of underutilized labor and materials, increased competition in the marketplace, and corporate demands for operating above cost margins. Belgium's Sabena Airlines, for example, cut its labor force from 11,800 to 8,800 employees and reduced salaries by 10% to balance operating costs. In Italy, where personnel costs account for 72% of the total operating costs in the banking industry, more than 10% of the country's 320,000 bank employees have been cut from the payroll.

At British Petroleum, CEO Robert B. Horton chose a team of young executives to overhaul the way the total company operates in an attempt to break up the layers of management between the CEO and first-line managers. The committee abolished 80 standing committees and 6 of the 11 layers of management. Taking a direct-involvement role, Horton opted to fire, transfer and promote managers face-to-face, often using teleconferencing in this aspect of the reorganization process.

Faced with declining profits, Philips Corporation of Holland, Groupe Bull, Michelin, and Renault of France began addressing their top-heavy corporate structures by eliminating large numbers of higher-paid executives. Only those managers who were capable of shouldering broad responsibilities were retained, often covering several countries and product lines. These managers were those who have the skills and expertise to operate decisively in diverse environments and content areas. Groupe Bull, PepsiCo, and H. J. Heinz have reorganized their structures by eliminating national managers in favor of managers who are responsible for a region of nations. The *Euromanager* in transnational firms has become a highly paid executive who is capable of managing across national boundaries. Eliminating language-bound management in favor of an international corporate structure has resulted in great cost savings for many of these companies, but it also has placed a substantial demand to identify and retain those with the personal and interpersonal competence to manage such diversity in the new corporate structure.[2]

Moog Inc., a medium-sized company that manufactures electrohydraulic control products, had avoided layoffs for 11 years. It ultimately was forced to let some of its best engineers go, but because of an elaborate outplacement program, many of those same engineers were happy to return, some even leaving new jobs, because of the trust the company engendered.

Some firms such as Inland Steel Company have hired consultants to conduct the downsizing process as objectively as possible. IBM, a company that prided itself on never releasing employees, decided to bring in outside help to study incentives for getting employees to take early retirement in order to downsize.

The consultants suggested several creative and innovative plans over several years for employees who were willing to resign. For example, in 1989 a plan was presented that granted a five-year leave of absence for qualified employees, continued benefits, and permission to return to work for one hour and retire. Retirement incentives included two weeks' pay for every year of service up to 26 years of service. In addition, IBM "outsourced" personnel by encouraging suppliers to hire experienced IBM workers. IBM agreed to share costs over a negotiated time interval with the expectation that these workers would make the transition readily (in one to two years). The plan provided experienced IBM personnel to key supplier firms and community organizations that would not normally have the resources to attract this caliber of employee.

In 1993 IBM reduced its work force further, laying off workers for the first time in the company's history. The restructuring taking place today is probably the most significant to occur in the last 40 years. The various plans implemented by IBM resulted in a substantial reduction in force. Until 1993, IBM reduced its work force without technically laying off employees, although many feel they have been forced out through subtle pressures and in some cases threats of losing their jobs without benefits.

Pitney Bowes was faced with the same changes in its product lines as companies such as IBM. Pitney Bowes opted to deal with advancing technological change by a special training center to teach people at the old mechanical plants how to make the new electronic machines.

The experience of Polaroid perhaps best illustrates the options available to companies that want to cut back and still minimize negative effects on their workforces. Forced to make drastic cutbacks, Polaroid created early-retirement packages, switched employees to other jobs, gave severance payments of one month for every year of service, and continued the benefits of even short-term employees for several years. Outplacement offices were set up to help laid-off workers seek employment by giving them resume and interviewing courses and secretarial assistance in their job searches. The end result was a 33% reduction in force at Polaroid. Rather than feeling anxious and guilty about surviving, most of those employees who remained felt reasonably secure as a result of the individualized consideration shown by the way Polaroid reduced the numbers in its work force. Underlying the plan was the goal of providing alternative strategies that were more suitable to the needs of Polaroid employees. Clearly, an important benefit of such efforts is the level of trust that remaining employees have with the organization's leadership, what might be called *residual trust*.

At the Olga Company, a small fine-quality women's clothing manufacturer, the CEO directly addressed employees about to be laid off and explained the economic problems the company faced. He asked the employees what they would do to run the firm if they had his job. Through these discussions, the company found out about a little-known state program that supplemented workers' pay through job-sharing programs. Employees were retained but cut to four-day weeks, with government covering the fifth day's pay. Now the practice of meeting with employees (who are called "associates") has become institutionalized at Olga.

Only a few examples have been presented so far of the many reduction-in-force options available to organizations. The best options are those that match the company using them and the image that the organization wants to maintain. The proper handling of the difficult times associated with a reduction in force affects the level of trust in an organization's leadership and its idealized influence. A vision of a leaner organization is also important, one that is slimmer to increase the firm's potential to compete in years to come. It is apparent from this brief review that individualized consideration and intellectual stimulation are both critical leadership qualities that can facilitate the change process associated with corporate restructuring, reorganization, and downsizing—which ultimately affect the idealized influence maintained by leaders who are enduring reorganization efforts.

Reshaping and Resizing

Reshaping and resizing the corporate structure is a challenge to even the best-managed firms. Management of human resources is at the core of implementing and integrating the reshaping process. Resizing proactively influences a company's shape and size in relation to developing a market niche and long-term objectives.[3] The reshaping process must be a carefully studied and systematic plan to:

1. expand parts of the firm into new markets or new areas of the current market niche,
2. shrink parts of the firm that have dried up the market niche or can no longer function efficiently, and
3. leave some parts of the firm intact where the niche remains viable and where performed functions are necessary to support the firm.

Some of the goals of a systematic reshaping include more diversified capability in multiple markets, greater precision of effort, and delegation of authority to managers to make site-based decisions. Both efficiency and effectiveness goals can be realized through reduced costs and increased revenues; however, management must face new demands to integrate the diverse operations and functions of the new organizational form, taking some of the lessons discussed earlier about the MFT leader. Greater precision of effort means that much of the redundancy and buffer support is cut away from the streamlined organization. Slack resources are scarce, and a single decision can have a much greater effect on the organization's vitality. New demands are placed on a reduced number of managers to empower those close to implementation with the authority for necessary action. Empowered managers must take on authority and accountability for decisions, often without guidance from above.

Reorganization creates new structures while eliminating old ones. These changes have a major impact on employees, requiring managers to take on new roles and develop new HR strategies that are better suited to the reorganized system. From the company's point of view, the HR strategy itself must be transformed. Such a transformation often requires a broader concept of employee value and how that value is maintained and enhanced over time. The transformation process typically results in changes in connected areas such as job design, performance expectations and appraisal, compensation, and training. This chapter focuses on both the general transformations necessary in the HR strategy as well as specific issues in staffing and compensation practices. Before we describe these practices, let us view a general philosophy of reorganization, which can operate as an overview of transformation.

Philosophy and Approaches to Reorganization

Reorganization involves some of the most extreme decisions that a company's leadership firm needs to make. This is especially true of decisions to downsize by companies that either have a history of growth and layoff avoidance or must decide whether to enter unfamiliar markets through acquisition. Such a decision often becomes necessary to (a) restore the organization's health by cutting away those layers that are needlessly absorbing the firm's prosperity or (b) attain valued diversity. Diagnosing the problem is a critical first step in determining the course of action or strategy to pursue. Of course, awareness will become a critical aspect of whether the organization and its membership move to make the changes possible.

Modern corporate reorganization can and perhaps should be viewed as an ongoing process—one that continually renews and revitalizes the organization. The decision to restructure has a history of being viewed as a one-time, static reaction to extreme market forces characterizing passive management by exception (MBE-P). Now it is seen as more than a discrete period of time or a stage that an organization might have to endure. During the last decade, a variety of companies have engaged in systematic reshaping and resizing as a matter of ongoing, dynamic strategy. Rather than being seen as a singular and onerous change, it is often seen as a set of continuous, refreshing transitions. This new perspective is consistent with the idea of continuous improvement or total quality management as discussed in Chapter 7.[4]

As a dynamic force, reorganization requires the attention and involvement of management at all levels. At GTE's Telephone Operations North, the ongoing nature of reorganization has become a positive force within the firm. GTE has worked to establish an internal climate in which those who are beginning their careers develop realistic expectations that help them prepare for restructuring well in advance. The planning retirement options (PROS) program is offered to selected professionals and managers to develop positive alternatives to continued employment, with early retirement as a viable possibility. Employees are invited into the PROS program when total age plus years of service equals 76, at which time the firm begins the process of educating and involving employees. Through trust and rapport with the HR staff, PROS participants are jointly involved in the study and dissemination of information on changes in tax laws, financial possibilities, and various retirement-related matters.[5]

Visionary leadership is at the core of the transformational process that characterizes continuous improvement. As such, leadership must provide a clear and exciting direction for an organization. The CEO must assume a significant role in the strategy and implementation of reorganization. It is through the alignment of vision and purpose that the organization is able to undergo a metamorphosis from chaos to convergence and then reorientation.[6] Idealized influence and inspirational motivation provide the core values and domain decisions that are needed to face chaos and uncertainty with an even approach and steady reformation. Clearly, the demands placed on top management are strong as the process of transformation is undertaken. Leadership competence is crucial during several phases of corporate reorganization if the process is to be successful in reaching strategic goals.

The general phases of the transformation process are shown in Figure 9.1. The figure suggests a typical initial decline in productivity and morale resulting from corporate reorganization.[7] The figure also suggests that a critical period exists that profoundly determines the course that the changed part of the organization will take during its recovery and revitalization. Management, particularly at top levels, can directly affect the direction of HR productivity at this critical period of transition. Top management must be able to visualize the dynamic phases of reshaping and resizing throughout each part of the corporation. Like any successful team effort, there must be effective lateral and downward communication, diagnostic problem solving, and continuous adjustment as the needs of the organization and its work force shift.

Through intellectual stimulation, the "old ways of doing things" must be questioned and often transformed to address new realities and structures. The new organization must learn to move away from old assumptions that may bond the organization to ineffective strategies and practices.

Successful reorganization follows a pattern of involvement. Management must be involved at all levels and in each phase of the transformation. The following section describes some of the guiding principles of the diagnosis and planning phases. Next, some of the important details of maintaining and developing the corporate culture during the critical period of reorganization are identified.

Reorganizing Corporate Structure

The initial phases of reorganization of corporate structure require extensive diagnosis and planning. A set of principles has traditionally been used to guide the development of corporate structure. Table 9.1 shows a set of principles that have been used for several decades and remain critical to the effectiveness of modern companies.[8] However, these principles are being viewed differently than in decades past to provide intellectually stimulating alternatives. Revision of their meaning is what reorganization is all about. These principles can be applied on both a macrolevel and a microlevel in the design of the organization and its HR practices and policies.

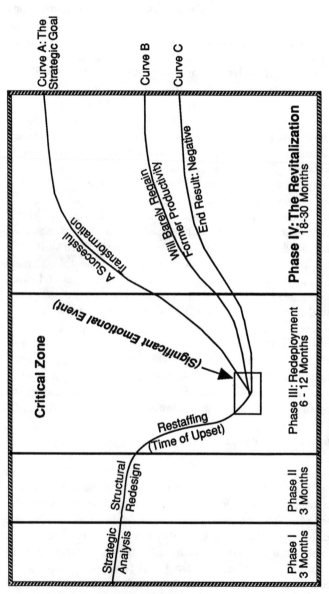

Figure 9.1 Organization Transformation

SOURCE: Ahler & Marshall (1990). © Marshall Group Inc. Used by permission.

TABLE 9.1 Guiding Principles of Organization and Reorganization

Principle of the **Objective**	Every part of an organization must align with the overall mission and vision of what the organization wants to become or that part of the organization becomes a useless, perhaps even counterproductive, entity.
Principle of **Level of Effort**	The "Archimedes Principle" implies that organizations seek the level of the leadership's working capacity. Effort expended will generally be concomitant with the preceding level of effort.
Principle of **Specialization**	Each division, area, and position should have a primary focus and function that segregates its activities with regard to the organization's overall objectives.
Principle of **Coordination**	Functions and positions with common objectives should be coupled to secure integration of effort. Management should link units by a system of correspondence and communication, as well as multifunctional coordination.
Principles of **Authority and Accountability**	There must be a clear line of authority and a defined area of responsibility. Leaders are accountable for their followers' acts.
Principle of **Definition**	Units and positions should be accurately titled so that communication channels and contributions can be clearly identified.
Principle of **Span of Control**	The span of management control should be neither too broad nor too narrow. Span of control should narrow up the hierarchy with more complexity in coordinating functions. It is a function of the capability of followers and how well they have been developed.
Principle of **Command Levels**	The number of levels of management should be minimized. Unnecessary levels in the organizational hierarchy inhibit and filter the upward and downward flow of information.
Principles of **Delegation and Empowerment**	Responsibility and authority should be delegated to the position closest to required action. Those who are closest to information about implementation should have the competence and power to make action-oriented decisions.
Principle of **Centralization and Decentralization**	Certain responsibilities and authority, but not all, should be centralized within the structure to accumulate and distribute information about results and objectives in the most efficient, effective, and comprehensive manner.
Principles of **Functional Growth and Balance**	As the organization grows, the functions performed increase in scope and complexity. Efforts must be made to keep the structure simple and balanced in size, strength, and authority. Diversification must be managed.
Principle of **Continuity**	Organization and reorganization is a continuous process. Growth and elimination are ongoing processes necessary to remain competitive. This means that to remain successful, organizations must be fit to their environment and inspired to go beyond conventional expectations and standards for performance.

The principles in Table 9.1 describe the optimum structural deployment of human resources as well as some of the necessary linkages in communication and authority. Whether designed according to a matrix structure, a linchpin system in which members belong to overlapping groups, a goal-driven strategy, or a lattice of commitments among members across various boundaries, these principles have direct implications for planning and managing organizational reshaping and resizing. The role of management in expressing the overall corporate mission is embodied in the principles of the objective, level of effort, specialization, and coordination as displayed in Table 9.1. The diagnostic phase of reorganization should begin with these principles in order to study how corporate goals are diffused throughout the firm. Old views of specialization and coordination are being usurped by modern views of a broadened realm of knowledge, responsibility, and commitment for each job, in line with the ultimate goal of developing the self-defining employee (see Chapter 2), as well as the transformational leader.

During the planning phase, reorganization is often focused on the principle of authority and accountability, the principle of definition, the principle of span of control, and the principle of command levels. Through these principles, managerial roles are defined in terms of breadth and depth of authority. These principles are particularly amenable to direct control by the organization, so they are usually the first approached in reorganization planning. Note, however, that successful transformation requires the corporation to attend to all of the principles throughout the process. In other words, these principles must be considered as a whole, with changes in one principle area interacting with others. Reorganization must be viewed as a dynamic, total change process. Modern firms are redefining these principles for a new era in management. New ideas about managerial span of control, breadth, and the nature of authority, coupled with a massive de-leveling of organizations themselves, are replacing outmoded practices.

The implementation phase of the reorganization often focuses on the principles of centralization and empowerment. Many organizations have taken a very discerning view of which parts of the system should and should not be centralized. Decision making has become decentralized in most diversified organizations, and the concept of empowerment is closely tied to the basic philosophy of reshaping and resizing. The decentralization of decision making is consistent with pushing the authority for action to where a problem occurs. Yet centralization of purchasing decisions to decrease redundancies and to enhance economy of scales also occurs in many reorganization efforts. Nonetheless, in terms of better customer relations, confidence is needed to give employees the authority to address customer needs at the point and moment of contact. Thus it is the employee's responsibility to diagnose the needs of the customer and to address them, although back-up often exists in the organization to address unusual problems.

During all phases of transformation, the principle of functional growth and balance and the principle of continuity affect the process. As organizations grow in size, they tend to become differentiated in terms of functions and goals. This diversity has the benefits of stimulating creativity and providing the ability to respond to a broad range of challenges. Units can learn and develop as a part of their own experiences as well as those of other units. However, diversity also must also be channeled efficiently to minimize duplication of effort and to maintain alignment with the global vision of the whole organization. Management is the integrating glue that binds diverse parts of the firm. However, when the glue becomes an unyielding, permanent bond, the ability of the organization to transform to meet new problems and challenges diminishes or ceases altogether.

Coins issued by the government of Colombia are inscribed with the words *Liberdad y Orden*. Colombia, ironically, may lack enough of either, but the balance of liberty and order is essential to all successful organizations. Excessive integration stifles an organization's creative development. It also limits how entrepreneurial employees can operate within the system. Some highly progressive companies are unwilling to confine the responsibilities or even the activities of employees. On the other hand, an excess of diversity and flexibility can result in conflict and chaos. Although a great deal of creativity might be born out of high diversity, it can be effectively and efficiently channeled only by an integrated system of managing contributions. Reorganization will inevitably affect the balance of integration and differentiation as some of the traditional support structures and overly hardened glue is stripped away. However, through careful reintegration, alignment, maintenance of the organization's core cultural values, and the stabilizing effects of a strong corporate vision, the path to revitalization can remain clear, providing needed predictability and stability through various stages of the reorganization process.

Reorganization and Corporate Culture

Corporate culture plays a decisive integrating role in any reorganization effort. The direction that the firm takes at the critical period in the transformation process depends on effective leadership of the corporate culture. Core beliefs, values, norms, and traditions form a pattern of corporate activity that affects the implementation of the organizational strategy and the way the corporate mission is communicated. The core values define where, how, and why a firm competes in the marketplace. The personal identity of employees is linked to the symbols and traditions of the corporation's cultural identity. Also, the organizational power distribution is constituted in its culture. The longer a management team has been in place, the greater the homogeneity of beliefs and values and, concomitantly, the greater the resistance to any disruptions to that homogeneity and balance.[9] However, the process of intellectual stimulation discussed throughout this book is critical to considering alternative options and courses of action. The transformational leader's salutary effect on the corporate culture is well documented. Although the transactional leader works within the confines of the organization's culture, the transformational leader also works to change the corporate culture, particularly before and during significant periods of reorganization.[10]

A fundamental requirement of successful transformation is the corporate leaders' awareness that the firm is entering uncharted territory, whether the reorganization involves acquisition or diminution. Corporate leaders must examine the organization's culture—its beliefs, values, traditions, and assumptions—during all phases of the transformation process. Difficult questions must be asked during these phases including:

- What are the tacit assumptions and expectations in the organization, and where do they originate?
- What are the values that flow from the particular nature of the industry? What issues about technology, legal environment, labor-management relations, competition, and economics face our employees?
- What stories, legends, and myths about the organization's history are in circulation? How are corporate successes and misfortunes explained by employees?
- What is truly valued behavior in this organization? What are the critical skills for success, and how does the evaluational reward system now relate to them?
- What effects do recruitment, training, and promotion have on the organization's culture? How does the selection process enhance the fit between employees and the organization?
- How are new employees socialized and oriented into the existing culture? Who are the role models? What cues do HR practices convey to employees? What values are communicated in training programs?
- What is the degree of employee involvement in the organization at all levels and within all processes? Are any subcultures at odds with the desired corporate culture?

Key newcomers to leadership positions must become quickly sensitized to future ideals folklore, rituals, symbols of the culture, and the meanings attached to them. Like the tenured members of management, they must learn to guard against the inevitable cultural clash that accompanies even minor structural changes. They must be prepared to provide a compelling explanation of the corporation's present problems and future actions as well as clear messages about the modes and norms of behavior that will be successful and rewarded in the new organizational culture. Both the new and old leadership must recognize that they may go through a period of learning how to run the new organization. Cultural differences between the new and old organizations should be identified and kept distinct: Attempts to carry over all aspects of one culture to another usually are unrealistic, although it is generally important that the core values of successful organizations be translated in support of the new organizational form.

Culture is unique to a particular organization at a particular point in time.[11] A company's culture may be symbolically displayed in the high-tech art or antique furniture of the corporate headquarters. It may just as readily be displayed through the integrity shown in relationships developed between the company and its employees. The culture is engendered through the folklore that develops within—the "war stories," both mythical and factual, that employees tell one another and new workers. Indeed, it is often the uncommon and unexpected actions that the company takes that form the basis of its culture. The stories that employees tell one another are not about the mundane events of the workplace, but about some significant interaction between a leader and his or her followers. Events concerning individualized consideration (or inconsideration) become the myths based in fact that transcend departments and sometimes carry over from generation to generation of employee cohorts, particularly during times of crisis, chaos, and transformation—as is typical with any significant organizational restructuring. Traditions and key events combine to form a cultural identity that workers attach to the firm as a part of their personal identities. These identities are communicated to the outside world, attracting or discouraging other talented people who are considering the organization as a place of employment. Information about the internal corporate culture also may affect perceptions of consumers about the firm's products or services.

HR groups encounter extensive difficulties when organizations experience any rapid change that the organization is unprepared to handle. Dilemmas have been well documented with regard to rapid introduction of technology and when new acquisitions are laid at the feet of management staffs who have little or no knowledge and experience in the new areas.[12] Reorganization alters the corporate culture but not necessarily the underlying core values and beliefs. In this sense, the changes must be managed in much the same way that a firm manages a strategy for entering new markets. Usually the management system can be adapted to cope with extreme change, but it is the altered-culture effect on people that is paramount in the success of any organizational transformation. Also important is the distinction that corporate reorganization may no longer be seen as an isolated event, but as part of continuous change and improvement.

Human Resource Strategy

Many firms are becoming transformed from a model of control of human resources to one of mutual commitment between employees and organization. We see this transition paralleling a change from more transactional to more transformational management strategies. HR policies designed to elicit trust and commitment are represented by a leaner, more flexible leadership that strives for idealized influence. This model is identified by broadly defined job responsibilities, ambitious performance expectations replacing minimum work standards, more direct involvement of employees in the decision-making process, and new compensation and evaluation policies based on skill acquisition.

Richard Walton has described the transition from a control to a commitment model of HR strategy.[13] He illustrates the success of a business organized by an identifiable product line that divides employees into 10- to 15-member, self-supervising work teams. Each team is collectively responsible for a set of related tasks, and each team member has the training to perform all of the tasks for which the team is accountable. Pay reflects the level of mastery of requisite skills. Workers have the assurance that management will go to great lengths to provide continued employment by committing to them priority in training, retraining, and repositioning as old jobs are eliminated and new ones are created. Employees are briefed on issues such as market share and product costs. Some organizations, such as Corning Glass, require that all workers be skilled in at least three job families. In its new plant in Conklin, New York, General Electric (recently sold to Martin Marietta) required similar transferability of worker skills, which goes hand-in-hand with flexible manufacturing processes. Such HR policies provide the basis for continuous reorganization, change, and development.

The contrast between a control and a commitment model of HR strategy is shown in Table 9.2 for 11 strategic areas. According to

Walton, those organizations undergoing this transformation have begun to report upward leaps in plant quality, lower warranty costs, reduced waste, higher machine usage, reduced operating costs, decreased needs for support personnel, and reduced turnover and absenteeism. In addition, many managers have reported a morale boost resulting from the value placed on HR development and heightened self-esteem. These managers are stimulated by the challenge of reducing adversarial relations with unions and broadening the agenda for joint problem solving, planning, and employee consultation.

The transition or transformation from a control to a commitment model requires altered mind-sets for both managers and workers. Much intellectual stimulation and inspirational leadership is likely to be needed. Changes of mind-set may be very difficult because of deep-seated assumptions about people and management. At the heart of a traditional model is an overt belief in efficacy yoked to establishing order, exercising control, and emphasizing efficiency. Employee voices are traditionally heard through the union representative or the occasional attitude survey. Supervisors in control-oriented companies tend to sustain an "us against them" perception of employee behavior that may be quite resistant to change.

The control model was exemplified by one company's recent campaign to document "airtight cases" against employees who had excessive absenteeism or below-standard performance: Many managers were pleased by and recognized for their ingenuity in finding evidence of employee misconduct and workers who showed lack of initiative. Such policies make the job of management more defined and may even save some legal fees. However, the message of mistrust and the damage to morale is more than offset financially by grievances, violations of plant rules, insubordination, and sabotage. This is a clear example of management by exception gone awry. Mistrust among employees is a natural consequence of such actions by management.

Ultimately, the commitment model places a requirement on first-line supervisors to move from a directive to a facilitative, developmental, and instructive role (individualized consideration). Unfortunately, many first-line supervisors are reluctant to give away the expertise that separates them from line workers. They may even resist new titles such as "team adviser," "individual contributor," or "sponsor" that blur the traditional chain of command. The transformation must be more than just a token change such as a simple team development or management lip service to a quality-improvement program.

Attempts to overreach too soon also may be counterproductive to transformation. Corporate rejuvenation takes time: A highly committed

TABLE 9.2 Transformation From a Control to a Commitment Model of Human Resource Strategy

Strategic Area	Control Model	Commitment Model
Theme	To establish order, exercise control, and achieve efficiency of operations and people.	To foster commitment with the expected results of efficiency and effectiveness.
Philosophy	Obligation to stockholders.	Expanded obligation to stockholders, employees, customers, and public.
Employee Focus	Individual attention given to job performance.	Individual attention and rewards as compensation for responsibility of improving organizational performance.
Job Design	Narrow, fixed jobs; concern for individual performance; separate thinking and doing.	Broad, flexible jobs; concern for team performance; combined thinking and doing in multifunctional teams.
Organizational Structure	Many layers of management; control based on rules and position of authority.	Few layers of management; control based on shared goals, values, traditions, and expertise.
Status Symbols	Distributed to reinforce hierarchy of positions.	Minimized to reduce emphasis on hierarchical structure.
Performance Expectations	Minimum standards monitored for the job.	Focus on excellence, dynamic personal competence, skill, expertise, and striving toward continuous improvement.
Compensation Policies	Incentives based on individual performance; equity based on comparison of jobs in the organization; attempts at cost reduction focus on hourly payroll reduction.	Incentives based on team performance; equity based on comparison of employee skills and expertise; attempts to cut costs focus on equality of sacrifice.
Employment Assurance	Employees considered to be variable costs.	Layoffs avoided; training, retraining, and cross-training programs developed; assistance provided to obtain reemployment.

Employee Participation	Provide narrow information on a "need to know" basis; information obtained from employees by attitude surveys and grievance procedures.	Provide broad information on a variety of issues; extensive sharing of business data; participation encouraged on wide range of corporate governance issues.
Labor Relations	Adversarial; emphasis on conflicts of interest regarding specific agendas in collective bargaining; traditional union leader, manager, and worker roles maintained.	Mutuality in labor relations; emphasis on joint planning and problem solving on expanded agendas; union leaders, managers, and workers redefine their respective roles within the context of a global organizational vision.

SOURCE: Adapted from Walton, R. E. (1985a). From control to commitment in the workplace. *Harvard Business Review* (March-April), pp. 77-84; Koys, D. J., Armacost, R. L., & Charalambides, L. C. (1990). Organizational resizing and human resource management. *Advanced Management Journal, 55*(3), 30-46.

organization is not created overnight. In one plant, managers permitted too much employee participation in pay decisions. In another organization, management downplayed the role of first-line supervision, a critical link in the chain of command. One company overemphasized flexibility of skills at the expense of mastery of critical operations.

Each organization must diagnose where it stands on the control-commitment continuum to determine how prepared it is for change, how change should be pursued, and the time frame in which change can be expected. Change may be initiated by a compelling vision of what the organization could be like if it were to undergo reorganization. Steps in the process of change can be reinforced by transactional CR leadership that rewards the adoption of new skills and behaviors and the elimination of old approaches. Intellectual stimulation will be required to provide new and more appropriate methods for addressing unanticipated challenges in the market. Inspirational motivation will be used to challenge and elevate employee expectations that the changes must be undertaken and that the goals are achievable. And, throughout this reorganization process, having empathy for those who are not quite ready for or prepared to change will go far in building a committed work force.

Despite the inherent difficulties, a growing number of manufacturing companies—not least among them automobile manufacturers—have begun to move from a control to a commitment model of HR strategy. These companies are removing levels of plant hierarchy, increasing managers' spans of control, and integrating TQM with production activity from the highest to the lowest organizational levels. By combining design with production and maintenance and, in some companies, even combining some of these functional areas with marketing, organizations have opened new career paths to workers who had been in dead-end jobs. These changes are most dramatically witnessed in GM's Saturn project.

In other industries, similar changes are rapidly underway. For example, Hyatt Hotel employees are strongly encouraged to develop novel ideas for business outside the basic hotel field. The company has a program that provides entrepreneurial employees with start-up capital (but no equity) to begin ventures such as party catering, retirement-apartment complexes, sporting-equipment rental shops, a major-event planning service, and even a disco that did not meet with total management approval. Providing the freedom to use the expertise gained in the hotel business has resulted in strong belief in the company's commitment to employees' taking charge of their own work and their own futures, as well as achieving substantial economic return on venture capital.[14]

Creative Contributions

The commitment model of HR strategy is designed to build teamwork and allow for a much broader and greater range of creativity. When committed workers operate in a team environment, innovation is stimulated by interactions as the task is done.[15] Ideas flow from employee to employee in a system characterized by trust and willingness to listen and learn. Such environments require at least a Model II environment of team player as described in Chapter 2. Individuals must see the potential for personal gain as inextricably linked to the gains of the teams—a goal of the transformational leader (Chapter 1).

The best reshaped companies are those that have found ways to weave the innovative and entrepreneurial spirit back into the organization. The essence of a commitment model of human resources is that the ideas of workers at all levels are sought out by management and, once found, are listened to by management. Of course, managers still must question ideas, but they can do so in a constructive fashion. Management also must champion those ideas that are deemed appropriate for the organization and its mission, even when they are inconsistent with the current organization's course. Top innovators have a talent for crossing organizational lines to tap employee creativity. Control organizations tend to trample ideas by bureaucratic rules and constraints, but transformationally led organizations nurture sprouting ideas through individualized consideration and intellectual stimulation. Employees who strongly believe that management cares about their ideas and treats them fairly are the most motivated.

A high-commitment model of human resources requires fundamental management shifts toward a teamwork strategy. The "bucket-brigade" or linear model of product development introduced in Chapter 5 can now be replaced by a dynamic interdepartmental and multifunctional process or system. In the bucket-brigade model, someone in R&D has an idea that is passed to the engineering department, which converts it into a design. Manufacturing gets a set of specifications and figures out how to make it. The finished product is handed to marketing and finance. Bucket-brigade approaches are easy to track, and it is not difficult to identify where failure has occurred when something goes wrong. If the product is too expensive or too difficult to manufacture, then blame can be fixed and the problem can be pushed back to its origin. The outcome is often slow development, high cost, and poor quality—or something that customers do not really want. Motivation exists only to get the idea past the next link in the bucket brigade.

Many companies take a *fast-cycle approach* to product development in which it is possible to respond quickly to customer preferences and make necessary adjustments. Using the teamwork approach, extensive interdepartmental communication is the top priority. A multifunctional team consisting of experts from each functional area of marketing, engineering, production, and finance constantly monitors the progress of product development and makes adjustments as required. Problems are often anticipated long before they occur, thus moving up the full-range of leadership model (Chapter 1) from more reactive to proactive leadership behavior.

Even though Japanese car makers showed that they could take a new car to market in three years, U.S. and European automakers usually required five or more, evidence that the vertical control system and bucket brigades that organized most Western companies were deeply ingrained in the mind-sets of many top managers. Creating a synergistic teamwork system in which employee involvement flourishes may still remain a dominating hurdle for many organizations. Nevertheless, the HR staff can begin the transformational process by merely providing information to employees about both internal and external customer needs. Managers seeking a TQM system, emphasizing both speed and quality of reaction to customer needs, can be urged to become coaches and facilitators who listen and provide resources to put ideas into action. They retain the control to make decisions and are linked to a wider range of input.

The "Lion's Den" program is an intellectually stimulating technique that some companies have selected over more popular brainstorming and quality-circle programs. It provides a modicum of structure to a process of freethinking that, without any framework, often goes awry or fails to provide needed results. The Lion's Den is a process that takes place during a restricted time period (usually 30 minutes) at the beginning of traditional management meetings. The concept encourages creativity and shows organizations how to channel the random energy of small groups into productive change. It creates a refreshing, informal environment in which people can more willingly participate in the team. The Lion's Den is a metaphor for a procedure that is used to relieve fears of being vulnerable in problem-solving groups when marginal ideas are put forth.

Two groups enter the meeting: "lambs" and "lions." The lambs are employees who raise an issue with the listening lions by asking, "How can we . . . ?" Both groups are composed of a range of employees from executives to entry-level workers, rotated on a weekly basis. Much of the time is spent reframing the question element of the problem presented. For example, employees from customer service might present a problem of unrealistic consumer expectations about a product. The lions hear the presentation and try to force a visual representation (usually on flipcharts). The lions question the assumptions and information that the lambs use to frame the problem. The lions actively become part of the solution seeking a process that is beneficial to all units of the organization. The lions fiercely attack the problem in a high-energy approach under limited time constraints. After listening to the lions' suggestions, lambs ultimately choose a preferred solution.

The Lion's Den is based on the following basic principles:

- Employees' ideas are the most important asset of any organization.
- Systematic and collaborative problem-solving sessions foster a norm of cooperation and teamwork. The structure provides the framework within which to explore new ideas as well as the opportunity to criticize constructively.
- The process helps leaders at different levels recognize that it is always their job to see that the right decision is made, but that it is not always their job to make the right decision.
- Units can help one another with their most serious problems and possibly uncover assumptions that may not otherwise be examined in an intellectually stimulating manner.

Groups that use the intellectually stimulating Lion's Den (or GE's similar Work-Out) have reported dramatic accelerations in the flow of creative solutions and a heightened sense of morale, commitment, and involvement. Norms of collaboration and information sharing tend to become strengthened throughout the organization. However, it is essential that members trust one another enough to engage in such discussions. Idealized influence is crucial to the successful processing of problems when obtaining employees' true opinions is absolutely necessary.

Compensation and Continuity of Employee Behavior

So far, employee contributions have been in the forefront of this chapter with minimal regard for the way in which organizations compensate their people for useful inputs. The compensation strategy sends a clear-cut message about the organization's view of people, perhaps more so than any other corporate policy. For many decades, employees were compensated for their loyalties, position, and tenure in the organization. This approach is being supplanted by one of several new compensation systems that have more far-reaching motivational potential. HR experts have referred to these compensation systems as being related to a corporation's fundamental HR management philosophy. In this sense, organizational rewards can follow an inducement philosophy, an involvement philosophy, or an investment philosophy of HR management.[16]

The inducement philosophy is based on the concept of motivation through rewards and punishments. Most often concerned with rewards, companies following this philosophy tend to emphasize pay and benefits, perquisites, or assignment to nontraditional work environments as inducement to perform and remain with the firm. Such companies follow this strategy when they downsize by offering rewards for resignation or control labor costs with selective layoffs. This inducement philosophy is most closely linked to our full-range of leadership concept of transactional CR leadership and management by exception.

The investment philosophy is built around extensive training and development. Companies that hold this transformational philosophy place a premium on the long-term education of employees and often take on a paternalistic family persona. These companies tend to avoid layoffs; when reduction in force is necessary, they try to create a supplemental workforce by techniques such as sabbaticals, and using ex-employees as independent contractors. This philosophy is most often found in large companies concerned with product differentiation, development, and customer maintenance. This philosophy of investment is more closely linked to our concept of individualized consideration.

The involvement philosophy is built around extensive training and self-managed work teams. Employees are motivated by the stimulation of autonomy, responsibility, variety, and being able to see their contribution to the final product or outcome of the work. It is the work itself that is intrinsically motivating. These companies try to develop such breadth of employee skills so that potential layoff can be forestalled by reassignment or laid-off employees can be helped to find work elsewhere. This philosophy of involvement is most common where innovation and flexibility are required for corporate success and calls for all four of the Four I's of transformational leadership.

These philosophies are directly linked to a company's compensation practices. Some of these practices are geared toward controlling employees, while others are used to gain employee commitment over time. The evaluation of actual contribution or direct links between rewards and performance is a relatively new business practice. Spurred partly by advances in the technology for accurate measurement of contributions and performance, many modern organizations have concluded that a direct tie between pay and performance is the only way to motivate executives—or all employees in some firms. The pay-for-performance concept, following the fundamental HR philosophy of inducement, is embodied by the elaborate employee-appraisal systems at companies such as Baxter Travenol and Citicorp. The compensation system is designed with short-term objectives in mind and with the purpose of stimulating rapid motivational impact. Pay for individual performance has become the most technologically advanced motivational tool within the control model of HR strategy.

Transformational models take on a very different view of compensation. Basic philosophies of involvement and investment are linked to the commitment model of HR strategy. The involvement philosophy is commonly focused on medium time frame objectives. Compensation expert George Milkovich reports that employee-involvement strategies make use of group rather than individual rewards such as gain sharing, profit sharing, and stock options. Companies such as Dana Corporation and Ford Motor have reevaluated their approach to contribution and employee equity in attempting to move toward an involvement strategy.[17]

The investment philosophy of HR management focuses within the organizational reward system on the long term by emphasizing learning by and development of employees. Aspects of commitment are extended to both the employee and the firm to enhance human capability as a long-term investment. In this approach, people are paid for the number of different jobs they are able to do rather than simply their effort and responsibility and the working conditions of their current jobs. Skill-based evaluation procedures alter traditional compensation systems in several important ways that are quite amenable to corporate reorganization. Compensable factors are reevaluated as to their relative importance. Entire jobs may be redefined. Marketing skills, for example, may become a more important part of a job than technical knowledge. Or the entire job may be broadened to include an entirely new set of compensable skills.

The transformation to a skill-based compensation system makes use of the teamwork concept. Replacing former job-evaluation committees, job-expert teams comprise experts and job incumbents who are charged with much more than a mere comparison of internal jobs along salary lines. They study the progression of job families, career paths, activities, skills, knowledge, and accountability in order to consolidate and regroup jobs into new progressions and interrelationships. A new, more generic set of job roles emerges that clearly defines the skills and knowledge required for success. The result is greater work force flexibility and productivity, fewer job classifications, higher employee motivation to acquire additional skills, reduced turf battles within job families, and improved morale. Perhaps most important, the system sends a message to employees about what is valued in the organization.

Most firms use some form of performance appraisal to evaluate individual employee productivity. Technological advances in performance appraisal have proliferated over the last decade. Some of these techniques could be most closely identified with an inducement philosophy because they are tied to purity in measurement of individual achievement. Others are more closely related to the investment or the involvement philosophies. One technique, the objective judgment quotient (OJQ), seems to be applicable to any of these philosophies. OJQ is based on the idea that employees should be evaluated by not only a supervisor, but also an entire sphere of people who have knowledge of the person's performance. This sphere of appraisal might comprise multiple levels of supervision, peers or co-workers, and the employee's self-evaluation, thus constituting a 360° evaluation framework. Employees are given the opportunity to nominate from four to nine colleagues who are familiar enough with them to make judgments about productivity, problem solving, creativity, leadership, and interpersonal relations. Judgments by multiple levels of supervision by peers and self-appraisal are entered into an equation that appropriately weights the evaluations and provides overall meaningful scores. Comparisons of self to others as well as peers to supervisors can indicate numerous issues that should be explicitly identified. Some of the companies that instituted OJQ, such as Levi Strauss and some sections of Florida Power and Light Co., were initially concerned that the method could lead to problems of inflated evaluations or backstabbing. However, the system seems to have none of those problems and tends to involve everyone in the appraisal process. At least for some companies, it has been well received by management and employees alike. For this type of system to work, however, the appropriate culture still must be in place and include a high level of trust.

Corporate restructuring is driven by rapidly changing technological, marketing, and societal conditions. A variety of principles are available to guide the transformational efforts. Many strategies in the corporate reward and discipline systems also have evolved to motivate employee performance. Linked to basic HR philosophy, variations and combinations of the inducement, involvement, and investment can produce powerful effects on the organization's future, whether short-, medium-, or long-term. These philosophies are usually widely diffused in the organization and range from how the firm attempts to motivate customers to buy its product or services to how it motivates employees to provide them. It typically emanates from the beliefs of top management. In general, it often reflects the philosophy of human nature held by the firm's top leader. No "best" philosophy exists for organizations to follow. The philosophy must be adjoined in a consistent fashion to a culture that represents top management's views, organizational goals, and employee involvement.

There is a wide diversity of organizational structures, cultures, and related HR practices. Corporations that are leaders within their industries in terms of market share and are recognized as being some of the best places to work—although diverse in structure, culture, and philosophies—share certain common HR practices.[18] Many of these best-managed corporations exhibit the following transformational leadership and CR practices:

1. They create the image "This organization is a special place to work."
2. They make people feel that they are part of a family or a team.
3. They encourage open communication, share information, and take time to listen to employees' views and complaints.
4. They nurture the culture by hiring certain "types" of people and by promoting from within.
5. They stress quality and a shared focus on excellence.
6. They share in the profits or ownership of the company and develop performance-appraisal and compensation policies that stimulate both individual creativity and teamwork.
7. They reduce the distinctions between management and workers, encourage people to relate to one another as partners or associates rather than as superiors and subordinates, and eliminate perquisites for managers that cause resentment in other workers.
8. They help employees with personal problems such as health care, work schedules, savings, daycare, physical fitness, and substance abuse.
9. They focus on expanding skills and compensating or reimbursing those who improve their value to the organization—that is, they practice their investment philosophy in human resources.
10. They avoid layoffs by attempting to relocate or retrain; when a reduction in force (RIF) is necessary, they provide outplacement, incentives to resign, fairness in RIF techniques, and possibilities for part-time earnings through consultancy, independent contracting, and sabbaticals.

Strong organizational cultures are those with the transformational leader's clarity of vision and integrity in the philosophy of its top management. HR practices and the relationships that companies develop with their employees ultimately reflect that philosophy. It is that vision which carries the firm through transition and reorganization. And yet the same strong or monolithic culture can prevent an organization from changing when needed. Consequently, a strong culture is not necessarily synonymous with success. Of course, it depends on whether the strength of a culture provides the basis for being both flexible and self-critical.

As we approach the next century, the most successful companies will be those that can best envision corporate reorganization as a naturally occurring transition. Organizations that struggle to avoid change probably will not survive.

Notes

1. For a broad discussion of change in corporate makeup, see Drucker, P. F. (1988). The coming of the new organization. *Harvard Business Review, 66*(1), 45-53; Frame, R. M., Nielsen, W. R., & Pate, L. E. (1989). Creating excellence out of crises: Organizational transformation at the Chicago Tribune. *Journal of Applied Behavioral Science, 25*(2), 109-122; Rose, F. (1990). A new age for business. *Fortune, 12*, 156-164.

2. For more information on specific corporate experiences in shifting toward new markets and internal restructuring, see Chaumeil, M. (1990). Fired! Now Europe is singing the white-collar blues. *Business Week, 3190*, 70-71; Nulty, P. (1990). Batman shakes BP to bedrock. *Fortune, 122*(13), 155-162; Nonaka, I. (1988, Spring). Creating organizational order out of chaos: Self-renewal in Japanese firms. *California Management Review*, pp. 57-73; Rossant, J. (1990). As profits plunge, DeBenedetti cries "Basta." *Business Week, 3189*, 52.

3. Koys, D. J., Armacost, R. L., & Charalambides, L. D. (1990). Organizational resizing and human resource management. *SAM Advanced Management Journal, 55*(3), 30, 46. This article provides an overview of many of the resizing issues inherent in the HR function. It also enhanced some of the ideas in this chapter and inspired the birth of others.

4. For more information on TQM, see Breisch, W. E., & Breisch, R. E. (1990, May). Employee involvement. *Quality*, pp. 49-51.

5. Hill, R. E., & Dwyer, P. C. (1990, September). Grooming workers for early retirement. *HR Magazine*, pp. 59-63.

6. Tushman, M. L., & Romanelli, R. (1985). Organizational evolution: A metamorphosis model of convergence and reorientation. *Research in Organizational Behavior, 7*, 171-222. This article provides a theoretical basis for understanding change in organizations, including (a) issues about core belief and value systems and (b) propositions about the necessity for discontinuity in real change.

7. For more discussion of restructuring and the transformation model shown here, see Ahler, P. G., & Marshall, R. B. (1990). Staying afloat during restructuring storms. *HR Magazine, 35*(10), 68-73.

8. Dougherty, D. C. (1989). *Strategic organization planning: Downsizing for survival*. New York: Quorum. This book is an excellent source for specific suggestions on how to relate principles of organization to corporate restructuring. See also Jaques, E. (1989). *Requisite organization*. Arlington, VA: Cason Hall.

9. Tushman & Romanelli (1985).

10. See Bass, B. M. (1985). *Leadership and performance beyond expectations*. New York: Free Press.

11. Succinct discussion of radical transformation is found in Allaire, Y., & Firsirotu, M. (1985, Spring). How to implement radical strategies in large organizations. *Sloan Management Review,* pp. 19-27. Many of the issues concerned with corporate culture discussed in this chapter were extracted from this source.

12. HR problems resulting from rapid technological change and corporate acquisition are documented in Rossetti, D. K., & DeZoort, F. A. (1989, Autumn). Organizational adaptation to technology innovation. *SAM Advanced Management Journal,* pp. 29-33; Tichy, N. M. (1984). Managing organizational transformations. *Human Resource Management, 22*(1-2), 45-60.

13. Walton's description of the transformation toward a high-commitment organization is cataloged in two visionary articles: Walton, R. E. (1985a). From control to commitment in the workplace. *Harvard Business Review* (March-April), pp. 77-84; Walton, R. E. (1985b). Toward a strategy of eliciting employee commitment based on policies of mutuality. In R. E. Walton & P. R. Lawrence (Eds.), *HRM Trends & Challenges.* Cambridge, MA: Harvard Business School Press.

14. Ellis, J. E. (1990, December 10). Feeling stuck at Hyatt? Create a new business. *Business Week,* p. 195.

15. For further information on teamwork innovations in high-commitment companies, see Bookman, R. (1990). Ignite team spirit in tired lions. *HR Magazine, 36*(6), 106-108; Mitchell, R. (1989, June 16). Nurturing those ideas. *Business Week,* pp. 106-118.

16. HR philosophies of inducement, involvement, and investment are identified in Dyer, L., & Hodler, G. W. (1989). A strategic perspective of human resource management. In L. Dyer (Ed.), *Human resource management: Evolving roles and responsibilities.* Washington, DC: BNA/ASPA.

17. For a review of current compensation strategies, see Milkovich, G. T. (1991). A strategic perspective on compensation management. In K. Rowland & G. Ferris (Eds.), *Research in human resource management* (Vol. 6). Greenwich, CT: JAI. Also, other innovative compensation techniques and ways to implement them can be found in Beer, M., & Spector, B. (1985). Corporatewide transformations in human resource management. In R. E. Walton & P. R. Lawrence (Eds.), *HRM trends and challenges.* Cambridge, MA: Harvard Business School Press; Esquibel, O., Ning, J., & Sugg, J. (1990). New salary system supports changing culture. *HR Magazine, 35*(10), 43-48; Krajci, T. J. (1990). Pay that rewards knowledge. *HR Magazine, 35*(10), 58-60.

18. For detailed information on many relevant companies, see Levering, R. (1988). *A great place to work.* New York: Avon; Levering R., Moskowitz, M., & Katz, M. (1985). *The 100 best companies to work for in America.* New York: Addison-Wesley.

APPENDIX A
TECHNIQUES FOR REDUCTION IN FORCE (RIF)

BASIS OF RIF TECHNIQUE	ADVANTAGES	DISADVANTAGES
TENURE Date of hire is criterion. "Last in, first out"	o An objective method perceived as fair. o Simple to administer. o Retains valuable expertise.	- Management has no control over selection. - Skill & performance have no bearing. - Personnel "bumping" may occur which takes more time and often causes confusion.
POSITION The organization evaluates how the position will be used.	o Staffing is based on business plan. o Nonessential positions are eliminated.	- Decisions interpreted as political. - Valuable employees terminated while less experienced are retained. - No guidelines for partial reduction within a position held by multiple personnel.
EMPLOYMENT STATUS Temporary and part-time employees are cut first.	o Well received by remaining employees.	- Full-time employees may hold the positions which need to be eliminated. - Difficult to deal with cyclical demands with strictly full-time workforce.
EARLY RETIREMENT INDUCEMENTS Employees leave on voluntary basis with enhanced retirement inducements. Often called "golden handshakes."	o Management becomes privy to information otherwise undisclosed--people planning to move or just stay home may volunteer to leave. o Effective method for maintaining morale	- Unpopular with management since there is a loss of control over who leaves and stays. - Often viewed as age discrimination and must be administered without a hint of coercion.
OUTPLACEMENT PACKAGES A voluntary separation program. Packages include attractive termination inducements, professional career transition counseling, and assistance in securing employment with suppliers/customers through "outsourcing".	o In the long term, this is the most effective method for organizational health and employee morale. o Management maintains cost control through development of programs that are attractive, but not expensive.	- HR department must ensure consistent application, with no hint of intentional or incidental discrimination. - Management has no control over selection. - Valuable employees may be terminated while inexperienced stay.

Strategy	Advantages	Disadvantages
WORK PERFORMANCE Who leaves and who stays is based on work performance.	o Effective for business plan. o Fair when there is a partial reduction within one position. o Workers on current formal reprimand are selected to leave first.	- Complex to administer. - Requires a valid performance appraisal system to be in place. - Favors only a performance appraisal system which results in overall numeric rating.
JOB SHARING An equitable distribution of work responsibility for one full-time job, usually between two employees who each work part-time.	o Retains more valuable expertise. o Minimizes involuntary terminations. o Heeds both the company's legal and business responsibilities.	- Difficult to implement and administer. - Takes more time and may cause confusion for managers. - Requires 100% team effort by employees.
SABBATICALS & LEAVE OF ABSENCE Employees leave for a specific period of time. Frequently all or some of the benefits are suspended; however, seniority is retained for benefit determination and promotional opportunities upon their return to work.	o Well received by remaining employees. o Beneficial in dealing with cyclical demands. o Costs are controlled through attractive programs which are not expensive. o Valuable expertise is retained.	- HR department must ensure consistent application of return-to-work policy.
SUPPLEMENTARY WORKFORCE Employees participating in voluntary separation program are hired as independent consultants or temporary employees.	o Staffing based on cyclical demand is easy. o Individuals with necessary expertise are readily available without taxing the resources of the organization.	- HR department must ensure fair market value for services rendered are maintained. - Decisions interpreted as political.
COMBINATION A hierarchial approach which includes a combination of these strategies.	o Retains more valuable expertise. o Minimizes involuntary terminations. o Heeds both the company's legal and business responsibilities.	- Difficult to implement and administer. - Takes more time and causes confusion for employees. - Issues of unfairness can arise.

10

Conclusion and Implications

BRUCE J. AVOLIO

BERNARD M. BASS

Center for Leadership Studies,
School of Management, SUNY Binghamton

EXECUTIVE SUMMARY

In this final chapter, we will highlight the central points raised in the preceding chapters. We also will pull together all of the pieces of the full-range of leadership model by integrating the core areas covered in each chapter. By the end of this chapter, you should thoroughly understand the following: (a) that individual and organizational transformations at multiple levels must be fully led; (b) at various points, and for a variety of good reasons, each and every point along the full-range model may be an appropriate style or method for positively effecting change in organizations; (c) there are times to improve and there are times to back off; and (d) what one does and when will depend on the context and contingencies being confronted by the organization.

We hope to have brought some new ways of thinking about change, development, and improvement for organizations, as well as individuals. In doing so, we have looked toward the future by expanding the full range of leadership to encompass the challenges and opportunities organizations will face into the next millennium.

Introduction

The chapters in this book cover many topics that are pertinent to the full-range of leadership model described in Chapter 1. It was our intent to apply the full-range model across multiple levels of analysis to highlight its characteristics, strengths, and limitations. In this regard, we evaluated the full-range model with respect to development, individual, group, and organizational decision making, information processing, communication, change restructuring, total quality issues, and human resource policies and strategies.

We serve several purposes by discussing the full range of leadership at multiple levels of analysis. First, we can demonstrate how a comprehensive framework of leadership-influence processes can explain the impact of leadership itself at the individual, dyad, group, and organizational levels. Second, through our discussion and application of the model, we hope to eliminate misunderstanding or confusion about what each construct in the full-range model represents. Third, we hope to integrate individual, team, and organizational development and change within a common framework to facilitate strategic plans for development in each area. Finally, to fully explain organizational behavior, we must examine the relationships of individuals and groups to one another and within the organizational context and culture, suggesting that the individual variables we observe can be considered as being within intermediate states in a network of dynamic interactions. This parallels arguments by quantum physicists, who suggest that to understand the individual elements, we must evaluate the overall process by which the elements meet, interact, and average. This seems to be good advice for studying a field even more elusive than the origins of the universe—leadership!

Links to the Full-Range Model of Leadership

One way to link these various chapters together is by first showing the full-range leadership model as we did in Chapter 1. The full-range model provides a way of thinking and ultimately the actions required for all levels of individual group and organizational change. We have attempted to use the full-range model as a lens for viewing development and change at multiple levels of analysis. Firmly establishing this framework in the reader's mind was Chapter 1's main objective.

Delegation to Develop Others

In Chapter 2, Kuhnert integrated the Four I's of transformational leadership with a rather nontraditional view of delegation and individual development. Separating the stages of individual development into three levels or models, he highlighted differences between individuals who operate at varying levels of maturity and linked those differences to the strategies a leader can use to elevate followers at varying maturity levels to higher levels of potential. Diagnosing followers with respect to their respective stages of development helps the leader determine the appropriate tasks to provide for followers at various points in their careers. A key point of this chapter is that leaders who operate at a higher level of moral development exhibit a strong inner sense of purpose and ability to delay their own needs for the common good of the group. Furthermore, Kuhnert and his colleagues have argued that to be transformational one must operate at a Model III level of development, which he called the *self-defining* leader.

Delegation of work is viewed in this chapter as having two purposes. First, it can facilitate the leader's development, as well as the accomplishment of task-specific goals; second, leaders delegate appropriate assignments to further their followers' personal development. By enlarging areas of responsibility commensurate with the follower's needs and capabilities, the leader can systematically move followers to higher levels of development and potential. Taken to its logical extreme, we would expect organizations having a culture of advancing their followers' moral development to operate at the highest levels of ethical standards, and we would expect that they do the same for performance.

The developmental framework provided by Kuhnert can help explain why certain followers are unable to comprehend a particular moral or ethical position recommended by the leader, and how their lack of capability could result in confusion and potential conflict. For example, a leader may not understand why a follower is unwilling to trade off his or her own needs for the group's needs. It is important to recognize that it is not an unwillingness based on intent; it may instead result from an inability to understand the merits of delaying gratification. Leaders who operate at higher levels of moral development also can operate at lower levels and thus should understand why some associates simply cannot see the merits of working toward a group goal or vision. It will be important for the leader in such a case to work on advancing followers' levels of maturity. If not attended, a follower's inability to appreciate group needs can lead to a disruption in the team-building process. The developmental framework provided in Chapter 2 offers leaders the opportunity to address this problem more fully, as well as to provide some basis for working with followers to move them to the required levels of maturity in a team-based environment.

In sum, Chapter 2 has at least two critical messages. First, delegation is an effective tool for developing leaders and their followers to higher levels of ability, motivation, and overall potential, thus moving both leaders and followers up the full range of leadership. Second, to be transformational, leaders will need to be developed to higher levels of cognitive and moral development. The evidence is clear that leaders who are able to consider the needs of others and to balance the demands of the present with the opportunities of the future are at higher levels of maturity and can be identified as self-defining and transformational.

Direct and Indirect Leadership

Chapter 3 by Yammarino takes an alternative view of the leadership process by examining the influence that leaders have on followers across several levels (individual, team, department, and organization) or from a distance. This chapter highlights the need to examine leadership and its direct and indirect influences at multiple levels of analysis. In doing so, the characteristics of the leader's actions and behavior take on a different quality, if one is comparing them at the individual, team, and organizational levels.

Often, leadership has been viewed as a direct process whereby leaders influence their immediate followers—a process that is typically viewed from the top down in most organizations. In Chapter 3, the process of leadership is examined with respect to the indirect effects that leaders have on followers and how those effects accrue through consecutive levels of management or when levels are skipped in the downward or upward influence process cycle.

A key issue regarding the indirect effects of leadership is that leaders must consider the behaviors or actions they display with their associates and how those behaviors or actions are interpreted by others subsequently at lower, lateral, or sometimes higher organizational levels. The behaviors and actions of leaders can have a second-order or ripple effect, depending on how followers at a distance from the leader interpret the leaders' actions, words, and behaviors, which are often filtered by others within the organization. This suggests that all leaders must broaden their range of analysis to include the impact of their actions on followers who directly report to them, subsequent followers at lower levels, and other constituent groups both inside and outside the organization who can be affected or influenced by the leader. Much is still yet to be learned regarding these indirect effects, because the bulk of previous leadership research has primarily concentrated on leadership as a direct leader and follower interaction, although political scientists, for example, in their studies of the presidency, have focused on the indirect effects of the president on his various constituencies. Leaders can likely have a more significant effect on their organization if they consider the potential range of indirect effects that accrue from their actions.

One obvious recommendation for leaders is to realize that any message they consider extremely important should be communicated in several ways and through several channels to ensure that its accuracy and reliability are maintained at all subsequent levels. As we suggest in our full-range training workshop, the leader is considered the keeper of the vision and is responsible for reminding colleagues of the central purpose of that vision. Information, behaviors, and actions regarding the vision can become distorted as it is communicated from one organizational layer to the next. Transformational leaders must remain aware of the direct and indirect effects their vision may have on close and more distant units. The walk-around manager and the open-door manager illustrate efforts by senior transformational leaders to provide opportunities for sharing the vision which ordinarily can only be done indirectly.

The Cascade

Related to the above suggestions is the idea that leaders also can influence followers by the behaviors they model with both immediate followers and their larger public. Bass, Waldman, Avolio, and Bebb have referred to the indirect effects of leadership that cascade from one organizational level to another as the *falling dominoes effect*.[1] These authors argue that transformational leaders can set the pace or direction in the organizational culture, which can indirectly affect the way in which organizational members operate at ever lower organizational levels. Similarly, upper-level leaders who are inactive or who simply react to problems may be sending a message to their followers to avoid problems at all costs. "If you want to be successful here, then keep a low profile. Do as little as possible. Don't take any risks." Particularly likely to serve as role models for their followers are those leaders who have idealized influence, leaders whom followers seek to identify with and emulate.

The Organization's Culture

Finally, it is particularly important that leaders consider their effects on followers through the design of their organizations and the impact the design has on the culture at multiple levels in their organizations. The culture of an organization often reflects many salient attributes and characteristics of top-level leaders. Consequently, the most effective leaders will underscore what is important and critical to the organization's success in clear and concise terms so that it becomes an ingrained part of the operating culture. For instance, if innovation is a top priority in an organization, then leaders must build mechanisms in the culture to ensure that such innovation is stimulated among colleagues who may or may not have direct contact with the leader on a daily basis. Thus recognition and support from others for being innovative can be built into the operating procedure and norms of the organization as well as into the strategic human resource (HR) policy as suggested in Chapter 9 by Kroeck. By affecting the culture in this manner, leaders can affect the level of innovation observed with colleagues who directly report to the leader, as well as colleagues at a distance, both hierarchically and laterally. Emphasis on innovation and the support needed to achieve it can become the doctrine continuously communicated by the top leaders in the organization both in what they say and in what they do as role models.

In turn, the extent to which the culture is assimilated by followers will have both direct and indirect effects on the behavior of those who work directly for the leader, as well as those individuals from outside the unit who interact with followers of the leader, such as colleagues within the larger organization, external customers, and so forth. Transformational leaders realize that their influence can be multiplied outward by the role behaviors they model, the symbols they choose, and the visions they advocate. Indirect effects also can occur by which followers develop so that they can influence the leader's thinking, even without reporting directly to the leader. Hence the indirect process of influence can be top-down, lateral, or bottom-up. Such indirect processes of leadership also can include the full range of leadership factors. In fact, one might argue that extremely bad and extremely good leadership is likely to be communicated rather quickly through the direct and indirect processes discussed above. In sum, Chapter 3 highlights many of the channels that a leader can use to communicate his or her message. Although not directly addressed, it is important to note that how these channels have been used in the past and the nature of the communicated information will affect how successful a current leader is in communicating his or her message either directly or indirectly to colleagues within the organization, as well as to outside constituencies.

Team Leadership

Chapter 4 by Atwater and Bass provides a comprehensive review of the basic principles of small group and team behavior that are relevant to the transformational leader. The authors examine critical areas with respect to team formation, development, and performance, including characteristics of the context, task, individual, team, leader, leader and follower interaction, and conflict. For each subarea, Atwater and Bass discuss basic principles regarding individual and team behavior, incorporating into their analysis the impact of transactional and transformational leadership on the individual and team process. Basic principles regarding team behavior are examined within the context of the leadership model and revised accordingly based on the full-range leadership framework. For instance, being individually considerate in addressing the needs of team members requires leaders who are capable of accurately diagnosing the developmental levels of followers and then providing them with appropriate challenges. In the team setting, this task has become more difficult when team members' backgrounds are diverse. Moreover, many teams are temporary in nature, thus requiring the leader to complete his or her analysis of individual and group needs rapidly. Nevertheless, the individualized consideration shown by team leaders is expected to help maximize the development and performance of individual team members in the short term for temporary teams and in the long term for permanent groups.

Encouraging team members to examine the assumptions they use to solve problems is also extremely important. Team members often come from very different backgrounds and must work together to solve problems. Establishing a norm within the team to accept diverse points of view using intellectual stimulation becomes critical to team success. Understanding differences in the assumptions, perspective, and methods used to solve problems is an important requirement of the team leader.

Aligning a diverse set of views, needs, and aspirations around a central mission is another challenge that confronts the leader, so he or she will need to use inspirational motivation effectively to align the team around a vision, even if it is sometimes only for the short term. The team leader must work to keep the team on track, reminding members of the need to work together to achieve the vision. It is very easy for team members to drift apart because of internal pressures, the desire to avoid conflict, and the urge for individual recognition and reward.

Along the lines discussed above, the chapter by Atwater and Bass attempts to integrate what we know about team behavior in general with a relatively new form of team structure and alternative conceptions of leadership, including, in large part, transformational leadership. The chapter is highly structured, offering the opportunity to examine each area delineated above—for example, type of task and leadership style—while offering basic principles and commentary to help guide team leaders in more effective use of their teams. In addition to presenting much that is immediately applicable, this chapter provides a broad range of suggestions for further action, research, and development.

The Multifunctional Team

Chapter 5 by Waldman extends the examination of team leadership to leadership in multifunctional team (MFT) settings. The chapter calls attention to the growing need for using MFTs in research-and-development (R&D) or other innovation-based settings. The de-layering of organizations, the move toward placing greater emphasis on interdisciplinary work teams, and the total quality thrust in organizations today are some of the key driving forces behind MFTs' development. As problems have become more complex and the demand for quicker innovation increases, organizations are moving quickly toward new organizational forms that depend heavily on team-based structure. Increasingly, leaders are working with teams comprising members from different departments who have multiple roles and responsibilities. Functional line authority is diminishing, resulting in MFT leaders having to use less-traditional influence strategies. The demands for more effective leadership are growing with the advent of team-based structures in organizations.

In contrast to the more general discussion on team leadership presented by Atwater and Bass, Waldman focuses on the nature of MFTs with respect to the unique qualities and challenges required of leaders, particularly those responsible for innovation and R&D teams. Waldman analyzes the leadership function at different levels in the organization. Thus, the leadership behavior of upper-level managers needs to change when working with MFTs rather than working with more traditional departments. Questions such as how the decision-making structure within a group changes when one shifts to an MFT, are addressed in this chapter. As in the previous chapter by Atwater and Bass, there is a concerted effort to integrate the full-range model of leadership with the discussion of MFTs. Implications for team structure, communication, authority, rewards, selection, and culture are discussed, keeping in mind many of the principles delineated by Atwater and Bass' chapter, coupled with the full-range leadership model.

In sum, Chapters 4 and 5 provide a comprehensive analysis of team leadership from the perspective of traditional principles of team behavior and functioning, as well as by application of MFTs to the challenges confronting organizations today. The discussion of MFTs and leadership provides an alternative look at organizational design, which will likely become the norm in future organizations rather than being added to existing structures. We are likely witnessing an evolutionary change in organizational systems and structure because of the changing demands of both internal and external markets, the nature and characteristics of the work force, improved technology, and the globalization of organizations. We probably are in a transition stage between the old hierarchical structure of organizations and the new flattened form of organizational structure that is more flexible and reactive to change. The full-range model can support this transition to a more effective organizational form and be a significant part of the new framework of leadership that will make up future organizations.

In Chapter 6, Bass's central goal was to show how the transformational leadership model and its diffusion would affect both decision-making processes and the strategies used to collect and disseminate information throughout organizations. For instance, leaders who are more individually considerate are likely to open channels of communication that were previously unavailable to them. On the other hand, leaders who manage by exception or who are laissez-faire may directly or inadvertently restrict the flow of information through the organization. For example, leaders who actively manage by exception by frequently focusing on mistakes may develop a cadre of associates who are unwilling to offer new and perhaps risky ideas. Even less active laissez-faire leaders may simply fail to pick up relevant information or may send cues to others that they are not interested in receiving new information and ideas to advance or improve their work. These alterations in information-processing channels will affect the way such leaders diagnose problems, the information gathered, the choices considered appropriate, and their ultimate decisions. In the same vein, intellectually stimulating leaders will help followers uncover possibilities that have not been previously considered, which may alter the choices deemed appropriate for an organization to pursue. By questioning assumptions in a constructive manner, they may move followers to seek out information that would not otherwise be uncovered. In turn, that information may change followers' ways of approaching the decisions that leaders must make. In all these efforts the leaders must remain aware of both the forward and backward flows of decision processes.

In Chapter 7, Avolio provides a framework for linking the full range of leadership to total quality and continuous process improvement (CPI) efforts. This chapter begins with a brief history of the areas of leadership and quality, highlighting the parallels that exist between the full range of leadership behaviors and the principles discussed in the area of total quality and CPI. Avolio argues that both areas—leadership and quality—have neglected the other, and he suggests that their alliance would benefit both leadership development and the development of high-quality work systems. One parallel drawn in this chapter between these two areas suggests that the development of systems and the development of individuals can be viewed as similar, often parallel, and mutually supportive processes. Thus what we have learned over the last 40 years in the psychology of life-span development at an individual level also can be applied to the effective development of leaders as well as total quality systems. A key goal highlighted in this chapter is the need to develop systems and individuals to higher levels of potential in order to furnish an organization with CPI resources. This builds on Kuhnert's notion of advancing moral development. To improve, both systems and individuals must be provided with clear directions and targeted end points, or desired future end points. Organizations, like individuals, can be supplied with appropriate benchmarks for their points of reference in their respective developmental plans for achievement. For the individual, as well as the organization, the vision becomes a critical component in the development process.

In sum, organizations must take a closer look at the impact of the full range of transformational leadership on efforts now underway in the area of total quality. Minimally, a training program we conduct that focuses on the full range should emphasize changes in behavior and organizational culture that complement the implementation of a total quality-improvement program. It is clear that total-quality efforts represent a way of thinking as well as a way of doing that is compatible with the full-range model. For example, it is difficult to conceive of CPI without considering the developmental component of individualized consideration. Similarly, seeking out and solving problems that are inhibiting performance quality is at the core of what we recommend as part of being an intellectually stimulating leader. Having a vision and inspiring others to accept that vision with respect to the type of performance one expects, the culture and context in which the performance will occur, and the expectations one desires is threaded throughout TQM writings. Coupled with all of this, top-level leaders must have the trust and respect of their colleagues to make this all happen. And most important, they themselves must model what is necessary to be a total quality organization and what represents the core of idealized influence, as well as the Four I's of transformational leadership.

Along these lines, senior management must realize that the demands of a total-quality organization on its members necessitate a transformational leadership orientation toward followers and customers. A culture must be created that supports both the continuous development of individuals and the development of systems in order to achieve the highest level of potential. This will require a complete analysis of the way the organization conducts business. To accomplish this, leaders in the organization must encourage and even insist that their followers question the status quo, substituting strategies to seek improvement. Intellectual stimulation coupled with the other three I's of transformational leadership will become a key part of the leadership culture, with each remaining component also being seen as an essential ingredient in the success of the total quality-improvement effort. When properly integrated, the results of aligning transformational leadership with total-quality efforts should have a dramatic impact on an organization's level of effectiveness.

Transforming Organizations

In Chapter 8, Leanne and David Atwater provide a framework for examining organizational transformations, selecting several well-known benchmark companies to highlight an extensive range of innovative HR strategies. Many of the strategies reviewed in that chapter are directly or indirectly relevant to changes that are currently underway and anticipated in many organizations throughout the United States, Europe, Asia, and elsewhere.

Several major characteristics underlying each benchmark company were reviewed, including the emphasis placed on total quality efforts, the ability of the organization to respond to and eventually anticipate the changing needs of the market (that is, being market-driven), the ease with which the culture of these respective organizations entertains new and innovative approaches (or what Peter Senge refers to as the *learning organization*),[2] and the level and type of resources each organization allocates to the development of its human resource pool. All of these organizations have undergone substantial reorganization within the last 5 to 10 years to confront rapid ongoing changes in their respective markets.

The authors emphasize the importance of building innovative HR strategies to stimulate the development and continuous improvement of individuals and organizations. Many of this section's suggestions for innovative strategies for handling human resources are consistent with earlier recommendations regarding the alignment of leadership with total quality and the development of human resources to higher levels of potential. Further, these suggestions provide the groundwork for recommendations made by Kroeck in Chapter 9. Each benchmark firm reported by Atwater and Atwater exhibits a deep respect for the individual, which is reflected in both the culture and the procedures used to develop human resources.

All of the benchmark firms reviewed by Atwater and Atwater have demonstrated the ability and willingness to advance the boundaries of their disciplines, whether they be technical, structural, or behavioral boundaries, in order to remain in the forefront of their fields. In some organizations, such as Motorola, a major crisis moved the organization to its current strategic position in the global marketplace—and a commitment to be the best in its field, as well as to continuously improve its people and overall performance capacity. Each benchmark company has consistently been considered by its employees as a highly desirable organization to work for and in which to establish lifelong careers.

These benchmark organizations are also similar in providing a broad range of growth opportunities for their employees to excel and perform at the boundaries of their own respective disciplines. Numerous strategies regarding selection, training, compensation, and benefits have been modeled by other organizations within their respective industries, underscoring the innovativeness of their HR policies and practices.

In Chapter 9, Kroeck examines *downsizing*, a difficult period in any organization's history. This period is dealt with by applying the full-range model and, in particular, the Four I's of transformational leadership. Similar to points raised in Chapter 8, this chapter reviews several innovative HR strategies for downsizing an organization that can help minimize its impact on the remaining work force and can often turn a threat into an opportunity.

Kroeck introduces the idea of reshaping and resizing organizations to demonstrate how traditional approaches to downsizing are often analogous to the managing-by-exception leadership style: Correct the problem after it has become noticeable! Resizing and reshaping the organization on a continuous basis (known as *right sizing*) offers a radical shift in strategic HR thinking about how an organization maintains the appropriate numbers and quality of people to deal with current challenges and future opportunities. For example, articulating a vision of the future state for an organization provides that organization with the opportunity to consider the resources (human or otherwise) required to address the vision. Without a vision, the organization is simply moving forward without any strategy of using its human resources to address the challenges envisioned 2, 5, or 20 years into the future. Downsizing is most severe and radical when corporate decision makers cannot look beyond the current challenges and problems that confront an organization to envision the type of organization that will remain.

Corning, which was one of the benchmark companies identified in Chapter 8, works to anticipate the changing requirements and demands on its work force by training its employees to handle a much broader range of job responsibilities. For example, in its plant in Blacksburg, Virginia, all employees must learn three different jobs after being with the organization for only two years. In a similar way, the General Electric company required that all employees at its state-of-the-art plant in Binghamton, New York (recently acquired by Martin Marietta), after three years be able to do every job required in manufacturing. Such strategies reduce the potential for obsolescence, increase employees' understanding of the challenges confronting co-workers, and reduce the need to downsize the organization during hard times. This represents a very dramatic step that organizational leaders can take to anticipate future change and challenges.

The new thinking in this chapter concerning downsizing is consistent with the message in Chapter 7 on TQM and CPI. Reorganization must become a natural part of the way an organization conducts its business. Waiting until layoffs must occur reflects a more passive than effective use of human resources. It sends a very distinct message: "We screwed up." In other chapters we have seen that such strategies, although sometimes necessary, clearly do not produce optimal performance. Achieving the right use of human resources is an ideal, one that is similar to those suggested in our discussions of idealized influence, one of the Four I's of transformational leadership.

How an organization treats its work force in more difficult periods will significantly affect its culture and the level of trust its employees have in its leadership. How the leadership handles reorganization or downsizing will likely become part of the stories that undergird the culture into the future. In a basic transactional sense, was the transition and its impact on employees handled fairly? Were individual needs factored into the process? Did top management listen? Did it seek alternatives to a reduction in force? How did it maintain the motivation of those who remained? Ultimately, could it be trusted again in better times? Many examples exist and are given that show that organizations that go through these difficult periods can gain enormous inner strength, depending on how they handle the changes.

As indicated by Kroeck in Chapter 9, moving from a control to a commitment model of human resources will require new thinking about the issues of downsizing and reorganization. How an organization handles downsizing and layoffs will affect the long-term commitment of its employees. Not only will the commitment of the employees who remain be affected, but also equally influenced will be the qualities of future employees who are attracted to the organization.

Appraising the Transformations

The transformations sought in this book at all organizational levels can be appraised by a broad spectrum of techniques, including passive or subjective forms of observation and diary keeping, well-structured survey techniques, and more standard measures of individual and organizational performance.

In such appraisals, several significant points must be made. First, one must link constructs that are targeted for change to the type of evaluation procedure most likely to capture the change process and its impact on individuals, groups, or the organization. For example, intellectual stimulation can be observed as a behavioral change in leaders, as well as a policy change with respect to the support for new innovative projects through the allocation of resources. Intellectual stimulation also may be assessed by analyzing how leaders structure their meetings, as well as by examining external customers' satisfaction with how well the organization solved customer problems.

In the same way, individualized consideration can be determined by observing how the leader treats followers and how the organization processes complaints from employees and handles its HR policies and procedures. The essential point here is that the transformation desired must be examined where and when it is most likely to occur. Moreover, the sequencing of measures with respect to the timing of impact is a critical issue to be considered when measuring change in individuals, teams, or organizations. Specifically, some behavioral changes may occur over a brief period of several months, while changes in values may take substantially longer, with significant changes in the culture of an organization taking three to five years, depending on the organization's size, market, and challenges, as well as its leaders' coverage and persistence.[3]

We can effectively monitor the transformational process, assess it, and make recommendations for future changes in strategic HR management. Note that any concerted effort to evaluate the change process will itself probably affect individuals and the organization. Specifically, by pursuing a comprehensive evaluation plan, the organization signals to its work force the value it places on the intervention and the desire for change. Such attention to evaluation can actually provide an impetus for change. Evaluation can also help direct and redirect the process of change in ways that are similar to those discussed in Chapter 7, which examined the alliance of leadership and total quality improvement.

To summarize, the chapters in this book point to some of the areas where the diffusion of transformational leadership in particular can be both observed and stimulated. As more managers and supervisors receive training in the full-range leadership development, more of the transformations in HR strategies outlined in these respective chapters are likely to be observed. All managers must realize, however, that a change in leadership philosophy and orientation, as it is currently underway in many organizations, will affect not only the interactions between leaders and followers, but also the culture and the institutional policies that govern the organization. The model of leadership that we present in our full-range workshop represents a way of thinking and a philosophy that can be generalized to all facets of HR development. Thus the real impact of this program and other efforts to enhance the full range of leadership will be observed in many forms, including changes in culture, policies, and procedures that will occur as the entire organization moves toward the Four I's of transformational leadership.

The development of a vision with inspirational motivation that is 2, 5, or 10 years in the future alters the landscape on which leaders make their decisions. Significant changes in the organization, its structure, and culture can occur as a critical number of managers shift their time horizons away from addressing problems of the moment to potential opportunities for the future. Managers who operate in a purely transactional culture will approach decisions with a different lens for interpreting and using information to reach a decision as compared to managers from a culture that is characterized by the Four I's of transformational leadership. Projects that go beyond the immediate budget cycle or that have little immediate payoff may never be considered. The development of new technology, processes, and procedures will require a more far-reaching perspective that takes an organization beyond its current constraints to imagine future possibilities. The intermediate technology that is required to get us to the levels envisioned for the future often is not yet available, thus even these intermediate steps must be envisioned to achieve the long-term vision. Thus establishing such a vision itself provides the opportunity to work through scenarios that otherwise would not have been considered. Those processes of envisioning, generating and disseminating information, and decision making simply cannot occur effectively under transactional leadership.

To summarize, the introduction of the Four I's into a manager's portfolio of leadership behaviors will have a significant effect on an organization's culture, the behavior of its members, and the way decisions ranging from routine tasks to nonroutine exploratory ventures are processed at all levels within the leader's organizational unit, as well as within the organization. Simply reconsidering the assumptions on which decisions are based can have a dramatic ripple effect throughout the organization, just as will the alignment of organizational members around a central vision. Finally, the promotion of innovative thinking can lead to the search for information and choices that have not been previously considered, which by itself could have a dramatic impact on the decision-making processes within an organization.

Notes

1. Bass, B. M., Waldman, D. A., Avolio, B. J., & Bebb, M. (1987). Transformational leaders: The falling dominoes effect. *Group and Organization Studies, 12,* 73-87.
2. Senge, P. M. (1990). *The fifth discipline: The art and practice of the learning organization.* New York: Doubleday.
3. Schein, E. H. (1990). Organizational culture. *American Psychologist, 45,* 109-119.

Author Index

218

Subject Index

About the Editors

Bruce J. Avolio (Ph.D., University of Akron, 1982) is Director of Graduate Programs in the School of Management at the State University of New York (SUNY) at Binghamton and Professor in the Organizational Behavior and Human Resource Management Group. He has published many articles on transformational leadership and conducted training and organizational development programs throughout North America and Europe. He is the coauthor of the Multifactor Leadership Questionnaire, the principal survey instrument used to measure transformational leadership.

Bernard M. Bass (Ph.D., Ohio State University, 1949) is Distinguished Professor Emeritus of Management and Director of the Center for Leadership Studies at SUNY Binghamton. He is responsible for 22 books and more than 300 articles on leadership, organizational psychology, international management, and related subjects. For the past decade he has concentrated on theory, research, and training in transformational leadership. He was founding editor of the *Leadership Quarterly*, has served as consultant to many Fortune 500 companies, and has conducted workshops and seminars in more than 40 countries. His most recent books include *Bass and Stogdill's Handbook of Leadership* (1990), *Advances in Organizational Psychology: An International Review* (1987), and *Leadership and Performance Beyond Expectations* (1985).

About the Authors

David C. Atwater (M.A., San Diego State University) has more than 20 years of experience in personnel research and extensive work in selection, classification, development, and validation of noncognitive selection instruments. His current interests include training research and evaluation of transformational leadership training. He has published in the professional literature and in U.S. government technical publications. He currently is in private practice in Phoenix, Arizona.

Leanne E. Atwater (Ph.D., Claremont Graduate School) is Assistant Professor of Management at Arizona State University-West and a Corresponding Fellow of the Center for Leadership Studies. Her research interests include leadership, power, upward feedback, and self-perception accuracy. She consults in a variety of areas, including leadership and organizational communication.

K. Galen Kroeck is Associate Professor of Management at Florida International University in Miami, Director of Doctoral Studies in the College of Business Administration, and Chairman of the Florida International University Research Council. He has written many magazine and journal articles and college textbooks on human resource management. He is president of OPD Management Consultants and has worked in a consulting capacity with private and public organizations in the United States and many international companies.

Karl W. Kuhnert (Ph.D., Kansas State University) is Associate Professor of Industrial/Organizational Psychology at the University of Georgia. His research interests include organizational leadership, job security, and organizational change. His recent publications include "Leadership Theory in Postmodern Organizations" (in R. T. Golembiewski, *Handbook of Organizational Behavior*, 1993) and "Integrating Skill Acquisition and Perspective-Taking Capacity in the Development of Leaders" (with Craig Russell), *Leadership Quarterly*.

Francis J. Yammarino (Ph.D., State University of New York at Buffalo) is Associate Professor of Management and Fellow of the Center for Leadership Studies at SUNY Binghamton. He has published many articles in management and social science journals, is coauthor of *Theory Testing in Organizational Behavior: The Varient Approach*, Senior Editor of the *Leadership Quarterly*, and on the editorial review board of *Group and Organization Management*. His research interests include superior-subordinate relationships, transformational leadership, their impacts on employee outcomes, and multiple levels of analysis issues. He has served widely as a consultant.

David A. Waldman is Associate Professor of Management at Concordia University, Montreal. He has published more than 40 articles on leadership and the management of work performance. His current interests include leadership and human resources issues surrounding the effective implementation of total quality management. He has actively consulted in both the public and private sectors in the United States and Canada.